Travels from Dostoevsky's Siberia

Encounters with Polish Literary Exiles

Studies in Comparative Literature and Intellectual History

Series Editor
Galin Tihanov
(Queen Mary, University of London)

Travels from Dostoevsky's Siberia

Encounters with Polish Literary Exiles

ELIZABETH A. BLAKE

BOSTON
2019

Library of Congress Control Number: 2019941831

ISBN 978-1-64469-021-5 (hardcover)
ISBN 978-1-64469-022-2 (paper)
ISBN 978-1-64469-023-9 (electronic)

Cover design by Ivan Grave.
Book design by Lapiz Publishing Services.
Published by Academic Studies Press in 2019.
1577 Beacon St.
Brookline, MA 02446
press@academicstudiespress.com
www.academicstudiespress.com

To my mom, Eleanor, and my grandpa, Bill, for their love surpassing understanding

We need the storm, the whirlwind, and the earthquake. The feeling of the nation must be quickened; the conscience of the nation must be roused; the propriety of the nation must be startled; the hypocrisy of the nation must be exposed; and its crimes against God and man must be proclaimed and denounced.

—Frederick Douglass

We must publicly condemn the very idea of certain peoples' slaughter of others! Being silent about vice—driving it into your core only so that it does not protrude outward—we are implanting it, and it will rise up still a thousand fold in the future.

—Aleksandr Solzhenitsyn

Table of Contents

Acknowledgments

As is frequently the case with my larger writing projects, this book is the result of a collaborative effort put forth over several years, so I wish to share my appreciation for the research support extended to me by the international academic community. It was many years ago that Caryl Emerson saw the value of Józef Bogusławski's remembrances and thought that I should translate them, but it was Robert L. Jackson who pointed out to me that the manuscript lay in Jagiellonian University's library. Having received a professional development leave from the Department of Languages, Literatures, and Cultures under the direction of Annie Smart at Saint Louis University, I conducted research at Jagiellonian University, the Czartoryski Museum, and the National Museum in Krakow, with the support of Krzysztof Frysztacki and in consultation with Henryk Głębocki and Janusz Pezda. A Fulbright-Hays U. S. Department of Education grant and a Mellon grant from Saint Louis University's College of Arts and Sciences supported research in Russia at the manuscript division of the Russian National Library and at the Dostoevsky Museum in St. Petersburg, where consultations with the Deputy Director, Boris Tikhomirov, advanced my research on Siberia. Support from American Councils in the form of an Advanced Research Fellowship for Russia and Poland, funded by the U. S. Department of State (Title VIII) allowed me to conduct further archival research and to consult with a Dostoevsky scholar specializing in his Siberian period, Viktor Vainerman.

Summer housing grants at the Summer Research Laboratory on Russia, Eastern Europe, and Eurasia at University of Illinois Urbana-Champaign allowed me to obtain background research on Dostoevsky's Siberia and Polish resources with the aid of Slavic Reference librarians Joseph Lenkart and Jan Adamczyk, with whom I have consulted for many years on translation issues, locating resources, and obtaining access to materials. This project grew out of research undertaken in connection with presentations at Washington University in St. Louis, at the invitation of Nicole Svobodny and Anika Walke, as part of the Eurasian Studies Divan and the workshop "On the Move: Migration and Mobility in East and Central Europe and Eurasia." The Center for Intercultural Studies at Saint Louis University under the leadership of Michał Rozbicki has supported the dissemination of this research in lectures and publications. I also greatly appreciate the funding for research and the subvention offered by Dean Chris Duncan and Associate Dean Donna LaVoie of the College of Arts and Sciences at Saint Louis University as well as the University's provost leave granted by Provost Nancy Brickhouse. The following have also helped connect me with valuable resources in the field: Ivan Esaulov, Timothy O'Connor, Valentina Gavrilova, Jarosław Moklak, and Jacek Lubecki. In addition, I would like to thank the readers of my manuscript with Academic Studies Press as well as the editors who worked with me, since their comments led to improvements in the initial submission.

As always, I wish to express my great appreciation for my loving husband Ruben, who has supported me personally and professionally, through separations for research trips and many bends in the road for almost thirty years. Finally, I must extend a big thank you to my amazingly strong, resilient, and intelligent daughter Isabella for her forbearance during the long periods of traveling, writing, and translating as well as to her brother, my sweet Raphael, whose sense of joy, humor, and generosity are completely incommensurate with the suffering he has borne in his short life. I dedicate this book to two family members whose positive influence I appreciated too late—my mother Eleanor J. Blake and my grandfather William H. Blake—whom I have in some sense lost but who remain with me in my work, partly because of their loving attention to my education.

A Note on the Text

For the Russian text, although the notes and bibliographical references follow the Library of Congress system, a simplified version has been adopted elsewhere, e.g., with the elimination of ' and " to replace the soft and hard signs in Russian as well as with common spellings favored over adherence to the LC system (i.e. with endings in –skii converted to –sky).

Throughout the introductions and notes, the references to Dostoevsky's oeuvre cite the following academic edition of his collected works:

Pss Dostoevskii, F. M. *Polnoe sobranie sochinenii v tridtsati tomakh.* 30 vols. Leningrad: Nauka, 1972–90.

Unless otherwise cited, much of the information in the notes is gleaned from the research collected in three reference sources on Polish exiles:

Urw Djakow, Włodzimierz, et al. *Uczestnicy ruchów wolnościowych w latach 1832–1855 (Królestwo Polskie).* Wroclaw: Wydawnictwo Polskiej Akademii Nauk, 1990.

ZpIR Śliwowska, Wiktoria. *Zesłancy polscy w Imperium Rosyjskim w pierwszej połowie XIX wieku.* Warsaw: Wydawictwo DiG, 1998.

UzS Śliwowska, Wiktoria. *Ucieczki z Sybiru.* Warsaw: Wydawnictwo Iskry, 2005.

The Russian State Military Historical Archive (RGVIA) gave permission for the reproduction of the two sketches included in this collection: Figure 1 (Fond 349, opis' 27, delo 1381) and Figure 2 (Fond 349, opis' 27, delo 1463).

Introduction

This present volume addressing political exile in Western Siberia in the middle of the nineteenth century seeks to introduce new avenues for understanding Fedor Dostoevsky's experience of incarceration and exile, which is not only represented in his autobiographical novel, *Notes from the House of the Dead* (1860–62), but also impacts his post-Siberian murder novels by providing insights into the criminal mind in *Crime and Punishment* (1866), capital punishment in *The Idiot* (1868), criminal conspiracy in *The Demons* (1871–72), and political theology in *The Brothers Karamazov* (1879–80). The three authors—Józef Bogusławski, Bronisław Zaleski, and Rufin Piotrowski—whose well-known published nineteenth-century works are represented in this collection, are Dostoevsky's contemporary peers in the Russian Empire who were arrested and deported to Siberia and Orenburg for their political activism.[1] Their personal witness to the experience of confinement in fortresses, deportation (in chains), a life of hard labor in a foreign criminal environment, and conscription into the military ranks supplement Dostoevsky's impressions of the Dead House with diverse depictions of the penal system in the empire of Nicholas I and its myriad means of torment, whose complexity explains "not only the possibility and the long survival of physical punishments" but also "the rather sporadic nature of the opposition to them."[2] Many insurgents from the Congress Kingdom of Poland, linked through the camaraderie of university days in Berlin or Dorpat or their participation in conspiratorial circles, sat awaiting

1 The Siberian and Orenburg exiles are not necessarily discussed as separate categories in official correspondence on Western Siberia or early historical research, such as Michał Janik's *Dzieje Polaków na Syberji* (Krakow: Nakładem Krakowskiej Spółki Wydawniczej, 1928).

2 Michel Foucault, *Discipline and Punish: The Birth of the Prison*, trans. Alan Sheridan (New York: Vintage Books, 1977), 55.

interrogations, beatings, and judgment in overcrowded prisons in Vilnius, Warsaw, and Modlin, from whence they were subsequently dispatched to Siberia, Orenburg, or the Caucasus—listed by Zaleski as the three main places of Polish exile. After having read the many ways in which these political exiles were detained, stripped of their birthrights, physically abused, psychologically intimidated, and persecuted as a group by criminals and officers alike for years, the mock executions endured by Poles and Russians before their deportation may seem less impactful than the years spent in Siberia practicing a patient forbearance in the midst of adversity—a coping strategy that Zaleski identifies as "the only path" forward.

Because these exiled authors are more deeply committed to regime change than Dostoevsky, the remembrances of Bogusławski, Zaleski, and Piotrowski follow in the tradition recognized by Paul Ricoeur as "attestation–protestation" whereby citizens observing historical events, such as the nation in captivity here, feel obligated to articulate a shared trauma.[3] These recollections also highlight the artistic talent of a neglected generation of exiles who came of age between two Polish armed insurrections of 1830 and 1863 (after which Polish and Lithuanian insurgents were sent *en masse* to Siberia) but before Alexander II's legal reforms impacted the imperial penal system.[4] The writers of this inter-revolutionary generation, implicated in uprisings across Europe—both inspired by French revolutionary movements, and emboldened by Aleksandr Herzen's subversive publications—provided stable employment for many agents of the Third Section under Nicholas I.[5] Thus, the arrests and deportation of both the Omsk and Orenburg exiles—especially Dostoevsky, the Ukrainian artist and poet

3 Paul Ricoeur, *Memory, History, Forgetting*, trans. Kathleen Blamey and David Pellauer (Chicago: University of Chicago Press, 2004), 259.

4 For example, the recent popular study *The House of the Dead: Siberian Exile under the Tsars* (New York: Vintage Books, 2016) by Daniel Beer focuses not on Dostoevsky's generation but on Polish exiles linked to the two uprisings, and Abby M. Schrader critically notes the tendency for historians of Russian penal systems to focus on the late imperial period in *Languages of the Lash: Corporal Punishment and Identity in Imperial Russia* (Dekalb: Northern Illinois University Press, 2002), 7. Bruce E. Adams concentrates on this period in his study *The Politics of Punishment: Prison Reform in Russia 1863–1917* (Dekalb: Northern Illinois University Press, 1996), while Andrew Gentes addresses the post-1863 exiles in *The Mass Deportation of Poles to Siberia, 1863–1880* (Cham, Sz.: Palgrave Macmillan, 2017).

5 Indeed, Herzen's co-editor Mikhail Bakunin, who was implicated in Polish subversive activities in the 1840s, was himself exiled to Tomsk (1857–59) where he met with the Petrashevets Feliks Toll' (E. H. Carr, *Michael Bakunin* [London: Macmillan, 1937], 226–27).

Taras Shevchenko, and the Polish-Lithuanian poet and playwright Edward Żeligowski—attest to the concerns of Nicholas I's regime regarding the ability of writers to disseminate politically subversive material, as Zaleski recognizes: "the Moscow government sent to various provinces situated in the depths of Russia, an entire circle of people busying themselves with our literary production."[6]

All the same, the authors of the texts represented here write candidly, in relative freedom, since Bogusławski indicates that he leaves his manuscript for posterity, Piotrowski works on his remembrances in Vienna, and Zaleski publishes in Paris. These authors are linked either through their connection to Dostoevsky's imprisonment in Omsk or through networks of conspirators that extend from Omsk to Orenburg through the political activities of the Omsk inmates—Bogusławski and the Petrashevtsy Dostoevsky and Sergei Durov—that are interwined with famous Russian, Polish, Lithuanian, and Ukrainian authors connected to the Orenburg Circle, including Bogusławski's co-conspirators Zaleski and Żeligowski, the Petrashevets Aleksei Pleshcheev, and Shevchenko. Indeed, Zaleski and Bogusławski were recidivist offenders, who were not only arrested together in 1839 in connection with a student group from Vilnius but then also shared the same cell after their subsequent arrest in 1846 for their links to the famous Jan Röhr conspiracy, while Pleshcheev, Durov, and Dostoevsky were victims of the infamous mock execution on Semenovsky Square.[7] Dostoevsky's first letter after his liberation from the Omsk fortress reinforces the connection between Omsk and Orenburg, since in reporting on nine of the deported Petrashevtsy, he includes a discussion of two who served in Orenburg—Pleshcheev and Vasily Golovinsky; furthermore, Dostoevsky corresponds with Pleshcheev from Semipalatinsk as early as 1857, even as he was working on *House of the Dead*.[8] Orenburg was such a common place of exile that Dostoevsky assumed that after his return from the mock execution, he would be assigned to a fortress in Orenburg, like his co-conspirator Pleshcheev. Yet, only after four years as a prisoner in Omsk was Dostoevsky released into the ranks to serve in the army, like Zaleski, but in the more isolated Semipalatinsk.

6 Bronislaw Zaleski, "Zmarli na wychodźstwie od 1861 roku: Żeligowski, Edward," in *Rocznik Towarzystwa Historyczno-Literackiego w Paryżu* (Paris: Księgarnia Luksemburgska, 1866), 370.

7 Polevoi Auditoriat deistvuiushchei pervoi armii s 1842 po 1856. Fond 16233, opis' 3, delo 2604. Rossiiskii gosudarstvennyi voenno-istoricheskii arkhiv.

8 A. E. Vrangel', *Vospominaniia o F. M. Dostoevskom v Sibiri 1854–56 gg.* (St. Petersburg: Tipografiia A. S. Suvorina, 1912), 52.

At times, the parallels between Dostoevsky's recollections and these accounts translated from Polish and French suggest a common experience, such as in the public display of deprivation of rights found in Dostoevsky and Bogusławski. In other words, Dostoevsky's brief description in a letter to his brother detailing how he was conveyed in a carriage through an abyss of people to the scaffold where he took leave of fellow Petrashevtsy after the reading of their death sentence shares similarities with Bogusławski's depiction of wearing a board with the inscription "malefactor" around his neck as he was paraded around Vilnius in a cart with his co-conspirators before being placed in the pillory (*Pss*, 28.1:162). In addition, Zaleski effectively summarizes the process by which some Petrashevtsy and Polish exiles were able to negotiate a return home under Alexander II by currying favor with local officials and superior officers and depending upon the camaraderie of fellow exiles, who helped the former conspirators navigate the processes of promotion and petitions that could eventually secure a release from the sentence of an exile. All the same, Zaleski, Piotrowski, and Bogusławski consciously divide themselves from the Russian officers in their critiques of their physically and verbally abusive captors, whose otherness is underscored with the pejorative term *Moskali* and whose cruelty was enhanced by a "pernicious upbringing in the corps" (which Zaleski concludes "sucked out their souls"). Their detailed descriptions of corrupt guards, depraved military culture, and strict hierarchical communities challenge penal and Siberian histories invoking *House of the Dead* to recognize that Dostoevsky's focus on his fictional narrator's ability to adapt to living among *Russian* peasant convicts necessarily impacts the historical record of the author's interaction with Polish political prisoners and military personnel in the prison fortress as well as in the town of Omsk.[9] Piotrowski's account of Omsk from his famous *Memoirs from a Stay in Siberia* offers further testimony clarifying the degree to which sympathetic officials in Western Siberia interacted with political exiles, on whose conduct they were expected to report.

This collection excludes a discussion of Eastern Siberia, not only because the realities specific to this region are significant enough to earn it a distinct position in the history of Siberian penal servitude but also because the political prisoners in Orenburg and Western Siberia were treated with

9 In *Wages of Evil: Dostoevsky and Punishment* (Evanston, Ill.: Northwestern University Press, 2012), Anna Schur notes the immediate impact of Dostoevsky's work on historical studies, such as N. M. Iadrintsev's *Russkaia obshchina v tiur'me i ssylke* (1872), which in its structure and focus on the humanity of the *Russian* common convicts follows the model of Dostoevsky's autobiographical novel (82).

a greater intent to rehabilitate, which is evident from Alexander II's decisions granting clemency to former Petrashevtsy and Polish political exiles in these regions. These translations of Bogusławski's manuscript and Zaleski's article provide information on Western Siberia between the revolutions that has not been as accessible as research on its Eastern counterpart, which is largely based on the writings of the prolific memoirist Agaton Giller, who arrived in 1855 in Irkutsk to serve his sentence in a Siberian battalion and proceeded to write several volumes about Siberia in addition to establishing a historical record of Polish and Lithuanian Siberian exiles, his *List of Polish Exiles before 1860.*[10] *A Siberian Memoir* and "Polish Exiles in Orenburg" provide a sense of the interaction between Russians and Poles that characterized for this western region both the journey on foot to fortresses through various local way stations as well as the ways in which they navigated accommodating and resisting cultural assimilation. Since Dostoevsky and his co-conspirator Durov were traveling by conveyance, they had more limited encounters with the filthy, vermin-infested, and overcrowded transit houses where civilian convicts broke their journeys on foot from Tobolsk to their assigned prison fortresses (*Pss*, 28.1:168–69). The Poles' empathy for local populations in their writings—for example, Old Believers, Circassians, and Kirgiz—distinguishes their remembrances from the well-known recollections of Baron Vrangel, *Memoirs about F. M. Dostoevsky in Siberia, 1854–1856* (1912), in which many members of the diverse Siberian population appear more as those whom the army sought to monitor or subdue.[11]

Intercultural Tensions and Camaraderie

Bogusławski, Zaleski, and Piotrowski do not reach as far as Eastern Siberia so they focus on Western Siberia and the border areas of the Orenburg line

10 For example, in his discussion of this period in *The House of the Dead*, Beer invokes Sergei Maksimov's *Sibir' i katorga* in 3 vols. (St. Petersburg: Tipografiia A. Transhelia, 1871), which draws heavily on Giller's writings, as is discussed in Elizabeth Blake's "Traumatic Mobility: Motivating Collective Authorship in Siberian Narratives of Polish Exiles from the Inter-Revolutionary Epoch (1832–1862)," in *Migration and Mobility in the Modern Age: Refugees, Travelers, and Traffickers in Europe and Eurasia*, ed. Anike Walke, Jan Musekamp, and Nicole Svobodny (Bloomington: Indiana University Press, 2016), 246.

11 Vrangel', *Vospominaniia o F. M. Dostoevskom*, 40–41. Dostoevsky and Vrangel were situated closer to the porous border with China where foreign prospectors crossed in search of gold, and a Tashkent khan prepared a large army to fight Russians along the Southern border.

with Bogusławski and Zaleski reserving their most elaborate critique for their soldier captors and military superiors even while their expressions of moral disgust at the surrounding drunkeness, debauchery, and savagery are aimed at the Russian military and convicts alike. Descriptions of Polish moral exceptionalism, while overtly maintained by Zaleski, pervade Bogusławski's recollections of the maltreatment dispersed throughout Russian military structures, including the corps of cadets which educated Dostoevsky. This structures fostered retributions instigated by petty jealousies, rewarded opportunistic informants, and maintained an indifferent leadership fearing reprisal more than injustice. Dostoevsky similarly recognizes such abuses linked to the military after his incarceration in Omsk when writing to his older brother that he fears only "people and tyranny," since "If you fall under a superior, who takes a disliking to you (there are such), he will pick on you, destroy you, or make service a misery" (*Pss*, 28.1:172). However, like Zaleski, Dostoevsky knew that he had to serve and advance in the military to the level of an officer in order to earn clemency from the tsar, so he does not express himself in his correspondence as elaborately as Zaleski, who explores the struggle between "the Polish idea—represented by prisoners fitted with fetters—with the idea of the Tsar dressed in purple and propped on a bayonet" representing a "universal lawlessness at the top." He maintains that "the absence of every fixed right, through always exceptional courts," allowed for an infinite variety of sentences to be confirmed by the tsar or his Viceroy of the Kingdom of Poland.

Zaleski's article, therefore, attests to the failure of the 1845 revisions of the penal code to address arbitrariness of punishment, because he concludes that the historically young Muscovite society operated on instinct and sensual urges without pretense to equality in law or justice, a foundational element of penal systems emerging at the turn of the nineteenth century.[12] Likewise, Piotrowski, who passed through Omsk about five years before Dostoevsky's arrival, impresses upon the reader of *Memoirs from a Stay in Siberia* that Governor General Petr Gorchakov individually had the power to dispatch the prisoner "to Tomsk, to the gubernia of Irkutsk, to Nerchinsk itself," and "The Martyrdom of Prior Sierocinski" indicates that this "true despot of Siberia" and "thug, executioner, and tyrant of the unfortunate slaves of 1831" exercised his privilege freely, thereby earning him the enmity of multiple generations of Polish prisoners. Bogusławski further holds Governor Gorchakov responsible for allowing Major Krivtsov

12 Schur, *Wages of Evil*, 83; Foucault, *Discipline and Punish*, 231–32.

a free hand in tormenting the prisoners in the Omsk stockade in a lawless criminal environment that tolerated the sexual assault of unsuspecting soldiers, guards passing counterfeit money, and prison officials' appropriation of inmates' property. His portrait of Major Krivtsov supplements the illustrations of his cruelties in *House of the Dead*, with references to a complicated man without conscience, clad in Mirecki's deerskin, sleeping on the Poles' leather pillow, but with some regrets over the flogging of Józef Żochowski.

In *Discipline and Punish*, Foucault identifies a "carceral net" that may effectively be applied to this imperial penal system which places "over the slightest illegality, the smallest irregularity, deviation or anomaly, the threat of delinquency."[13] Consequently, the authors in the Dead House particularly fear denunciation, since, as Zaleski observes, "there were as always denunciations and prosecutions," such as those resulting in Shevchenko's sudden arrest and deportation to the distant fortress of Novopetrovsk for painting or in Żeligowski's removal from Orenburg for traveling with Decembrist Prince Sergei Trubetskoi.[14] Indeed, Szymon Tokarzewski, Bogusławski, and Żochowski had been moved from the fortress at Ust-Kamenogorsk to the more austere conditions at Omsk because of letters and writings found in their possession. Although Bogusławski correctly identifies the corrupt Major Gusev (subsequently released from service) as the source of the trouble, Zaleski does not appreciate the degree to which Governor Vladimir Obruchev monitored political prisoners, as is evident from Obruchev's reports to St. Petersburg on the issue of reading materials in the possession of the Petrashevtsy.[15] In Dostoevsky's novel, the concerns over denunciation are attributed to Tokarzewski during a protest against the prison food: "They will begin to search for instigators, and if we are there, of course, they will shift the blame for the revolt to us first. Remember why we came here. They will simply be flogged, but we will be put on trial" (*Pss*, 4:203). Clearly, this was a valid concern in regard to Dostoevsky's "moral Quasimodo" Aristov, who acted as a perpetual informant. Yet, Bogusławski extends this potential

13 Foucault, *Discipline and Punish*, 297.

14 George S. N. Luckyj, *Young Ukraine: The Brotherhood of Saints Cyril and Methodius in Kiev, 1845–1847* (Ottawa: University of Ottawa Press), 66–68; Pavlo Zaitsev, *Taras Shevchenko: A Life*, ed. and trans. George S. N. Luckyj (Toronto: University of Toronto Press, 1988), 197–99; Zaleski, "Zmarli na wychodźstwie od 1861 roku: Żeligowski, Edward," 370.

15 O zloumyshlennikakh Petrashevskom, Speshneve, Mombelle, Dostoevskom, Iastrzhebskom, Tolle, Filipove, Akhsharumove, Deby 1, Deby 2, Timakovskom, Shaposhnikove, Khanykove, Pleshcheeve, Golovinskom, Kashkine, Evropeuse, Pal'me i Chernosvitove. Fond 395, opis' 285, delo 81. RGVIA.

threat to Dostoevsky with whom the Poles had severed all relations, since he "threatened us with the reporting and publication of our former conversations." Ironically, both Dostoevsky and Bogusławski had already displayed an admirable resistance to their interrogators' attempts to force them to incriminate fellow conspirators, as attested by Dostoevsky's evasive answers during his interrogation and by the official complaint that Bogusławski "concealed his actions and did not want to reveal Röhr's ill-intentioned ventures."[16]

Still, the deterioration of their intellectual dialogue reflects a more subtle but sustained ethnic conflict in the prison than Aristov's coordinated attack on the Catholic Christmas feast. It was likely Dostoevsky's admiration of the tsar that offended Bogusławski who notes the novelist's ambition to gain Constantinople for the Russian Empire as well as his desire to see historically Polish, Lithuanian, and Ukrainian lands under the authority of the tsar.[17] Both Zaleski and Bogusławski clarify that their failure to attribute the ideal of humanity embodied in Christ to the Russian tsar meant that they were regarded by Russians as soulless, since they were not properly educated in the veneration of the tsar, "the deity of the nation," through the instruction of the Orthodox priest attired in the vestments of Christ with chalice in hand. Bogusławski implies that Dostoevsky, having received this education in a cadet corps that rewards the blind fulfillment of duty, naturally honored the hand that fed him and so gave into Satan's tempting of Christ with the kingdoms of the world in exchange for worship (Luke 4:5–8). Furthermore, Bogusławski remains certain that Christ does not reside with Russian imperial authority, and by extension with the Orthodox Church reinforcing the tsar's secular power. As he clarifies with the case of Pantaleon Potocki, he sides with the Catholic priests who refuse absolution to informants for the state at a time when the law required Orthodox priests to disclose crimes against the state revealed in the confessional. In other words, such a political theology prevents Catholics in the empire from identifying Nicholas as sovereign in the Orthodox understanding, especially since in Zaleski's assessment Nicholas is the tsar who increasingly militarized the empire, kept track of all those he condemned to serve in his military, encouraged the lawlessness of abusive provincial authority figures, and disregarded requests of local officials in harshly regulating the fate of exiles from the imperial capital. All the same, the two Polish-Lithuanian authors share with Dostoevsky a

---

16 V. F. Ratch, 1830–1840. Fond 629, opis' 188, folio 45. Rossiiskaia natsional'naia biblioteka: Rukopisnyi otdel. See the 18th vol. of Dostoevsky's collected works for documents relating to his arrest and interrogations.

17 Blake, *Dostoevsky and the Catholic Underground* (Evanston, IL: Northwestern University Press, 2014), 31-32.

sense that their Siberian sentences represent the will of the tsar, not the fair application of an impartial legal code, so they all accept that their return home is predicated on persuading a single sovereign to change their fate which can be realized only through applications for clemency by persons of influence. The tsar's personal intervention in the case of Shevchenko—one that deprived the poet and painter of the right to draw, write, and sing—drives home for Zaleski the power of the tsar to impact the fate of the Orenburg exiles.

For the three Poles arriving from Ust-Kamenogorsk as well as for Mirecki and the additional four political prisoners implicated in the Krakow uprising of 1846 (Józef Anczykowski, Karol Bem, Ludwik Korczyński, and Jan Musiałowicz) who arrived in Omsk in 1850, a search for camaraderie led them to convince Major Krivtsov to allow them to live in a single prison hall alongside a Jewish inmate Isai, Circassians, and Karbadians, thereby isolating themselves from the Russian-speaking prison world.[18] This tendency to separate themselves from the general prison population, which Bogusławski notes increased the resentment and harassment against them in the fortress, shows how the Russian oppression shared by Poles, Circassians, and Karbadians created a common bond that transcended the linguistic divide. In his depiction of Nuru Shakhmurlu Oglu, detailing that "on his face and on his body you would certainly not find a piece of skin that was not broken" since "in his youth the bayonet was not a stranger to him," there is empathy for a fellow victim of the empire. All the same, this was not an equal partnership, as is disclosed by Bogusławski's admiration of the Circassians' "hail of fists" meeting the shaved heads of the Russian convicts, since the Circassians were appreciated for their muscle that protected the Poles from abuse. Zaleski's article is less forthcoming about Polish soldiers' interaction with the Kirgiz population, even though he published an illustrated collection *The Life of the Kirgiz Steppes* (1865), because he does not clarify the extent to which service in the tsar's army, particularly advancement and a return to Poland, often required the exiles to subdue the Kirgiz population for the tsar.

Instead, Zaleski, Piotrowski, and Bogusławski focus on Russo-Polish tensions with Zaleski asserting that following the foot of the Russian soldier expanding the empire ever eastward was "a Polish exile with his pining and

18 The sketch found in Bogusławski's manuscript helps establish the authenticity of the manuscript, since the arrangement of the bunks corresponds to a sketch from the Russian State Military Historical Archive (Fond 349, opis' 27, delo 1381) included as Figure 1. The sketch resembles the uppermost division of the lower right-hand barrack with a door on its left-hand side that leads to the door exiting the barrack into the courtyard.

his tear." Zaleski adds that Pugachev and his gang killed many of the Bar Confederates exiled to Orenburg and that during the reigns of Nicholas I and Alexander II "at almost every new stage it passed to us to pay with a victim or blood." Bogusławski's devotion to the national cause encourages him to alienate Poles who assimilated into Siberian society but to polonize the daughter of a Cossack colonel, whom he pays the compliment of naming "a Polish woman in the full sense of the word." Zaleski also appreciates Shevchenko's transformation from a "Little Russian" with "great hatred for the Polish nobility" to an artist capable of sharing with Zaleski's brethren "the entirely beautiful, wistful, and poetic side of the Ruthenian people"; Shevchenko's poem dedicated to Zaleski, "In the Days when We were Cossacks," reveals that the fraternal admiration was mutual. Since both Bogusławski and Zaleski consciously preserve the memory of fallen comrades, the footnotes to their translations provide important information about the location of more prominent political exiles within the history of the Polish-Lithuanian deportations in addition to directing the reader to additional readings on nineteenth-century Siberia.

Staging Punishment in the Carceral Continuum: Beyond the Knout and the Lash

In his exposé of the Stalinist penal system, *Gulag Archipelago*, Aleksandr Solzhenitsyn traces its complex structure, expanding the length of the empire, from the locale of the accused's arrest and interrogation to the network of camps through which the inmate sentenced to the gulag could expect to rotate. Bogusławski's recollections attest that the foundations for this vast "carceral continuum" existed in the imperial period, before the expansion of the railroad, and were a means by which the tsar's government, through more gentle means, employed detention, interrogation, surveillance, corporal punishment, isolation, and deportation to suppress dissent within its borders.[19] Depictions of imprisonment in multiple prison fortresses with political and common offenders (including infamous lifers) as well as long treks while chained to others in the cold of a Siberian winter in the midst of a struggle to survive illness and hunger allow the reader to envision the state's intentional torment of convicts, beyond the mental

19 In his chapter on the "art of punishing," Foucault discusses gentle means of correction before he concludes with "the carceral" that identifies the replacement of defined frontiers between "confinement, judicial punishment and institutions of discipline" with a continuum (*Discipline and Punish*, 104–31; 297).

anguish of standing on the scaffold or the physical abuse by the knout, bludgeon, rod, and lash. Even Siberian robbers knew to employ the environment to their advantage when leaving their victims naked and tied to a tree for the insects to eat them.[20] Piotrowski's *Memoirs from a Stay in Siberia* and Bogusławski's *A Siberian Memoir* clarify that the threats to their wellbeing began at the moment of arrest, confinement, and interrogation—that is, before the commencement of the arduous journey to Siberia. Torture drove inmates to suicide, prolonged confinement in the dark prison citadels and casements destabilized inmates' minds, and interrogators looking to earn promotions and medals seized the property of those they tormented and "buried for life in the mines!" What they failed to confiscate, those on the lower rungs of the penal hierarchy such as Reimers, Diagelev, or Gromov would be sure to pilfer. Since the variations in punishment differed widely according to class, economic, and ethnic distinctions as well as degree of offense, each of the authors encounters a distinct impression of the extensive disciplinary system in the Russian Empire.

Being a recidivist offender, Bogusławski understood the empire's use of false release to entrap the unsuspecting, as in the case of Aleksander Grzegorzewski who was set free after lengthy incarceration in a citadel, then asked to write an explanation of his activities to exonerate himself, and finally surprised with a Siberian sentence. Zaleski identifies such duplicity as a defining characteristic of Russian society with its citizens bearing "two different countenances" —that is, one "formal external shell" and "the other domestic," or genuine. The empty formal etiquette requiring the illusion of fair judgment and the condemned's satisfaction with the verdict in this "court of a free people" disgust Bogusławski who maintains that the Commission of Inquiry always finds enough guilty ones to enrich its members sufficiently, thereby challenging Solzhenitsyn's assumption that there was a clear distinction between those sentenced to hard labor under the tsars and the inmates of the gulag in that Dostoevsky's convicts were conscious of their guilt and the Soviet prisoners were convinced of their innocence.[21] Of course, Solzhenitsyn writes with more assurance about categories of good and evil, especially in his juxtaposition of the persecution of virtue and triumph of vice, whereas Zaleski states forthrightly that "in the life of our exiles not everything was purely spiritual or immaculate." Piotrowski provides a more hagiographic portrait of exiles in the account of

---

20 Vrangel', *Vospominaniia o F. M. Dostoevskom*, 123.

21 Aleksandr Solzhenitsyn, *Arkhipelag GULAG* (St. Petersburg: Izdatel'stvo Azbuka, 2017), 859.

the flogging of Abbé Sierociński by casting his crime of treason as a humanitarian attempt to liberate those captive on Russia's steppes, by emphasizing the force of his soul, by endowing him with a martyr's death, by displaying his dignified comportment when faced with a death that exposed his skeleton of broken bones, and by vilifying those who informed on him.

Still, between arrest and arrival in Omsk, lies the carceral continuum in *A Siberian Memoir* with the Omsk stockade signifying simply the locale of the most severe maltreatment, embodied in the corporal punishment of Żochowski, who died in the prison, and in the abuse of Mirecki at the hands of the drunken Major Krivtsov. While Piotrowski sought out maps to orient himself within the Siberian expanse, Bogusławski, himself, provides an overview of the settlements, towns, fortresses, mines, and battalions of soldiers, which also serves to map out the location of political conspirators, thereby displaying the extensive Polish community in exile, some of whom never return. Along his journey, Bogusławski elaborates on "the moans of the tormented and beaten" disseminating along the citadel's corridors, the sensation of being enclosed in the "Satan's sheds" for transport, surviving the cholera epidemic in Tobolsk, being shackled to a rod alongside other convicts for the march through rural stations, and the hungry maggots awaiting the prisoners at the filthy transit houses. He implicates the nations of the world in this punitive system, since they all send "tribute to Siberia" in the form of prisoners who become "naked and become gaunt without bread" while other arrivals (presumably explorers and managers of the mines) pass through in carriages, "supplied with everything—sometimes, they even have big money." His depictions of the tensions between Siberian settlers and the prisoners who marched through their small towns distinguish his narrative from the remembrances of those traveling by conveyance through similar spaces—for example, the Petrashevtsy and even Piotrowski who, although he rode in shackles to Omsk in a *kibitka*, still includes a common recollection of generous donations of food, money, and hospitality offered by various locals.[22] Zaleski even finds "a certain type of pleasure" in the torturous ride for the convict coming "from a cramped prison in which he most often spent two or three years," because he "breathed fresh air and had the heavenly vault over his head."

Despite his varied encounters with overpriced spoiled food, superstitious Old Believers, and unwed mothers on the journey from Tobolsk, Bogusławski prefers marching through small Siberian towns to confinement with the predatory groups of social outcasts who greeted him in

---

22 A *kibitka* is a covered sleigh or wagon and was associated by this time with deportation to Siberia.

Ust-Kamenogorsk and Omsk. After having encountered on the road university students throwing insults at his *kibitka* and the rumor that "traveling Poles flung cholera out of their pockets in the streets," Bogusławski must have been prepared to face some abuse in the prison courtyard. Although he does not focus on the peasant convicts to the same extent as the Russian author of *The House of the Dead*, he nevertheless highlights their aggression with general references to the "continuous plan for murdering Vaska," the convicts' hands stained with blood, volleys of curse words that drove Bogusławski into delirium, and the violent mass of brigands accompanying that "heinous" creature, the "walking corpse" Gromov. He admits to their mutual animosity and then attributes it to the brigands' decision to do as they pleased once they donned the prison garb and to reject an appeal to dignity with the challenge: "And what, do you think that you're God?" Although he may not affirm the convicts' potential for moral improvement, Bogusławski does maintain that the Third Section and certain prisons (Tiumen or Sevastopol) breed petty villains like Aristov and Gromov who then initiate the unsuspecting in their vice-ridden world, so in response to Dostoevsky's regeneration, Bogusławski posits degeneration. Thus, *A Siberian Memoir* confirms that Nicholas I effectively provided an additional carceral torment for the Petrashevtsy and the Polish insurgents of the nobility by forcing them, following their survival of confinement in the damp thick walls of his casements, into crowds of resentful hardened criminals populating the transit prisons, roadside stations, and fortresses.

For Bogusławski, whose health, like Durov's, was ruined by a life of hard labor in Omsk, the issue of workload is more central to his remembrances than it is to others'. From the first time clearing snow in Ust-Kamenogorsk to brickmaking at a location removed from the Omsk fortress, Bogusławski's accounts reveal that he did not have the same physical stamina as his comrades, such as Mirecki who had to clean out the cesspool at night. The detailed description of the brickmaking process—cleaning the ovens, gathering the clay, kneading it, making the bricks, and then removing them—emphasizes the arduous process of forced labor, while his passing out in a wheelbarrow only to awake to a uniform soaked in blood indicates that no physical abuse of prisoners was necessary in order to drive them beyond their physical limitations. Vaska's presence at the work allocation ensured that the Poles did not receive light tasks but were put to work making bricks in 1850, as a result of which Bogusławski counsels youth to learn the trade of a shoemaker, locksmith, blacksmith, or carpenter, so that, should they find themselves in a prison fortress, they would be able to conserve their strength. Fortune favored Bogusławski with the arrival of a tradesman, the painter Bem, who took Bogusławski on as his assistant, thereby alleviating his workload so as to ensure his survival. The frequency with which the author discusses work detail in the fortresses allows the reader to understand not only the tensions within the prison related to selection of assignments but also their importance for protecting those whose health was compromised by long-term issues, like Dostoevsky, Durov, and Bogusławski.

The portraits of military abuse provided by both Bogusławski and Zaleski illustrate the spectrum of harsh discipline that pervaded Siberian society beyond the walls of prison fortresses. For instance, Bogusławski recalls that during his visit to Semipalatinsk—the remote town near the Chinese border where Dostoevsky served in the military following his imprisonment—the separation of the political prisoners was strictly enforced according to regulations, Cossacks sat under military judgment, and a noncom was beaten by his superior for insolence until the noncom was "all drenched with coagulated blood from the shoulder blades to the knees." All the same, his eyewitness description of the birching's physical effects on the body and the subsequent removal of the pieces of the twigs stuck on the beaten body suggest that this open display of corporal punishment was not a common occurrence. Zaleski's account of the highly regulated life of the Siberian line battalions with their disciplined drilling, formal external rigidity, savage corporal punishment, and the careerism of their ambitious officers imparts a sense of daily challenges facing conscripts in the tsar's army corps. This view from within the ranks recorded by one of the Polish exiles flooding the battalions in the Caucasus and Orenburg betrays an outsider's disgust for the "muzzled" military society defined by discipline, there understood as "unconditional obedience" to one's commander. This regulated life during which political exiles were constantly monitored (as a result of which they were transferred, demoted, or promoted) was another means of correction in imperial Russia that has been researched well by Vladimir Diakov in a series of studies on army battalions, on Shevchenko's relationship with Polish conspirators, and on Siberian circles of contact among conspirators of Russian, Ukrainian, Belarusian, and Polish ethnicities.[23] By comparison, Baron Vrangel's portrait of sharing Eldorado briefly with Dostoevsky in the 1850s appears as a self-censored account of their military experiences. Still, published more than fifty years later, these

23 See, for example, Diakov's studies: *Deiateli russkogo i pol'skogo osvoboditel'nogo dvizheniia v tsarskoi armii 1856–1865 godov: Biobibliograficheskii slovar'*. (Moscow: Nauka, 1967) *Taras Shevchenko i ego pol'skie druz'ia*. (Moscow: Izadatel'stvo "Nauka," 1964) and "Polscy zesłańcy w Syberii Zachodniej i północnym Kazachstanie (1830–1862)," in *Polacy w Kazachstanie: Historia i współczesność*, ed. Stanisław Ciesielski and Antoni Kuczyński (Wrocław: Wydawnictwo Uniwersytetu Wrocławskiego, 1996), 45–68.

reminiscences include some comment on Vrangel's own official duties (such as the torture of an Old Believer), references to Dostoevsky's Omsk period introduced by a visit from the bewitching gypsy Vanka-Tanka (or "Fire"), and Dostoevsky's recollections of fellow Petrashevtsy Durov, Pleshcheev, and Grigorev (*Pss*, 4:222).[24]

Strategies for Coping and Surviving

Zaleski, Bogusławski, and Dostoevsky admit that self-discipline remains crucial to bearing the abuse and torture of confinement and forced military service in addition to the cold and hunger—hardships defining the Siberian experience. Although Zaleski praises the Poles' superior understanding with their "highly developed soul" and "hardening of the will," Bogusławski reveals on a personal level that faith in God and Adam Mickiewicz's verse (reminding him to conceal his emotions and quietly plan for destruction) kept him from despair when faced with adversity. Dostoevsky finds that retreating into himself and feigning indifference to the peasant convicts' taunts allowed him to maintain a sense of decency. Unlike Dostoevsky, Zaleski and Bogusławski also write of the consolation received from the "camaraderie of fellow brothers," thereby highlighting significant Polish and Lithuanian presence in the battalions and prisons on whose company they could depend to alleviate the loneliness of exile, to receive news from home, to obtain a lighter work detail, or to improve their living situation. Zaleski's fond recollection of Zygmunt Sierakowski's donations of milk to their gatherings suggests the importance of such fellowship, and his depiction of Father Zielonka displays the potential for a single charismatic individual to impact the local community through a life of service. On a more limited scale, Dostoevsky's friendship with Baron Vrangel in Semipalatinsk fulfills a similar role, since he writes his older brother to look after this man with a tender character, confides in Vrangel about his courtship of his first wife, and travels with him to other towns in Western Siberia (*Pss*, 28.1:205, 190–91).

By the time that Bogusławski arrived in Omsk in October 1849, he had built a friendship through adversity with Tokarzewski and Żochowski with their shared marches and hard labor in the fortresses at Ust-Kamenogorsk

24 A. E. Vrangel', *Vospominaniia o F. M. Dostoevskom*, 28–29, 36, 68–69. This escape is described by Dostoevsky, Bogusławski, and Tokarzewski, the latter of which dates it to 1853 in his *Siedem lat katorgi: Pamiętniki Szymona Tokarzewskiego 1846–1857 r.*, 2nd ed. (Warsaw: Gebethner i Wolff, 1918), 217.

and Omsk. A common language, experience, and sense of humor aid Tokarzewski and Bogusławski in overcoming adversity, as is evident from the bold laughter that greets Tokarzewski's failed bread experiment in Bolotna or their refuge in heartfelt laughter at the lockup in Ochair that contrasts strikingly with his wry comment at the sight of Bogusławski's shaved head in Omsk: "your own mother [. . .] would thrice proclaim that you are not her son." The tribulations that these two deportees shared from Tobolsk through Omsk inform their common language infused at times with Bogusławski's ironic commentary on impossible situations or ridiculous authority figures like the drunken Major Krivtsov with his colorful abusive language and habit of forcing prisoners to sleep on their left sides like Christ.

Traveling and exploring the steppes and villages of Siberia provided some solace for these exiles, as well, since the vast expanses, although sparsely populated and sometimes barren, embodied liberty to those whose lives otherwise were spent at hard labor or military drills. Dostoevsky's admiration of God's country, or the open steppe as viewed from the bank of the river Irtysh during his years of labor, prefigures his gambler's preference for the nomad's "Kirgiz tent" and Rodion Raskolnikov's equating of the Kirgiz steppe with a life of freedom and the age of Abraham (*Pss*, 4:178; 5:301; 6:421).[25] Dostoevsky encouraged a geographer of the steppe, Chokan Valikhanov—to whom he refers as "the first of your tribe, who has attained a European education"—to disseminate a native knowledge of the Kirgiz near whose settlement Dostoevsky lived while in Semipalatinsk (*Pss*, 28.1:249). Zaleski's aforementioned volume of striking sketches and descriptions of the culture of the steppes, displays how he creatively applied his artistic talent to preserve for posterity visual and written impressions of peoples inhabiting Russia's vast expanses. In his introduction, he, "an involuntary witness to the life of the sons of the steppe," concludes that the nine years he spent viewing this space while walking and riding on horseback gave him the opportunity to sketch it, since "The hours when I had a pencil in my hand were my best hours, those of contemplation and of forgetting a more than poignant sorrow."[26]

The steppe also represented a temptation to those who felt that they could no longer bear the burden of captivity or forced labor, because it

---

25 Robin Feuer Miller connects the chapter "Summertime" in *House of the Dead* to this second epilogue in *Crime and Punishment* with reference to the freedom of the Kirgiz steppe in *Dostoevsky's Unfinished Journey* (New Haven, Conn.: Yale University Press, 2007), 42.

26 Bronislas Zaleski, *La vie des steppes kirghizes: Descriptions, récits & contes* (Paris: J. B. Vasseur, Libraire-Éditeur, 1865), 1.

encouraged deportees to believe that they could safely escape and conceal themselves in Russia's vast expanses. In *House of the Dead*, springtime is associated with the temptation of a Romanticized vagabondage, since "God's people run from the stockade and save themselves in the forest" where "at night they calmly conceal themselves somewhere in the forest or field, without any big care and without prison melancholy, like forest birds parting from the night with only the heavenly stars under God's eye" (*Pss*, 4:174). Although this sense of adventure is apparent as well in Piotrowski's narrative, in its references to the "immense steppes of Siberia" and Count de Benyovszki's successful escape, the penalty for failure is more elaborately displayed when the discovery of Father Sierociński's plan to flee through the Kirgiz steppe to India ends in the conspirators being flogged to death. Still, this only sets the stage for Piotrowski's successful flight across the Russian border, as he depicts in *Memoirs from a Stay in Siberia*, and also provides the reader with an understanding of the triumphant welcome that greeted Bakunin when he arrived in London after having fled Eastern Siberia. Zaleski also celebrates Count de Benyovszki's adventure but nevertheless includes the famous failed escape attempt by Wincenty Migurski and his wife from the Orenburg region.[27] Furthermore, the denunciation of Bogusławski, Żochowski, and Tokarzewski—that is, their being vulnerable to being implicated in corresponding with Paris and London in a plan to arm Kirgiz soldiers for an attack on the fortress—suggests that Russian military officers understood the danger of locating political exiles in a region with Circassians and Kirgiz, since all of these groups longed for freedom from Russian occupying forces.

Many prisoners and deported soldiers, however, chose a more quotidian escapism in literature, journals, and newspapers that could be collected over years as well as personal letters passing through friendly hands. Bogusławski recalls having taken books on the road with them from the fine library in Tobolsk left by a liberated Polish exile and relates the kindness of a generous woman in Ust-Kamenogorsk, who subscribed to a newspaper for the sake of the Polish inmates and allowed their loved ones to send their letters addressed to her.[28] Books circulated in Omsk, since Dostoevsky there read novels by Charles Dickens while Durov read novels by Alexander Dumas, *père* and Eugène Sue, and Bogusławski even reports a heated argument between himself and Dostoevsky about *The Wandering Jew* that

27 Both of these are recalled in Maksimov's *Sibir' i katorga* (3:74–79).

28 This is a footnote in the sixth installment of "Wspomnienia Sybiraka: Pamiętniki Józefa Bogusławskiego," *Nowa Reforma* 254 (1896): 1.

required Durov's mediation.[29] Upon his release from prison, Dostoevsky immediately asked his brother for a series of books—the Quran, Immanuel Kant's *Critique of Pure Reason*, and Friedrich Hegel's *History of Philosophy*—while Vrangel recollects that Dostoevsky read Pushkin aloud and notes that they were translating Hegel (*Pss*, 28.1:173).[30] Zaleski also recalls a small library in Orenburg having developed from a departed exile's collection that circulated among the Poles, which not only "often strengthened their spirits and even allowed them to educate themselves" but also impacted the knowledge of Polish literature in the local community. Zaleski even became a librarian in the Orenburg Public Library, where he worked on the library catalogue and made important acquisitions for their collection.[31] Zaleski's article provides a published writer's perspective on the intellectual life in Orenburg—its lectures, library, literary salon, and reading material—thereby confirming the active intellectual exchange in remote Siberian environs. Of course, the circulation of such materials, often with the help of the local civilians, built community among different ethnicities, especially those literate in more than one language. For example, the Russian poet and Petrashevets Pleshcheev translated the poetry of fellow exiles connected to Zaleski's Orenburg circle—Shevchenko and Żeligowski. Thus, readings and discussions influenced the manuscripts, notebooks, and diaries they kept, and sometimes concealed, since literary allusions made their way into the prose and poetry composed in exile and beyond.

Some Shared Ground

In attempting to assess how this collection contributes to scholars' knowledge of Dostoevsky's Siberia, it is necessary to consider the impact of genre that shapes the *House of the Dead*, as Jacques Catteau discusses in a summary of various readings of the novel: as "a documentary novel," "descriptive scenes of a Siberian prison," or "a series of sketches with psychological studies and inserted stories" owing to Russian literature of the 1850s and 1860s that includes several similar historico-literary examples—for instance, Ivan Turgenev's *A Hunter's Notes* or Leo Tolstoy's *Sevastopol Sketches*.[32]

---

29 Blake, *Dostoevsky and the Catholic Underground*, 37–38.

30 Vrangel', *Vospominaniia o F. M. Dostoevskom*, 33–34.

31 L. N. Bol'shakov, *Orenburgskaia Shevchenkovskaia entsiklopediia: Tiur'ma. Soldatchina. Ssylka. Entsiklopediia odinnadtsati let 1847–1858* (Orenburg: Pechatnyi dom "DIMUR," 1997), 136.

32 Jacques Catteau, "De la structure de la Maison des Morts de F. M. Dostoevskij," *Revue des études slaves* 54, no. 1–2 (1982): 64.

Exploring the common ground shared by the Polish remembrances and *House of the Dead* is complicated not only by form and language but also by the condition in which the remembrances were left, published, or read for posterity. The fragmented nature of Gorianchikov's exerpts "written in insanity" is never concealed from the reader, and the extent to which the novel reflects Dostoevsky's experience in his first two years in the fortress suggests that there exists in the author's mind no intent to provide a holistic portrait of his incarceration (*Pss*, 4:8). This period remains the focus of the Omsk segment in Bogusławski's manuscript as well, presumably because he passes away before completing it and before most of it appeared in print, either selectively in the chapter "Imprisonment and exile of the year 1848" of the historian Eustachy Heleniusz Iwanowski's *Remembrances of Polish Times, Long Ago and More Recent* (1894), or in installments in *New Reform* in 1896. Bogusławski's fellow inmate, Tokarzewski, is thought not only to have edited the published account but also to have drawn on them for his own more widely circulated *Seven Years of Hard Labor* (1907), which primarily focuses on the same period of imprisonment as Bogusławski's text and includes references to *House of the Dead*.[33] Presenting a similar period but in fictional form, Dostoevsky not only protects himself from the censor but also employs artistic license to create and shape his impressions of the fortress under the guise of Gorianchikov's memoirs. Still, writing and editing the novel in St. Petersburg in the midst of formerly exiled writers in the early 1860s and reading them to the public alongside Shevchenko, Dostoevsky knew that he could depend upon his readership to associate the novel with his own term of hard labor (*katorga*) in Siberia.[34]

Piotrowski, Bogusławski, and Tokarzewski rely on movement through geographic space to organize their narratives; for instance, *A Siberian Memoir*, after briefly connecting Bogusławski to the famous Szymon Konarski circle with his first arrest, subsequently traces the conspirator's journey after his second arrest from Vilnius to Omsk. His discussion of imprisonment and

---

33 For a summary of competing theories regarding Tokarzewski's impact on Bogusławski's published "Recollections of a Siberian Exile" and Bogusławski's presence in *Seven Years*, see Śliwowska (*UzS*, 350–53).

34 Joseph Frank, *Dostoevsky: The Stir of Liberation, 1860–1865* (Princeton University Press, 1986); V. Anisov and Ė. Sereda, *Litopys zhyttia i tvorchosti T. H. Shevshenka* (Kiev: Derzhavne vyd-vo khudozh. lit-ry, 1959), 347; it is worth noting that the Russian State Archive of Literature and Art has in its catalogue an 1857 letter written by Shevchenko in Novopetrovsk in the envelope of Dostoevsky's wife: T. G. Shevchenko, pis′mo k F. P. Tolstomu, grafu. 1 konvert A. G. Dostoevskoi. Fond 212, opis′ 1, ed. khr. 279.

the Commission of Inquiry particularly allows his recollections to stand out from those of Zaleski, Dostoevsky, and Vrangel who concentrate more on a single locale. Bogusławski perspicaciously analyzes systemic abuses of authority and so understands that the members of such commissions benefit professionally and financially from incarcerating those defending freedom and, therefore, *pro forma* fulfill their obligations to the state. Dostoevsky's novel, on the other hand, traps the reader within the prison world and employs temporal phrases to mark progression through the narrative in a way likened to "circles of hell."[35] In other words, aside from the introduction explaining the discovery of the ex-convict narrator's papers in a small town in the remote edges of free Siberia where merchants flourish, champagne flows, and the caviar is excellent, the reader remains in the prison world created by the deceased narrator Gorianchikov and contained in a manuscript of prison notes "somewhere" entitled, "Scenes from the House of the Dead" (*Pss*, 4:8). References to champagne, watermelon, forest berries, nuts, dried pineapple, honey brought from Orenburg, and apricots and raisins from Bukhara or Kokan in Vrangel's memoirs suggest that Dostoevsky draws on their Eldorado in Semipalatinsk for this image of abundance in this Siberian town.[36] Yet, as Catteau remarks, having entered Gorianchikov's prison world in the first part of the novel, the reader progresses through only a month of time in its eleven chapters with the chronology of the second part being only vaguely marked by various references to Easter, springtime, the first summer, the arrival of new Polish prisoners, Mirecky's release, and Gorianchikov's liberation.[37] Since Dostoevsky arrived in the camp at the Omsk fortress in January 1850, his first Christmas spent in the prison is the same one described by Bogusławski (although the dates of the Catholic and Orthodox celebrations differ) when the Poles have arranged to celebrate in their new quarters shared with Isai, the Circassians, and the Karbadians.

Dostoevsky's discussion of the Polish prisoners does not reflect the timeframe of his Omsk period, especially since the most prominent personage of Mirecki leaves less than two years after Dostoevsky's arrival. Also, the four Poles—Anczykowski, Bem, Korczyński, and Musiałowicz—treated as late arrivals in *House of the Dead* serve more time with Dostoevsky than Mirecki, since they serve at least two or three years of Dostoevsky's four-year prison term.[38] Their minor roles in the three extant remembrances of

35 Catteau, "De la structure de la Maison des Morts," 66.

36 Vrangel', *Vospominaniia o F. M. Dostoevskom*, 43, 49–50, 101.

37 Catteau, "De la structure de la Maison des Morts," 66.

38 N. F. Budanova and G. M. Fridlender, eds., *Letopis' zhizni i tvorchestva F. M. Dostoevskogo v trekh tomakh 1821–1881,* 3 vols. (St. Petersburg: Gumanitarnoe agentstvo "Akademicheskii proekt," 1995), 1:184, 187.

Omsk suggest that they did not share many experiences significant for the authors' recollections (especially since at least Bem shared work assignments with Tokarzewski and Bogusławski) rather than their absence from the prison itself. Although the timeline of *House of the Dead* does not correspond to Dostoevsky's prison experience, he does provide a sense that Major Krivtsov was removed and judged for his abusive behavior in the winter of 1852, whereas Bogusławski never shows this progression of time in his discussion of the hardships in Omsk even though he is not released until July 1855.[39] Perhaps because Dostoevsky reaches his narrator's departure from the prison world, he can show the improvement of his character's lot that mirrors his own experience. For instance, in a parallel to Gorianchikov, who has friends among the soldiers serving in town providing him with money and reading material, Dostoevsky receives money from Evgeny Iakushkin in the winter of 1853, chats with him about literature, and gives Iakushkin a letter to deliver to his brother Mikhail (*Pss*, 4:229).[40] The portion of *A Siberian Memoir* taking place in Omsk, however, seems to favor not dynamic movement through time but more physiological sketches (frequently associated in fiction with the Natural School of the 1840s), like those of fellow Polish exiles, Prince Gorchakov (and the Omsk affair), Commandant de Grave's wife Anna Andreevna, Major Krivtsov, Dostoevsky, Durov, Aristov, and Gromov. All the same, the pages on Omsk in *A Siberian Memoir* share common scenes with *House of the Dead*, such as the convicts' food protest, the beating of Żochowski (predating Dostoevsky's arrival in Omsk), and the attempted escape of Aristov, Kotlar, and Kuleshov—an event dated after the replacement of Major Krivtsov and related to Gorianchikov by a Polish inmate. Zaleski's "Polish Exiles in Orenburg," like Dostoevsky's novel, does not attempt to develop a clear chronology of the author's many years in exile but instead Zaleski provides a broad overview of the region's deportees and refers sporadically to famous exiles such as Shevchenko, the Petrashevtsy, and Migurski in discussions of the hazards of military life that they shared with Dostoevsky, which lie beyond the scope of his novel focused on peasant convicts.

The recollections of these former political prisoners to some extent similarly assess the administrators residing in Omsk with Governor Gorchakov being more intimidating and distant while de Grave is kind, displays empathy at Piotrowski's loss of freedom, and is considered by Dostoevsky to be "a very decent man" (*Pss*, 4:213; 28.1:169). Furthermore, Dostoevsky shares Bogusławski's and Tokarzewski's admiration for Anna de Grave, calling

39 Ibid., 1:189.

40 Ibid., 1:190; Frank, *Dostoevsky: The Stir of Liberation*, 84.

her his "good acquaintance" as well as a "noble and intelligent woman," and visits the de Graves when he passes through Omsk on his return from Siberia (*Pss*, 28.1:284). Bogusławski provides greater detail about Anna Andreevna whose kind and charitable nature coupled with her power over men enabled her to alleviate some hardships of the Polish prisoners, whom she joyfully greeted in the prison and generously fed in her own home. Tokarzewski especially remembers her charity and her hospitality when the prisoners were painting the home of the de Graves.[41] For Bogusławski, she is a good example of the extent to which the prominent social set in Omsk could harm or help the *unfortunates* (as the Siberians called prisoners), as the political exiles in Siberia understood well. Of course, in a more general fashion, the victimization of the less fortunate by petty tyrants are portrayed in Vrangel's memoirs as well and inform Dostoevsky's Siberian novel, *The Village of Stepanchikovo and Its Inhabitants*.

Common Language

The divide between Russian and other Slavic identities in Siberia inevitably appears on the linguistic level of the texts with cursing and insults recorded in Russian, in Polish transliteration, or in Polish and French translations. Frequently, the Polish exiles were able to overcome the language barrier with Russian soldiers and inmates, and Bogusławski, especially, had experience with Russian from his first term of exile, when sentenced to civil service in Tambov, so his unpublished manuscript contains quotes in Russian when relaying the direct speech of various native speakers in Siberia, Russian proverbs, and local measurements. All the same, at crucial moments language presents an obstacle to cross-cultural communication, such as in the case of Żochowski's outburst or the Cossacks' discussion of the defeat of Hungary—with both instances resulting in harsh measures for the political offenders. Despite the mixture of languages (Russian, Polish, and French) in the texts, there exists evidence of a common experience of exile in the Russian Empire that extends beyond the generic forms characteristic of prison or exile literature—for example, images of liberty or the organizing motif of homeland—that suggests the authors, often indirectly, address common political, philosophical, and theological issues like situatedness of suppressed minority populations in the empire, capital punishment, the parameters of self-determination, the privilege of martyrdom,

41 Tokarzewski, *Siedem lat katorgi*, 184–86.

the temptation of depravity, and the civilizing potential of volition. For instance, Bogusławski admits that he passed his time in Tobolsk pursuing the reason "why a man born a man will become an animal further in life"—an interest he shared with Dostoevsky—but Bogusławski also cautiously draws the unpopular conclusion that capital punishment may be more humane than the torments inflicted by some carceral systems.

In the Polish-Lithuanian memoirs, concepts common to multiple authors' experiences of Siberia can receive a more cynical treatment than they do in Dostoevsky's novel. For example, both Dostoevsky and Bogusławski conceive of *changes of place*—that event regularly occurring in a convoy when a naive prisoner agrees in exchange for payment to take the place of a prisoner assigned to a harsher sentence—in different manners. Whereas in *House of the Dead* this might subject a prisoner to ridicule (*Pss*, 4:59), in *A Siberian Memoir* it allows hardened lifers to con the unsuspecting so that those choosing to remain nameless—thus, "Forgetful Ivans," "Nameless Ivans," and "Fatherless Ivans" can be found in every convoy.[42] In addition, a similar language of incarceration functions disparately in the narratives of Dostoevsky and Bogusławski, so the offensive appellation of "vagabond" (a reference to a category of Siberian prisoners) that Krivtsov hurls at Żochowski becomes Dostoevsky's image of a convict with the potential of a Robinson Crusoe, who, seduced by the promise of adventure, is born to wander and, hence, quits the confines of the prison or settlement (*Pss*, 4:174). Moreover, while the environs—the bright sun over the frozen expanse, the prison courtyard, the flowing Irtysh, and the Russian steppe—can spark the natural ebullience of the political exiles stifled by the pungent air in the barracks, the natural setting also invokes Bogusławski's comparison of their march to the Israelites' wanderings, but without the hope of the promised land (since only captivity awaits them), and therefore stands in bitter contrast to Dostoevsky's aforementioned depiction of the Kirgiz steppe as a modern representation of the age of Abraham.

Indeed, Dostoevsky, Zaleski, and Bogusławski even have unique ways of combining life and death imagery to name this hell to which they had been condemned. The deceased Gorianchikov has conveniently entitled his convict's notes "Scenes from the House of the Dead," so the first chapter coopts the title "House of the Dead" from which Dostoevsky's prison receives its appellation—a combination of death and domesticity (*Pss*, 4:8). Of course,

42 Zaleski finds the transit prisons particularly dangerous, as well, since murderers, knowing their sentences cannot be extended for yet another kill, will commit the same crime again in order to remain at a prison while an investigation is conducted so that they can execute a plan arranged beforehand.

the 150 convicts—primarily peasants—housed here are not dead like those in Nikolai Gogol's *Dead Souls*, however much Dostoevsky depends upon its dark humor to impact the reading of his portrayal of living in this Siberian prison.[43] Likely, he hoped that his readership would recognize the despair of those abandoned and forgotten by friends so well articulated by a prisoner in a novel he read while in the fortress—*The Posthumous Papers of the Pickwick Club*: "If I lay dead at the bottom of the deepest mine in the world, tight screwed down and soldered in my coffin, rotting in the dark and filthy ditch that drags its slime along beneath the foundations of this prison, I could not be more forgotten or unheeded than I am here. I am a dead man—dead to society, without the pity they bestow on those whose souls have passed to judgment."[44] Dostoevsky's famous letter to the Decembrist's wife, Natalia Fonvizina, refers to a similar resentful sorrow when describing the "past grief" that overwhelms the exile upon the return to his homeland: "It is similar to scales, on which you will weigh and learn the real weight of all that you suffered, endured, lost and that which good people took from us" (*Pss*, 28.1:176). The phrase "House of the Dead" therefore expresses the famous author's fears of being forgotten and socially ostracized by his former circle of friends. Zaleski's and Bogusławski's epithets, on the other hand, underscore the hostility of their surroundings, since Bogusławski's "grave of the living" and Zaleski's "living grave" emphasize that the prisoners live in edifices designed to be their final resting places, thereby highlighting the malevolence of certain Russian guards, soldiers, and officials. It also reminds the reader that although Polish graves are scattered throughout Siberia and along the Orenburg line, these exiles constitute a living presence in the country's memory and can come back from the grave with the help of testimonies like Agaton Giller's *Polish Graves in Irkutsk* (1864).

In addition, the exiles espouse a political theology, more overt in some texts than others, that allow them to appeal to a Christian God who will not forget those in abandoned Siberian graves, those whom Zaleski counts in the thousands and likens to saints or martyrs in the Early Christian tradition. Zaleski's and Piotrowski's discussions of the persecution, even torture, of priests further demonstrates the exiles' attachment to the religious as a protected group and the way in which empathy for their plight was shared by believers across many faiths. Gatherings for mass, fellowship, and holiday celebrations included in Bogusławski's remembrances show how his faith impacts how he marks time (with references to Christmas and Good

43 Catteau, "De la structure de la Maison des Morts," 64.

44 Charles Dickens, *The Pickwick Papers* (Oxford: Oxford University Press, 1986), 532.

Friday), establishes friendships, and develops his resilience in hostile environments. Even though Bogusławski situates their Siberian trials within the Old Testament exilic tradition, as an observant Catholic he discloses a more personal faith shaped by the Enlightenment when equating God not only with salvific compassion but with the empowering gift of human volition that serves as a shield against despair in times of adversity that shatter deeply held convictions. This evidently conflicted with Dostoevsky's support for the tsar as God's representative and for Russia in her holy war in the Crimea, especially since in his Siberian poem, "On the European Events in the Year 1854," the triumph of the two-headed eagle in Constantinople is to continue Russia's expansions thereby supporting a renaissance in the East at the expense of the Catholic West's defense of the Turks and Muhammad. Bogusławski's arguments with the Russian novelist over the status of lands in the Russian Empire as well as their opposing viewpoints on the war are part of a national discussion, to which the more liberal Pleshcheev also contributes his own poem "After Reading the Newspapers," concluding that despite his love for his homeland, there is no room in his soul to stoke the flames of hatred for other tribes nor to rejoice over national victories on blood-soaked battlefields.

Also, transcending the linguistic divide are the writers' horror at scandalous murders committed by infamous criminals, intriguing fascinations with the physical processes of torture, and strong desires for escaping the strictly regulated life of the prison or military and for freeing oneself from shackles. The authors of all these texts believe that they represented a civilizing force in the area because of the dissolute life of the peasant convicts, the lack of moral foundation among youth, and capricious military authorities. The young men enjoyed the attention of prominent local women, the novelty of encountering the multiethnic groups populating Siberian prisons and villages, and even exploring remote regions. However, none of these deportees, like many others before them, was forced to make his home in these regions, so all of them resisted integration into the greater community, especially since they did not marry local women. Although the courtship of his first wife occupied much of Dostoevsky's leisure time in Semipalatinsk, such a pursuit would be controversial in the Polish-Lithuanian exile community, as is evident from Bogusławski's comments about his comrades in Tara, which equate their marriages to Siberian women with forever abandoning their national cause and its native sons. Yet, their lack of connection to their assigned geographic spaces of exile allowed them the freedom to return home when they received their amnesty—an event that provided them with a better opportunity to preserve and circulate accounts of what they had witnessed in notes, letters, and manuscripts, which were published in a number of European cities or maintained in private collections by co-conspirators and loved ones.

The narratives of this generation of *unfortunates* from the western edge of the empire, popularly understood to be victims of its corrupt judiciary, can contribute to cultural knowledge about famous Russian deportees such as the Decembrists and the Petrashevtsy with whom the circles of exiles represented here interacted. As a result of either shared experience or common language, Polish and Russian authors impact each others' semantics, concerns, and artistic expression, so Bogusławski's "mare" (or plank to which the victims of the knout) provides context for Raskolnikov's dreamt childhood in which a drunken peasant Mikolka lashes and beats a mare in the presence of an imagined but inconsolable child-Raskolnikov. Since the inscription on the plank around Bogusławski's neck was the word malefactor or *zloumyshlennik* (an appellation shared by the Petrashevtsy), the second sentence of *Notes from Underground*—"I am a spiteful man [*Ia zloi chelovek*]"—may be seen as the malcontented anti-hero's mockery of that category of prisoner so feared by the Third Section (*Pss*, 5:99). Zaleski's anecdote about Nicholas I's adoption of the Fourierian concept of the phalanstery for his battalions governed by force suggests an additional motivation for the Underground Man's hatred of the Crystal Palace. In other words, this collection is intended not only to provide the reader with a greater understanding of the Siberian experience for the inter-revolutionary generation but also to enrich the reader's encounter with Dostoevsky's post-confinement writings.

A Siberian Memoir about the Dead House

A Few Words on Józef Bogusławski

As a representation of this generation coming to age in the middle of the nineteenth century, Józef Bogusławski's lasting witness to the lives and deaths of Poles in captivity, preserved in his unfinished manuscript, *A Siberian Memoir*, was so fascinating to his contemporaries that his fellow inmate, Tokarzewski, and a prominent historian of the period Eustachy Iwanowski borrowed from it. One of the Enthusiasts (Emilja Gosselin)— that famous Warsaw group of women who helped Citadel prisoners and returning Siberian exiles—has a note in its published version, "Recollections of a Siberian Exile: Memoirs of Józef Bogusławski," in the Krakow journal, *New Reform*.[1] Because of his connections to two famous subversive groups in Vilnius within the same decade and owing to his shared exile with Tokarzewski—arrested for his collusion with the famous charismatic conspirator, Father Piotr Ściegienny—Bogusławski had extensive knowledge about a number of prominent agitators in the Congress Kingdom before 1863 when he was writing or editing his text. All the same, political analysis does not overwhelm his narrative but discernibly impacts certain traumatic episodes such as experiences with the Commissions of Inquiry, being transported from the Warsaw citadel to Modlin, encounters with inmates numbering approximately 11,000 in the large prison in Tobolsk, their maltreatment by prison soldiers and officials in the Omsk fortress, and his arguments with Dostoevsky.[2] As an author, Bogusławski wants his reader to enjoy the characters he meets, to be intrigued

1 "Wspomnienia Sybiraka," 256:1. A more detailed publication history is available in Blake's "Traumatic Mobility," 247–53.

2 In *Vospominaniia o F. M. Dostoevskom*, Vrangel provides a depiction of the prison, including its wide variety of incarcerated people who thoroughly shock this impressionable youth (108–16); this is also the prison in which Dostoevsky first became acquainted with "convicted persons" who are by nature "coarse, irritable, and embittered" (*Pss*, 28.1:159).

by the twists of fate that guide this precarious journey, to be horrified by the commonplace violence in the prisons, and to feel empathy for those who do not live to see their homeland again. Since he writes after having returned from Siberia, his story is one of survival through forbearance of physical and psychological torment, but he does not dwell on injustices as elaborately as some of his compatriots. By including information about Mirecki's ability upon his arrival home to forgive the one who informed on him and about Tokarzewski's current profession in Warsaw, Bogusławski emphasizes their potential to overcome Siberian hardships as attested by their successful return to a beloved homeland. In short, Bogusławski consciously presents this manuscript as testament to a national history about the turbulent past that provides a sense of the human cost of the forced Russification of the Congress Kingdom, but, all the same, as an author he provides an entertaining reading of intriguing individuals, Russian cultural customs, Siberian (and Old Believer) traditions, his natural surroundings, and the prison world.

Biography

Józef Bogusławski was a nobleman from the Congress Kingdom of Poland who was first arrested in connection with a clandestine student group in Vilnius with ties to Dorpat University and Karol Hildebrandt, who through his contact with Franciszek Sawicz was linked with the infamous Szymon Konarski (executed in 1839 in Vilnius) and the Polish exiles of the Great Emigration in Paris. Konarski had helped form the Association of the Polish People, dedicated to brotherhood and freedom, and Sawicz along with Jan Zahorski supported a large cell of Konarski conspirators at the Medical-Surgical Academy in Vilnius.[3] Among the group of conspirators arrested as part of Hildebrandt's circle were Bogusławski, Bronisław Zaleski, and Edward Żeligowski; Bogusławski probably had several acquaintances among the more than dozen who were arrested or fled, especially since Konarski's complete network numbered at least one thousand.[4] In *A Siberian Memoir*, he writes that after his arrest he was not only imprisoned but beaten, for which

3 Although Vilnius University had been closed, the Medical division, renamed in 1832 as the Academy of Medicine, continued to operate under Nicholas I's efforts to "*dicatholiser*" and "*dipolaiser*" Lithuania, as is discussed in Wiesław Caban and Ryszard Matura, eds., *Bronisława Zaleskiego i Kajetana Cieszkowskiego nieznane relacje o powstaniu styczniowym* (Kielce: Wydawnictwo Wyższej Szkoły Pedagogicznej im. Jana Kochanowskiego, 1997), 17.

4 Witold Łukaszewicz, *Szymon Konarski (1808–1839)* (Warsaw: Książka, 1948), 132–33, 173; Caban and Matura, eds., *Bronisława Zaleskiego i Kajetana Cieszkowskiego nieznane relacje*, 27.

he blames Vice Governor Aleksei Trubetskoi, but it was Aleksandr Kavelin, the general adjutant from St. Petersburg, who in a report to the War Ministry wanted Bogusławski punished harshly.[5] After having been in Tambov for a few years, Bogusławski returned home in 1845 to his parents and sister.[6]

However, by the summer of 1846 he was sitting in a Vilnius jail cell with Zaleski and Doctor Anicety Renier for their contact with emissary Jan Röhr, who had asked a fellow acquaintance (Apollin Hofmeister) for an introduction to Bogusławski and Augustin Suzin (later sentenced to the Orenburg Corps).[7] Röhr not only confided to Bogusławski plans for an armed insurrection in Poznan, which the latter repeated to others, but Bogusławski also used his own horses to help Röhr attempt to flee across the border.[8] The military historian Vasilii Ratch's notes on Röhr's conspiracy provide a description of his activities in Vilnius, including Röhr's having disclosed his plans to Doctor Renier and Bronisław Zaleski and having convinced Hofmeister and Bogusławski that they had the resources to form an army.[9] Bogusławski received a harsher sentence than most of the others—ten years of hard labor in a fortress—likely because, as noted in his case file, he concealed his activities for a long time and was reluctant to admit Röhr's intentions.[10] Since the health of his prison mate Zaleski suffered during these years of incarceration and since Zaleski referred to "poor" Józef in his letters while in exile, Bogusławski's health had likely already been affected by the lengthy imprisonment in Vilnius so that by the time that he arrived in Omsk, he had earned the nickname "the sick one."[11] In Vilnius he was placed on the scaffold along with Hofmeister and Renier in 1848 and was dispatch from Tobolsk in the summer of that year to Ust-Kamenogorsk on foot in a group of convicts. He arrived in Ust-Kamenogorsk by fall of 1848 and spent about a year in this fortress before being sent to Omsk. He was released into the settlement in the Tobolsk

5 Kaveliny. Fond 947, opis' 1, delo 7, k. 63.

6 O litsakh, sostoiashchikh pod nadzorom politsii v Tobol'skoi Gubernii, 1855, Departament politsii ispolnitel'noi MVD. Fond 1286, opis' 16, delo 387, chast' 1/I, k. 411. Rossiiskii gosudarstvennyi istoricheskii arkhiv.

7 Śliwowska, *ZpIR*, 586.

8 V. F. Ratch, Fond 629, opis' 188, f. 43, 47.

9 Ibid., f. 42.

10 Ibid., f. 45.

11 Wiesław Caban, *Z Orenburga do Paryża: Bronisław Zaleski 1820–1880* (Kielce: Wydawnictwo Akademii Świętokrzyskiej, 2006), 38. Dostoevsky briefly describes his weakened condition in the first pages of the chapter "Comrades": "B-ki was sick, somewhat inclined to be a consumptive, irritable, and highly strung" (*my translation*; *Pss*, 4:209).

region in 1855 and returned to his homeland after the 1856 amnesty with ruined health, so he went for treatment to Carlsbad, where he worked on *A Siberian Memoir*. The introduction to his published memoirs has him dying in 1857, although Siberian deportee and historian Agaton Giller records that he died in 1859.[12]

Bogusławski the Author

Perhaps because Bogusławski was ill, even dying, while he was working on the manuscript, he admits the limitations of his recollections. He has forgotten much and can record only what he remembers from his own experiences and from the adventures of others he met on the road, in prisons, and in the towns. For instance, attesting to Zaleski's observations about storytelling in the Siberian prisons, Bogusławski regrets that the "beautiful memoirs" shared in Tobolsk—a main gathering point for fellow political prisoners—were not written down at the time, especially since Bogusławski claims that little of them remain in his memory even as he recollects unforgettable details. At other times, such as on the approach to Tomsk, Bogusławski vividly depicts the appearance and sound of the convicts in chains, "extremely badly and strangely clad," clattering, cursing, laughing, and blustering as they run, trying to keep warm in the bitter frost by the banks of the river Tom. His often impressionistic style allows the reader to become almost a fellow traveler on the deportees' journey—such as when they are being transported from the Warsaw Citadel to Modlin, and he depicts not only the chains, locks, and bolts that held them in a moving cage, but the shaft of light falling through the polluted window and the frightened faces and hands of men and women awakened by the tremendous rumbling of "Satan's sheds" winding through the city streets. He is even expansively eloquent when conveying a sense of the prison filth in Ust-Kamenogorsk as he recalls a foul-smelling hut, with "fumes of sweat, rot, and grease" and with a floor strewn with straw trampled into manure, in which were housed the "outcasts of society" with their glowing eyes and mocking smiles. In such passages, his tendency toward censorious imagery in depicting Russians conveys to the reader his disdain for many strata of

12 Bogusławski, "Wspomnienia Sybiraka," 249:1; Agaton Giller, "Lista wygnańców Polskich do roku 1860. Spisana przez Agatona Gillera na Syberyi," in *Album Muzeum Narodowego w Rapperswyll*, ed. Władysław Plater (Poznan: Nakładem J. K. Żupańskiego, 1872), 388; Śliwowska, *ZpIR*, 69.

Russian society, but Bogusławski here also uses such opportunities to advocate for his own values without overtly insisting on his moral superiority.

Bogusławski provides portraits of outrageous behaviors by the convicts with blood on their hands, by the informer Aristov, and by those involved with discovering and punishing those connected to the Omsk affair. His sensitivities are particularly shocked by Russian sexual mores—young unwed mothers with children, the debauchery of the syphilitic Gromov, and the licentiousness of the cadet corps. Moreover, it is clear from his assessment of Natalia Stefanovna, the wife of Krzyżanowski, that he expected from women an intellectual education as well as charitable kindness and generosity, which he discovers in the daughter of a Cossack Colonel Elizaveta Evgrafovna. He clearly has little respect for Siberians with their habit of price gouging and beliefs in omens and enchantments, so he finds the women especially trying—from the priest's daughter who seeks healing for her father from women folk healers and the "medicine man" Shelagin to the Old Believer who believes that she was ruined by his tobacco smoke. To some extent, this animosity is linked to his failure to tolerate a popular faith that infused Christianity with local legends and traditions, even though he supports the Old Believers' desire to maintain a religious community independent of the Russian Orthodox Church. Still, his attitude toward Isai Bemstein, that "superstitious Talmudist" who performed an *amusing* "ear-piercing" Sabbath ritual reflects an intolerant essentialism (yet less intense than that displayed in Dostoevsky's depiction of Isai's ceremony), but Bogusławski values Bemstein's learnedness more than the convicts who beat him, so for Bemstein's own survival he is included in the group of comrades who share the separate quarters enjoyed by the Poles, Kabardians, and Circassians. Although Bogusławski greatly appreciates his friends, the brave and forceful Circassians, who protected the Christmas feast, in their shared barrack Circassians along with the Kabardians (both not individually named in the sketch) were located in the two rows of bunks in middle of the room with Bemstein while the Poles occupied one row of bunks along the wall (and are named in the sketch in the following order: Żochowski, Bem, Anczykowski, Korczyński, Mirecki, Tokarzewski, Musiałowicz, and Bogusławski).

Thus, repeatedly in his narrative Bogusławski displays his noble privilege and shows that he holds his own compatriots in higher esteem than other ethnic and religious groups, even as he paternalistically characterizes Bemstein and the Circassians. For this reason, while acknowledging his imperfect comprehension of Russian, Bogusławski nevertheless perceives Cossacks as a group harassing the Polish political prisoners on the way to

Omsk and peasant convicts as a mass of brigands—an abusive type like the *Moskali*, but not individuated, so that the curses and "volley of abuse" hurled at him in the courtyard have no originating source. His personal disgust at their past crimes and their ethical system, characterized by a belief that a sentence of penal servitude exonerates the criminal from the crime, resembles the disbelief of Piotrowski and Zaleski upon the discovery of Russian convicts' ability to kill innocents in cold blood. Therefore, Gorianchikov's assessment that Polish political prisoners avoided Russian convicts and saw them as brutes without any redeeming human qualities seems an accurate assessment of Bogusławski's behavior (*Pss*, 4:210).[13] At the same time, Bogusławski responds to Dostoevsky's typing of Poles in *House of the Dead* with his own portrait of the villainous Russian nobleman Aristov, who landed himself in prison because he falsely relayed the discovery of a hotbed of political conspiracy to the highest ranking members of the Third Section, Count Aleksey Orlov and General Leontii Dubelt. Ridiculing the Russian nobility and a Third Section purported to be always seeking to discover the next major conspiracy, Bogusławski enjoys that Russia's chief investigators overlooked, and even financed, the spy in their midst. Aristov also stands out in Bogusławski's narrative owing to the rare appearance in Omsk of a prisoner from the Russian nobility, aside from the writers Durov and Dostoevsky, and so he can be established as representative of a class. For this reason, in Bogusławski's understanding Aristov was an informant by nature (like Major Gusev and possibly Dostoevsky), knew like other *Moskali* how to flatter his superiors in order to advance himself, and was so protected by his nobility that the executioner could not bring himself to insult his "noble skin" when Aristov was caught counterfeiting and preparing to escape. Such depictions demonstrate that like Dostoevsky, Bogusławski prioritized those who shared his ethnicity even while attempting to provide an accurate portrayal of Siberian and prison cultures.

Some Comparative Comments on the Manuscript of *A Siberian Memoir*

The manuscript *A Siberian Memoir*, donated by Iwanowski to Jagiellonian University Library in 1898, is obviously a clean copy of the original and is handwritten in black ink on lined paper in a hardcover medium brown

13 Even though Mirecki was Gorianchikov's interlocutor frequently in the novel, Mirecki left the prison more than two years before the conclusion of Dostoevsky's four years in the fortress.

notebook. Although for the most part it follows the published version, "Recollections of a Siberian Exile," the manuscript's lack of divisions in the text—few sentence breaks and paragraph divisions and no chapter delineations or titles—results in a continuous narrative that fills almost every page of the notebook. The parts omitted in the published version include some of the author's most scathing criticisms of Russian prison transports, sexual abuse, and venereal disease in the military, the exploitation of soldiers by illiterate newly commissioned officers, the convicts' mass harassment in Omsk, and Vaska's maltreatment of (and regrets over) Żochowski. Unlike "Recollections of a Siberian Exile," which contains attributions to two writers and is prefaced by several paragraphs describing its editing process, *A Siberian Memoir* does not openly maintain that it was edited by a secondary author.[14]

Except for the few pages on his first arrest, Bogusławski focuses his narrative on the account of his second exile, starting with his arrest and imprisonment in Vilnius, but he is also present as a remembering self when relating his own location in Carlsbad and when providing biographical information, often parenthetically, about the current situation of his

14 The first installment of "Recollections of a Siberian Exile" in the 1896 *New Reform* (*Nowa Reforma*) is prefaced with the following under the heading "An Introductory Word" (249:1):

> The author of the memoirs heretofore never published in print, Józef Bogusławski, is known from the history of Polish martyrology. Already in the year 1838, after his graduation in Dorpat, J. Bogusławski was sent for the Konarski affair to Tambov, where he remained until 1845. However, hardly had he returned to his nation, when already a year later, in the year 1846, he was imprisoned again, and in the year 1848 was exiled from Vilnius to forced labor in Siberia, together with Apollin Hofmeister and [Jan] Röhr, who in addition were sentenced to 1000 bludgeonings.
>
> The memoir, which we have before us, includes for the most part the period of Bogusławski's sojourn in Siberia. Images piercing with terror, an entire hell of suffering and torment, the unfortunate prisoner of the state admirably jotted down with commendable presence of mind and with an acquaintance with the human soul and relations governing the Russian society of those times. Bogusławski also traced the silhouettes of many prominent people, with whom he met in Siberia—which confers not a little historical value on these memoirs. Bogusławski's way of writing, his essential clarity of presentation, and his talent will engage the broadest sphere of readers, and for this reason we prepared his memoirs for publication.
>
> In the year 1855 Bogusławski returned to his nation, from where for the recuperation of his health he went to Carlsbad, where he also began to write his memoirs. On his return, he died, so it seems, in 1857 in Częstochowa. The Siberian Józef Tokarzewski copied and supplemented his memoirs. The present memoirs are a reprint of Tokarzewski's manuscript. Eustachy Heleniusz also recalls these memoirs in his work entitled *Remembrances of Polish Times* (II, pg. 108).

fellow Siberian exiles—that is, that they have died, fallen ill, or returned. Vacillating in the narrative between his Siberian sojourn and the period since his return, Bogusławski casually switches time frames, contextualizing the Siberian past with subsequent biographical details (deaths, illnesses, relocations, or professional advancements). Bogusławski's disclosures frequently allude to important biographical information that impacts historians' understanding of the interaction among groups of exiles following their return home. For instance, the fact that Bogusławski passed through Warsaw after his return where he encountered Officer Valichnovski, as is casually related in the midst of a remembrance of the Citadel transport, is an early indication that the author returns to a location where many former Siberians (including the prolific writers Tokarzewski and Giller) gathered to discuss plans of the future 1863 uprising and where Emilja Gosselin resided.[15] A further link to Gosselin lies in the reference to the "kind-hearted" comrade Bogusławski met in Tomsk, Ksawery Stobnicki, whose letter was found among Tokarzewski's possessions while they were in Ust-Kamenogorsk. Bogusławski then discloses that Stobnicki, after having left his wife and daughter in a Siberian grave, returned to Warsaw where he presently lies in a hospital (with no reference to his death in 1861 in the home of Gosselin). Moreover, the fact that Bogusławski's fellow Siberian baker, Aleksandr Grzegorzewski, died before the completion of the manuscript indicates that it is composed after his death in 1855. Such details situate the writing of this version of the text in a period that must follow Bogusławski's return to Poland in 1857 but do not include any biographical information that extends beyond Stobnicki's illness (1859–61) and certainly does not include references to the fate of those exiled again (Tokarzewski) or hanged (Józef Toczyski) for their participation in the 1863 uprising.[16]

This time frame excluding the fate of the conspirators of 1863 differentiates his manuscript from many of the Siberian remembrances that are shaped frequently by the deaths, imprisonments, or exiles of comrades connected to the 1863 uprising. Even Dostoevsky's writings in 1862–63, including *House of the Dead*'s portraits of Poles in the chapter "Comrades," reflect Russian writers' concerns over the growing unrest in Warsaw in the early 1860s, which is only briefly alluded to in "Recollections of a Siberian Exile," because

15 Śliwowska, *ZpIR*, 574. The name of Emilja Gosselin is linked to both Tokarzewski and Bogusławski, as discussed in Blake's "Traumatic Mobility," 252; Tokarzewski, *Siedem lat katorgi*, 8; Bogusławski, "Wspomnienia Sybiraka," 249:1.

16 If Bogusławski is the only author of the text, then he did not die in 1857 as his introduction to "Recollections of a Siberian Exile" states (249:1), but he could have died as Giller records in 1859, en route from Carlsbad to Częstochowa.

a massacre on Castle Square occurred on the day of Stobnicki's burial.[17] For this reason, in Bogusławski's personal reflections on Poland's native sons who survived their Siberian sentences, there exists a sense of optimism that the Congress Kingdom will not again experience to the same degree the trials and torments associated with those who died as a result of their dedication to the national cause or who still suffer from the physical scars of captivity. All the same, Bogusławski conveys to the reader the precarious situation in which those Polish nationalists, living under Nicholas I, frequently found themselves, by placing the abbreviation for a deceased Christian, *śp.* (meaning *świętej pamięci* or "dearly departed"), before their names. This serves as a reminder that those conspirators executed by the state, such as Konarski and Potocki, nevertheless have a sacred memory in the Christian tradition, and Bogusławski underscores this fact when recalling that the miller who informed on Potocki was told by a seminarian, subsequently sent to Siberia, that for this deed, the devils would bake him in the hell fires for eternity. In other recollections of the mortality of friends, as in the Ust-Kamenogorsk section, Bogusławski simply highlights the tragedy of those who died before their time such as Feliks Fijałkowski, whose death not only tears away at their circle of friends and but also reminds his comrades of their own fragility. The righteous Elizaveta, who perishes after Bogusławski's departure, also earns a place of respect in his narrative with the description of her body being escorted by prisoners to her eternal resting place.

Thus, Bogusławski includes accounts witnessed by others in his own remembrances of Siberia, and could even be drawing on published information for the current whereabouts of returning exiles, so *A Siberian Memoir* in some respects is limited neither to Siberia nor to his own memory. He focuses more on those who speak his native tongue, even in the depths of Russia, because he, like Zaleski, insists that his narrative is one that belongs to the annals of Polish history, including multiple generations of Poles who settled in Siberia, some of whom, in choosing to assimilate, lose their Polishness in his understanding. Whether by choice, language, or circumstance, Bogusławski appears, based on their narratives, more isolated from the Russian prisoners than the authors of *House of the Dead* or *Seven Years of Hard Labor*, owing to the Poles' separate barrack, an undisguised desire to remain apart from murderous convicts, and a growing hatred of his military captors, which influences his rapport with the leading author in the Omsk fortress, who comes to pity Bogusławski for his resentment borne of suffering (*Pss*, 4:209). At the beginning of his narrative, Bogusławski

17 Bogusławski, "Wspomnienia Sybiraka," 254:1.

infuses his recollections with more camaraderie and even humor, such as when he relates the nicknaming of the lieutenant colonel Zhuchkovsky after Morok, the animal tamer in Eugène Sue's novel *The Wandering Jew*—a literary reference employed but not appreciated by Tokarzewski in *Seven Years*.[18] By the end of his unfinished manuscript, however, Bogusławski remains more embittered, less because of the convicts' maltreatment and more because of the moral depravity he witnessed, especially at all levels of the military establishment. On the other hand, Tokarzewski's *Seven Years* contains more frequent inclusion of dialogue, diminutives, patriotic effusions, and hyperbolic expressions, thereby reflecting a nationalism more characteristic of a post-1863 world, likely owing to Tokarzewski's return a second time to Siberia (1864–82/83).[19] Therefore, *Seven Years* does not display the temporal links to the late 1850s present in *A Siberian Memoir*, but more consciously engages *House of the Dead* with selections from Dostoevsky's novel—including the more intolerant sections on the Poles from "Comrades" appearing in January 1863—in footnotes to the chapters taking place in Omsk, which frequently center on people in the fortress, for example, "Arrival in Omsk—Vaska," "Fedko," "The Schismatic," "Fedor Dostoevsky," and "The Relations of Poles with the Residents of Omsk."

Bogusławski's manuscript favors narrative description over dialogue, which reflects not only his habit of self-imposed isolation but also his separation as an author, owing to his treatment in Carlsbad soon after the amnesty, from a community of Siberian exiles, from which Tokarzewski and Dostoevsky benefited following their returns in Warsaw and St. Petersburg, respectively. This Siberian camaraderie remains a period removed from the present of the remembering self of the author, and, due to the unfinished nature of the manuscript, the author does not provide a closing frame to contextualize the remembrance but leaves the reader suspended in Omsk, whereas the narrator of *House of the Dead* is liberated and progresses to a Siberian settlement. Biographers of Dostoevsky can discern that parts from *House of the Dead* were written before his return and were informed by his *Siberian Notebook* (also known as *My Convict's Notebook*)—a collection of direct quotations of convicts' speech recorded in Omsk (likely 1852–53) and quotations written in Semipalatinsk.[20] Bogusławski refers a few times

18 Tokarzewski, *Siedem lat katorgi*, 34.

19 Ibid., 231; Tokarzewski alludes to his late editing of the manuscript, in his note in the conclusion of the second edition (1918) of *Seven Years*, which mentions that the author supplemented his Siberian manuscript with "specifics" recalled after 1882.

20 F. M. Dostoevskii, *Moia tetradka katorzhnaia (Sibirskaia tetrad')*, ed. V. P. Vladimirtsev and T. I. Ornatskaia (Krasnoiarsk: Krasnoiarskoe knizhnoe izdatel'stvo, 1985), 38–46.

to a correspondent as though he is pulling some of his recollections from letters he wrote while in Siberia, a habit that Vrangel more openly follows by including passages from dated letters in his remembrances. For example, Bogusławski's consciousness of fading memories is expressed at times not only through his allusions to his limitations as an author but also to his failure to immediately record events, such as on the approach to Omsk when he writes: "How I feel at this time that I should have written you!" Even more explicit is a passage following the depiction of the Omsk affair when he writes that he "tore off a little dried wormwood" from the common grave of the executed and "attached it for you to this letter." Bogusławski, thus, understands that he contributes only a single chapter to a national story, which he expects will be completed not only by the writings of his own comrades, especially Tomaszek and Teresa Bułhakowie, but by successive generations.

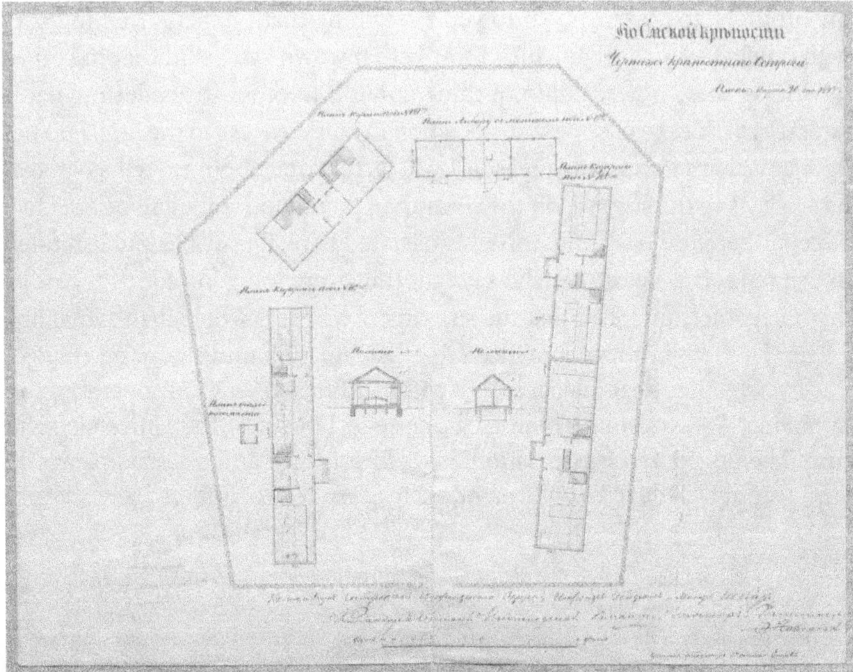

Fig. 1. The Omsk Fortress: Sketch of the Fortress Stockade (March 20, 1847) *Above Left*, Kitchen; *Above Right*, Storehouse with Icehouse; *Far Left*, Latrine; *Left and Right Middle*, Barracks

A Siberian Memoir of Józef Bogusławski[1]

Arrest and Deportation[2]

For several weeks I have been staying in Carlsbad; I have been staying here to fortify my health weakened by long suffering.[3] However, I am convinced that everything is in vain; one has to pass away. With this it follows that I want, my brothers, to make known to you everything that I experienced together with others as well as that which I saw with my own eyes. While sitting down to writing these notes, I did not think about it in order to render my name famous, in order to occupy some position in literature. As to the first, I do not have any claim and for this reason I will lecture you about myself as little as possible; as to the second, on the contrary, I do not feel myself to be talented. Accept, therefore I ask you, the facts narrated here; if possible, publish them in printed form. Let those who say that things are too good for us today, let them become convinced that the stroking of a bear is worse than scratching a tiger; let them become convinced that our situation underwent no change.

When the dear departed Szymon Konarski started operating in Lithuania, I was a young man at the time in Dorpat at the University, and since I belonged to the association, I was imprisoned and beaten; in a word I went through all degrees of torment, such as Trubetskoi inflicted on us.[4] After

1 This is a complete translation of: *Sybirski pamiętnik Józefa Bogusławskiego*, 1898. Rkps. 5912, III. Biblioteka Jagiellońska.

2 These divisions I have introduced to the manuscript, since it is a continuous manuscript with relatively few paragraph markers and no titled sections.

3 Carlsbad is a resort town located in Bohemia and known for its spas, where Bogusławski presumably went for his failing health after his return from Siberia.

4 This is a reference to the vice governor of Vilnius, Aleksei Trubetskoi, known for his cruel treatment of prisoners, who was the chairman of the Commission of Inquiry when Zaleski and Bogusławski were arrested.

all, this is not a new thing; so many people have already written about this, and many having returned today from exile certainly will write or also will leave notes, which only the succeeding generation will be able to supplement. So, I will pass over in silence the entire Vilniusian matter (I call it Vilniusian, because this old castle-town of Gediminas[5] was witness to a bloody drama played out at that time); I will pass over in silence about all that. I will tell you only that after the execution of the dear departed Konarski I was taken away to Tambov, handed over to the strict surveillance of the governor there, and afterwards was made use of by the civil service.[6] In Tambov I stayed until the year 1846 and toward spring only with the efforts of my father did I return to the district of Brześć to relax under the familial thatched roof. I did not think, riding from Tambov, that my stay in Lithuania would be so short, that new torments awaited me, and that I would once more for a long time have to be moved away, but that is what happened after all!

Scarcely had I welcomed the year 1846 when once again on March 14 I rode to Vilnius under a strong escort of gendarmes. You know without a doubt, what was the matter; ask about the details of Jan Rhör, whom you united with us.[7] In Vilnius I sat around until the year '48 under military judgment; together with Apollin Hofmeister and Doctor Renier I was placed on the scaffold in the pillory, but previously had been taken in a triumphal cart all around the streets of the city with a black board on my breast, on which one could read the inscription "malefactor."[8] From the pillory, dressed in a drab overcoat, with two red laths on my shoulders, I sat down in the *kibitka* and set off wandering to Siberia to penal servitude for 10 years.[9] In a dozen or so days

---

5 Gediminas was a fourteenth-century Lithuanian Grand Prince (c. 1275–1341) who consolidated the state into a regional power with the absorption of lands from Ukraine and Belarus (Daniel Stone, *The Polish-Lithuanian State, 1386–1795* [Seattle: University of Washington Press, 2001], 3).

6 Tambov, a city 260 miles southeast of Moscow, was a place of political exile for many Poles suspected of clandestine activities in the nineteenth century.

7 Jan Rhör (Röhr) was an emissary sent to Lithuania by Ludwik Mierosławski to prepare for an uprising in Poznan.

8 Agaton Giller's *Opisanie zabajkalskiej krainy w Syberyi* (Leipzig: F. A. Brockhaus, 1867) describes this same scene: "Jan Roehr [Rhör] was beaten with truncheons in the arsenal; other patriots—Józef Bogusławski, Apollin Hofmeister, Anicety Renier—were hauled around Vilnius in the wagon of delinquents, and afterwards on the scaffold their nobility was taken away, and the sentence was read" (2:77). Giller and Bogusławski use an alternative spelling to Apollin, but the names in the translation will adopt the standard spellings in Śliwowska's *Zesłancy polscy w Imperium Rosyjskim w pierwszej połowie XIX wieku*.

9 A *kibitka* is a closed carriage with only slits for windows, which was used to transport prisoners.

I greeted Tobolsk. Apollin Hofmeister set out to Orsk on the Orenburg line.[10] In a few weeks arrived Rhör, who was given 1000 bludgeons in Vilnius and who was sent afterwards to the mines in Nerchinsk for 12 years. Rhör did not amuse himself for long in Tobolsk; he left with a party for the road further, and I myself remained alone, awaiting what would happen to me. In May from Warsaw they brought Żochowski,[11] a professor who, like I, had been sentenced to 10 years of labor, and afterwards at the beginning of July [they brought] Dominik Chodakowski[12] (he died at the Ust-Kamenogorsk fortress[13]), Józef Toczyski[14] (currently in Warsaw in the position of bookkeeper in the trade service), Adolf Gruszecki,[15] Hippolit Raciborski[16] (both today with the good Prince Zygmunt Radziwiłł in Nieborów), and Aleksander Czerwiński[17] (he lives now in the countryside near Demblin). On the fourth day after the arrival of these five, more arrived—the following four: Szymon Tokarzewski (currently he is a shoemaker in Warsaw), Cyriak Accord[18] (he

---

10 V. F. Ratch. Fond 629, opis' 188, f. 40. Orsk, situated on the river Or (a tributary of the Ural River) was the location of a fort along the Orenburg line, where the famous artist Shevchenko spent part of his exile with the Petrashevets Aleksandr Khanykov (D'iakov, *Taras Shevchenko i ego polskie druz'ia*, 44).

11 The elderly and pious Józef Żochowski was a writer, editor, and librarian who was arrested for a public speech given in Warsaw in support of Polish insurgents (Śliwowska, *ZpIR*, 727–28); for a more detailed history see Blake, *Dostoevsky and the Catholic Underground*, 29–30.

12 Chodakowski is listed in Agaton Giller's "Lista wygnańców Polskich do roku 1860," because he was arrested in 1846, sat in the Warsaw citadel for two years, and was in the fortress at Modlin for 1.5 months (390–91).

13 This city, in present-day northeastern Kazakhstan, is described in Charles Herbert Cottrell's *Recollections of Siberia: In the Years 1840 and 1841* (London: John W. Parker, West Strand, 1842) as a small town that "lies in the valley three versts from the Ulba" with the fortress being "surrounded on one side by the Altai mountains" (186).

14 Toczyski was arrested in 1846 for participation in a secret organization and was sentenced to ten years of hard labor in Ust-Kamenogorsk (Śliwowska, *ZpIR*, 628–29).

15 Gruszecki was arrested in 1846 for participation in Stefan Dobrycz's conspiracy and sentenced to ten years hard labor at Ust-Kamenogorsk (Ibid., 197).

16 Tokarzewski's testimony, published in Djakow et al., ed., *Rewolucyjna konspiracja w Królestwie Polskim*, clarifies that Hippolit Raciborski introduced him to a book from Paris about the Association of Mutual Assistance, from which he understood that Raciborski was connected to Father Ściegienny (713). Raciborski was sentenced to hard labor in the mines of Eastern Siberia (Śliwowska, *ZpIR*, 491–92).

17 Czerwiński was also arrested in connection with Stefan Dobrycz's conspiracy in 1846 and was sentenced to hard labor, a term he spent in Ust-Kamenogorsk (Ibid., 117).

18 Accord had contact with the Towarzystwo Demokratyczne Polskie and helped organize a conspiracy for which he was sentenced to eight years to be spent in Ust-Kamenogorsk (Ibid., 31); his famous relative and author, Jakób Gieysztor, mentions Tokarzewski in his memoirs of the 1860s (Blake, *Dostoevsky and the Catholic Underground*, 238).

lives somewhere in Augustowski), August Karasiński[19] (in the countryside near Demblin), and Michał Korzeniowski[20] (he went back on his return to Irkutsk).[21] All of these four, not being members of the nobility, were punished with bludgeoning in Modlin, which I will mention a little later. They then brought Józef and Karol Rudnicki (the first a year after his arrival was released, and he returned from Krasnoyarsk where he had been in the settlement); about the second I have not heard to where he returned.[22] Later arrived Aleksander Grzegorzewski, sentenced to the mines for 18 years; he was in an iron factory under the name of Petrovska beyond Irkutsk, where he got confusion of the senses, then returned to Warsaw, and died.[23]

So then during July of '48 we were gathered in Tobolsk from 14 different directions.[24] The reacquaintance with comrades was very fast, and the commonality of suffering eliminated any secrets; we recounted to each other our mutual adventures to which I could certainly contribute whether in Vilnius or in Warsaw everything went according to the same procedure. The Commission of Inquiry, as in one place so in the other, was composed of base people, betrayers;

---

19 Bogusławski may have known Karasiński well from Ust-Kamenogorsk, where he was serving a sentence in the convict ranks for participation in an uprising (Śliwowska, *ZpIR*, 259–60).

20 Korzeniowski was arrested for contact with Accord and the intent to participate in an uprising, so in 1848 he was sentenced to hard labor, which he served in Ust-Kamenogorsk (Ibid., 288).

21 These eight prisoners were in Modlin together as of June 22, 1848, when a report was filed by its commandant (Polevoi Auditoriat deistvuiushchei 1oi armii s 1842 po 1856. Fond 16233, opis' 3, delo 2666. RGVIA).

22 Krasnoyarsk, one of the oldest and largest cities in Siberia, was a location of Polish exile to where at least a dozen of those on Giller's list were sentenced to be conscripted or to live in the settlement, where several of them died.

23 In a footnote in the original manuscript is the following explanation:
Brought to the Citadel with the Krakow affair, Grzegorzewski sat there almost a year, when he was released for lack of evidence. However, he had to remain in Warsaw and to respond at the ready, if the Commission of Inquiry were to summon him. In a few weeks General Storozhenko called him and asked very politely for him to give some explanation for the affair to which he belonged, since the Commission of Inquiry does not want to punish innocent people and needs to be well informed. Grzegorzewski, so caught up in the name of justice, answers in writing to the questions given to him and explains away the doubts of the most respected court. When they had extracted from him what they needed, they again took him to the Citadel, handed him over to be court-martialed, and took him away to Siberia. By then, Grzegorzewski already had the beginnings of insanity.

24 Tobolsk, in Western Siberia, enjoyed an international reputation in the nineteenth century for its famous prison fortress with legendary offenders as well as for being the point of departure from which common prisoners and political deportees were dispatched throughout Siberia.

it would be difficult for me to put down for you a precise description of these nefarious scoundrels. Nevertheless, I tell you do not look for honor, faith, conscience, noble-mindedness, heart, and soul in them; do not look for anything that is said to be innate to every human being, because your search will be in vain. Their hearts are those overgrown with the hair of a chrysalis, and their soul is the ruble. All thought, all reason of this group of scoundrels strove toward this single and main goal—how most frequently to discover the innocent (although only seemingly) and by this, to the farthest extent possible, maintain their position, since big money flowed there, and it rained crosses, ranks, medals, and awards. It was the wellspring of their base and ignoble gains. Every decent person must involuntarily recoil at the sight of these faces on whose forehead in immense letters, one can almost see branded the inscription "Villain." After all, such people were decisive for our fate, since to them was given every power, which they knew how to make use of and take advantage, and today each is a master of extensive domains, extorted from those who joined the defense of freedom and humanity and had to wandered about the world, or who also died for people and were buried for life in the mines! Everything, brothers of mine, happened identically—whether it was in Vilnius or in Warsaw.

Having chatted away with new colleagues, I learned about them, how they were judged by those who played this comedy with us. I will never forget how one of those new arrivals told me about the court-martial proceeding: "When I entered the hall," he said, "I found a large table, covered with a green cloth, along both sides of which were seated officers of various ranks; they looked like painted figurines, and their presence was necessary only for the formal etiquette instituted by order of the tsar. The chairman of the court, the General Commandant of the fortress, was there; however, the assessor plays the main role here.[25] He asks the questions; he devises the articles, or the imperial edicts, and the tsar's decisions, from which is composed the Russian law. Next, he writes the verdict and at that time the members of this supposed court attest to it with their signatures. Usually they ask the prisoner, who has been brought in, the question: 'What is your name?' Then they announce to him that by the order of the Prince Viceroy he is handed over to the court-martial; next they point out to him the members, and they ask if the defendant doesn't have an accusation against them. Finally, they inquire if he, himself, or also an attorney will be defending his case. It would appear that they want to judge fairly, that this is not a despotic court, but the court of a free people; meanwhile it is only

25 After the word "fortress" in the manuscript, the reference to the following footnote is noted: "Simowicz fell out of a carriage on Zakroczymska street [a major Warsaw street leading to the citadel] and was killed on the spot." In the version printed in *Nowa Reforma*, this "postscript" is attributed to Emilja Gosselin.

empty formal etiquette—throw out even one of the members, they will devise immediately a second similar to the ejected moron, and, demand an attorney, they will order you to choose one from a member of the court; in a word, all the legal formalities are fulfilled to the utmost. After all this, they still give you your testimony before the reading, they ask if you don't have something to add or to change, and finally they read, for example, the following contents: 'to deprive him of all rights and every possession, to lead him twice through the running of the gauntlet with 1,000 people, and to send him out to hard labor in Siberia for 10 years.'" Such was the content of the verdict of the newly acquainted colleague. Finally, they asked him if he were satisfied with the verdict. This was also a formality—as if the one sentenced were free according to such a verdict to appeal somewhere else! To such a question everyone agrees; it can only arouse a loud laugh in the one sentenced, and this was precisely the case with my new colleague who did not really like judges in general, in particular the chairman of the court. The latter ordered him to be decent in the presence of the tsar, hanging on the wall (that is his portrait, of course).

Also fine is the means of transport for the prisoners of the Citadel in Warsaw to Modlin; in Vilnius we did not have similar apparatuses. At the end of March in the year '48 the Citadel was emptied out completely; some ended their lives, some were transported to Siberia, some were hurried off to the Caucasus or the Orenburg line, and so a great number was emptied out. The Commission of Inquiry did not have anything more to do and so began to work on the population of the Citadel anew; the pretenses for this will never run dry, especially if someone has the same intention as the respected Lejchte, who always simply used to say that all are guilty; "I will seize any old one on the street, and he will be guilty!" So on Good Friday in 1848 in the evening, suddenly they transported at least 15, later in the night a second similar party, and still a third in the morning. Again the Commission works all day and night, again only the moans of the tormented and beaten disseminate along the corridors; then they began to bring in even more, and in the end they ran short of place for the newcomers and decided to transport some of them to Modlin. Then on April 28, around 9 in the evening on double watch in the prison courtyard stood two so-called "Satan's sheds."[26] They are rather large coaches divided into two halves by a wide

26 In the published version in *Nowa Reforma*, the following paragraph is inserted at this point:

> These are those wagons similar to the American invention, used in Pennsylvania to transport criminals with the goal of protecting them from the disgrace and mockery of the crowd, as well as not barring them from the road to rehabilitation. By us, it was used for another goal—for the deprivation of political prisoners of their sole and final consolation: commiseration and public sympathy.

corridor and along both sides are up to six small cages, in which it is only possible to sit; a small quantity of light falls into each guard house through a polluted little window in the form of a saucer from a teacup. Each of the prisoners, chained in short chains—but of the prescribed weight, occupied one of these guard houses to which Officer Valichnovski led him with a flashlight in hand.[27] I met him in Warsaw after my return; nature exerted itself in the marking of this scoundrel—his saurian eye, droopy lips, cheeks half overgrown with grey hair, and his monstrously long neck do not make a pleasant impression on every person. After the introduction to such a cell, the doors were closed with two sliding bolts and a lock, and when all six cells were already occupied, at that time an iron bar was stretched along all the doors, each individually screwed with the help of a key for each individual nut.

In this way on April 28, 1848 two wagons were stuffed with political prisoners—there were 24—because there were as many cells. It was already beginning to dawn, still some whispers were heard, and some emitted commands so that evidently everything whatsoever taking place outside was happening with haste. There was a great resemblance in everything to a gang of thieves, who left for the night prey, were late for whatever, and want recompense for lost time so as to escape the place where the crime was committed while it was still dark so that the light of daybreak did not illumine their base activities. There was a great resemblance in everything, however, as the most adroit thief does not always manage to escape unobserved; so, too, the guards of our 24 brothers did not manage to leave the Citadel, to pass through the side streets of Warsaw so that nobody saw them. Already the extraordinary rumble woke the residents of Zakroczymska street, and everyone saw the ramparts through the checkered pattern of the invigorating air at the top, where windows were locked on the higher storeys of some houses, from whence looked out the frightened faces of women in their nightcaps, men in their nightcaps, and even children, awakened

---

27 At the bottom of this page of the manuscript is a line, beneath which is found the following note:

> Members of the Commission of Inquiry almost all made a fortune. One of the squealers or scribblers from this Commission—Blumenfeld—built a brick house in Warsaw worth 200,000 złoty. Citizens, e.g., in the Krakow affair, transported to the Citadel, were for the most part well-to-do people; they took everything with them that they had in cash, thinking that they would be transported away immediately to Siberia. The Commission of Inquiry took the money from those brought over and judged; those condemned to confiscation could not even claim their property—in any case, it would come to nothing, because Mr. Official himself judged the case of Mr. Official, and so the Commission of Inquiry stole the money, and the gendarmes stole the food sent by the city for the prisoners.

from their sleep and in tears on account of it. Men and women extended their hands downwards and in this manner either pointed out or said farewell—it was difficult to make out, since it was not possible to hear.

For each of those being transported, the question came to mind—"Where next are they taking us?"—a question, which it was difficult to answer before they arrived at the first station, where they changed post horses and gave breakfast to the prisoners. At that time, inside of the large doors were these very little doors through which each one, having poked out his head, could see his sympathetic companion. After breakfast, they screwed the doors again and moved further down the road. Before us was Modlin, where, having arrived at about 10 in the morning, everyone was conducted to a lower casemate, where for the first time everyone came to know a plank bed and a faint outline of some of all that awaited us in the future. When everyone had gathered downstairs, a long warm greeting followed. Each person was more cheerful, and each person was glad to get rid of the sight of Morok (thus they called the gendarme Zhuchkovsky, since he dealt with the prisoners like Morok the tamer of wild animals in *The Wandering Jew*) and was glad that he found himself in the company of people living the same faith, the same convictions. It would be difficult to recount everything that happened there after such a connection to everyone in the same circle! A couple days later after the first transport approached a second composed of 22 all of whose names are Aleksander Grzegorzewski, Jacek Kochanowski, Michał Podgórski, Ksiądz Dominik Jasiński, Józef Leszczyński,[28] Józef Toczyski, Karol Rudnicki, Wiktor Domaradzki, Cyriak Accord, Dominik Chodakowski (died in the fortress of Ust-Kamienogorsk), Szymon Tokarzewski, Adolf Gruszecki, August Karasiński, Władysław Modrezejowski, Henryk Raciborski, Hipolit Raciborski, Jan Mikułowski, Ignacy Kostrzycki, Jan Mikoszewski, Konstanty Filipowski, Aleksander Grzybowski, Florijan Butwiłło, Aleksander Czerwiński, Michał Korzeniowski, Ksiądz Woroniec (73 years old), Franciszek Kamiński (died in Modlin), Ludwik Mazaraki, Aloizy Wenda, Feliks Jordan, Julian Jordan, Jan König, Józef Kośmiński, Władysław Kowalski, Ksiądz Tomasz Włodek, Józef Rudnicki, Władysław Pągowski, Benedykt Kosiewicz, Konstanty Brzosko, Szymon Czaplicki, Aleksander Raczyński, Stanisław Dudkiewicz, Mieczysław Zarębski, Jan Sobierański, Karol Mieczkowski, Ignacy Sobolewski, and Marcin Zientkiewicz.[29]

---

28 Tokarzewski marries Leszczyński's daughter, Halina, who edited his *Seven Years*, as the 1918 edition informs the reader; Tokarzewski's account identifies Leszczyński as his comrade from the Modlin citadel and discusses an incident from their shared imprisonment (231; 35–37).

29 This list resembles the one included in [Eustachy Iwanowski], *Wspomnienia polskich czasów dawnych i późniejszych*, 2 vols. (Lwów: w komisie księgarni Gubrynowicza i Schmidta, 1894), 2:109–10, and in Tokarzewski's *Siedem lat katorgi* (47–48).

Onward to Tobolsk

I came to know many of those above, since half arrived at Tobolsk and each of them narrated his adventures, which, if it had been possible to write them down, would have been beautiful memoirs, but in Tobolsk in the prison it was not appealing to think about this, and a while later in Omsk even less so, and today little remains in my memory. However, I have already begun recounting them without interruption, until I recount for you everything that only I remember. From my journey through Russia, I took away nothing. It was fast as lightning; it is true sometimes that seeing Babruysk, Berezina, Krasne, Mozhaysk, and Smolensk, the past, burdened with events, comes to mind. You withdraw to those turbulent years, in which we only just lived and whose events and history—written and recounted through collaboration—are preserved for us. In these recollections, there was no order, since there was no time for observations; everywhere contact was more significant—to make one see, saying in the words of the poet, statues that are cast, standing "like a haystack."[30] On the sixth day after the departure from Vilnius, I was already in Moscow, in that second capital of the Russian tsar. At that time cholera almost decimated the residents; hence the streets were empty and only the funeral processions went one after another. I counted about 60 going from the tollgate to the Kremlin, and around them extremely few people were gathered, since everyone out of fear was shut up at home. In a word, Moscow seemed somehow sad to me; I was not amazed either by its magnitude nor the beauty of its edifices, and for that reason I did not take away with me either recollections or impressions, such as I usually experience upon seeing something for the first time in life! From the Kremlin, I reached the office of the Main Administration, where having stayed for a couple of hours, I got two new gendarmes and headed farther down the road. Having departed at night, I was able to see even less of the city, which on my return, did not make such a bad appearance. In Nizhny Novgorod I found more similarities to our cities, more life, or rather more buzz and urban movement; it was before the bazaar, which has such fame throughout all Russia.

The two beautiful rivers Oka and Volga unite with each other here, and both of them were congested with ships on whose masts waved a multitude of elegant flags. The situation of the city, one may say, was rather beautiful.

30 This is part of a description of a church located in a region near the capital in Adam Mickiewicz's *Forefathers' Eve*.

The governor of Nizhny Novgorod seemed to me a rather decent man, he conversed with me for a long time, and in manner he was polite, sometimes to the point of affectation; he invited me to lunch and did not fear the anger of the tsar, since he dared to sit next to me, attired in the clothes of an arrestee. Kazan, the capital of some khanate of that name and not too spacious a city, has a university whose students, passing my *kibitka*, greeted me with an insulting word. Kazan also has a factory of knouts and whips—that foundation of that lever of state administration. In Perm, I already found some fellow countrymen: Henryk Woliński as a soldier, Dr. Jaroszewicz deported from Vilnius into the settlement, Skowroński—a clerk in the Building Commission, and some others.[31] I was received very hospitably and sincerely; I was entertained here, too, as in Kazan at all hours, after which I headed for Tobolsk. The capital of the province, built on the banks of the Irtysh, takes pride in its monument on display to Yermak, the conqueror of Siberia. Although I survived here for rather a long time, I could see nothing after all besides the walls of the prison in which I was immediately locked after arrival. Cholera struck Tobolsk; it was so very strong that up to 70 people died daily. The rumor that the Poles brought cholera disseminated like lightening throughout the city; there were even those who maintained that they saw with their own eyes how traveling Poles flung cholera out of their pockets in the streets. Next, they sent a delegation to the governor with the request that he condescend to have mercy on the people and that he order those Poles sent further sooner so that they did not kill people.

I do not know what would have happened with us, if we had not been locked in the prison; certainly, nobody caught sight of us. Sometimes similar incidents took place, and usually in those catastrophes Poles first fell under the knife of murderers. Similar scenes recurred in not just one place; people were incited to murder the innocent, whereupon judgments followed. The rich paid and were freed; the poorer, on the other hand, received the rod and the knout and rushed along on foot to penal servitude for many years. In Tobolsk in a short period of time fourteen of us were gathered. We would carry out the journey farther on foot, and from there onward also would pass from one extreme to another. There the *kibitka* like a swallow flew from place to place; here again we would strive like the sons of Isaak for the promised land! No doubt you have a mind to know, my brothers, how he made do for such a long time in Tobolsk? I examined crimes, which

31 Perm was a location to which political offenders were exiled; Petr Kropotkin provides the following description of the city: "the city is large, not bad-looking, and there are very small houses, but the silence and lack of people is intolerable" (*Sibirskie tetradi: 1862–1866* [Moscow: Common Place, 2016], 30).

here for the first time I confronted face to face. I traced the reason why a man born a man will become an animal further in life. And next I asked, did I want to reach that which would hold him back from crime? I finally adapted to life as it awaited me in the future. It was my exclusive occupation. So that I could more closely examine crime, as many times as possible I visited those who sat in shackles, chained to the wall for several years. I found there among them some Jew from Częstochowa. I thought that I would quickly learn something about him. Meanwhile my expectation was yet disappointed, because I maintained that he was innocent. He had already sat there for three years and died of cholera.

Also, there was some Kornev; he was a common bandit.[32] He murdered, it seems, for pleasure; about his past life he spoke with confident bragging. He remembered how, wanting to force a mother to confess where the money was hidden, he rent her infant before her eyes, as he then tormented the mother and so on. Kornev did not have a very wild look; he seemed to be very gentle. The first moments of his life passed under the eye of his parents, who were not as bad as he, he said; later on, having come to know some scoundrel sent to their village for settlement, he began to play cards and dice, and then drank a lot. Such a life pleased him a lot, and then not having the means for prolonging it, he began to steal. For theft, a few times he was not caught; however, he was released from capture for murder and continuing on so, received chains to Tobolsk. About improvement further in life he no longer thought; he wanted only to get out again into freedom and to avenge himself bloodily on those who deprived him of it. Kornev in prison began to counterfeit money; in his cell he made lead rubles, exchanging them with the help of the soldiers standing guard for genuine rubles. For all who were serving time that designated chains, they would advance in the same way—they would remain in the prison until death. Occasions of exchange happen all the same—parties of those newly arrived and departing change every week. The prison in Tobolsk almost continuously holds up to 1,000, and for this reason it is not very difficult for someone, who must serve his entire life in prison and has found someone with similar features, to leave him in his own place—albeit for big money—but the former succeeds to the place destined for the one who agreed to the familiar change. One shouldn't doubt that such changes take place often. I have known dozens of similar occasions, where even the measure of height

32 From his notes on Tobolsk in *Vospominaniia o F. M. Dostoevskom v Sibiri*, Wrangel recalls having seen the famous, "most enterprising and dangerous" Korenev, to whom eighteen murders were ascribed and who subsequently broke out of the prison and ran free for several weeks before being caught again (116–7).

was completely different, and, all the same, no one called attention to it; they usually considered it an error. In every party going on the road farther you find some Forgetful Ivans, Nameless Ivans, and Fatherless Ivans. These are the names adopted by those who do not want to disclose their real names. This is enough about Tobolsk, because before us there is still a lot of road and many different developments.

On August 11, 12 of my fellow colleagues were sent on a journey with a party of 70 convicts. I still remained with Józef Rudnicki. A few days before the departure of the party uniforms were handed out, complete with a cap sewn from gray cloth and a kind of robe, on the shoulders of which is sewn a square of a completely different color for the label, which is in a gray color. They allow two shirts in very coarse cloth, two pairs of ankle boots, and two small pouches, and I no longer know what purpose they could serve. The cloth used for the clothes is from a Siberian factory, and it is usually made in towns which make little use of wool, and more widely of the hair of beasts—which is still flimsy, also extremely weak, and rarely lasting, to such a degree that a certain little Russian known to me reflected very humorously about it, saying: "The rains may be still beyond the mountain, but the back is already wet." All the things issued were marked with the stamp "T. E. C. 1848 *goda*"—the letters denoted Tobolsk Expedition of Exiles.[33] Every day 3 silver copecks or 6 groszy were allocated to each person. I watched my departing comrades at 5 o'clock in the morning; all having to belong to this party stood on the square in a row. They inspected foremost whether the chains were intact and sturdy; next they looked at whether all parts of the uniform were there—this happens, since the prisoners either immediately play cards for them after taking them from the warehouse or also steal them from one another. Such on-site inspections from the beginning of the road took place at almost every station, then were slowly ceasing, and at last ceased completely. After the completed inspection of chains and things, a list of all the names was read out, and then we were ordered to approach the chain extended on the ground. There were short rails of iron at certain intervals connected with circles, on which were placed lots of hand chains. Into such hand chains they locked, rather screwed with a key in pairs, one on the left and one on the right hand. So prepared, a party sets off from Tobolsk every new week, week in and week out! Having taken leave of colleagues, I still remained some time in Tobolsk. I awaited the arrival of Ludwik Mazaraki, Aloizy Wenda, Benedykt Kossiewicz and Bokszański, with whom I had been dispatched. But later arrived: Feliks

33 *Goda* is the Polish transliteration of the Russian word for year.

and Julian Jordan, Mieczysław Zarębski, Józef Koźmiński, Jan König, and Stanisław Dutkiewicz.

The same story and the same order were retained for my departure from Tobolsk that took place with the dispatch of my previous fellow colleagues. In the same way, they handed us our uniforms, and in the same way they examined our chains and chained us in rods; in a word everything was performed completely identically. Those who lacked a place with the main chain were forged together with the help of the following apparatus: *a. b. c. d.* are collars whose links are locked each individually in a padlock as soon as they embrace the neck of a person; *e. f. g. h.* chains are joined by means of a circle. Poor, unfortunate are those, who must accomplish travel in a similar apparatus. Since often it happens that one of those locked in is constrained by circumstances, by necessity, and by the necessary out of necessity; the position of the walking man is changed to a position that is neither sitting nor standing, and at that time everyone else is forced to bend their heads down and to look at the ground as if they were looking for something. Then the third curses the fourth—in words that I am unable to repeat here—not one of them stops to think that this similar incident can happen to him and that the fourth will similarly curse him in turn. I must pause a moment here; we will set off farther, since it is necessary to recall the officer, who from Tobolsk escorts the party to the first night's lodging. He was an old invalid, older than 50, but he was only a second lieutenant. The tall, dry, and habitual drunk—a rare example for observation—was named Ivanov; he was dressed in a uniform, on which were stains, holes, and patches beyond measure. Then this Ivanov, with every party he conducted, collects money in the following way: after 10 versts of road there is some monastery, and there he orders the *starosta* (since every party has its own generally chosen *starosta*) to ask everyone, "Do you want to be freed from the chain?"[34] Oh who wouldn't want it? Naturally everybody agrees; it is necessary only to pay the officers, and the officer demands no more than 2 kopecks per mug (that means per person). He puts the chains in the wagon, and the prisoners, surrounded by soldiers, progress farther.

At the second station it is the very same story with small changes, e.g., the officer demands payment no longer by a mug but by nose, by man, by head, etc. At the departure from Tobolsk we had a little money, which had to be taken from us and which had to go to our place of destination so the officer had handed it over to the officers with a receipt. Wanting to

34 A verst is approximately 1.07 kilometers, and *starosta* may be translated as elder and is used to describe local leadership in various contexts.

lighten for them the weight and trouble of keeping another's money, we decided to take it away although to waste anything at all further took a proposal to Mr. Ivanov so that he gave back the money, but such a distribution was dismissed. "There is no way!" Mr. Ivanov recoiled. We did not stop with our persuading, promising him half a pint of vodka for such a courtesy. The vodka softened the officer a little, he was already dreaming about it, he began to haggle, and before long stood an agreement that Mr. Officer would give himself half a ruble of vodka, would give us the rest, and would wipe out the distribution. In the town of Abatsk, lying on the Irtysh, Mr. Officer gave us back the money and drank up half a ruble of vodka; the party relaxed for a moment, and again we set off farther. . . .

Beginning the Trek to Ust-Kamenogorsk through Tomsk

It was the first day of our pilgrimage and in no way did it differ from the next: every two days we were on the march, and on the third we were allocated rest—the monotony is horrendously boring. Everywhere is this same order (if it is suitable to name a similar state order). These same yellow-colored homes, called staging points, are surrounded by stockades, around which everywhere there are the same—or with a very small difference—homes and villages—villages cast upon the Barabinsk steppe and homes covered with sod or birch bark.

You will not catch sight of a single small tree there, which could shade a little rural house; you will not glimpse how we have that nice greenery and those various little gardens, where the village girls keep themselves, handing over rue, periwinkle, and southernwood from generation to generation. Everything there is unadorned; the entire desert is bare! And not just once, too, did the thought occur to me that our journey has many similarities to the journey of the Israelites, when they sought the promised land; with possibly only the difference being that they are poor and that only some are long wandering and are given to catch sight of that land, which is supposed to flow with milk and honey. We, on the other hand, likewise poor arrived at the place that had been promised us; we found the land, but the land was not really similar, since for us it did not flow with honey and milk, so it was bitter to eat it.[35] On the road leading to the fourth or fifth station from Tobolsk, one

35 A footnote for clarification appears in the printed version in the same column as this text which concludes chapter four:

> In the vicinity of Ust-Kamenogorsk and Omsk the steppes are overgrown with wormwood, owing to which, particularly in the spring when cows go out for green fodder, milk has an unpleasant bitterness.

of the prisoners fell sick with cholera. Who he was, I do not know; I know only that he was branded—maybe a robber or a thief, or maybe even less guilty! Then they let him loose from his chains, put him down in the wagon, and transported him, who had turned blue and was almost dying, to the station. Here it turned out that we spent the night; it was, it seems, a Turkish settlement by the name of Balakhaia Yurta.[36] They took him off the wagon, left him behind in the courtyard without help or rescue; no one approached him, because everyone feared cholera worse than fire. It was terrible to look at the sight of this poor being, evidently struggling with certain death. This man was fading, it is true, but he deserved some help all the same; having a little anodyne and drops of mint we gave this to him, both with sugar, and this brought him some relief. I am almost certain that if there had been both a doctor and a pharmacy, maybe there would have been more help. But it is possible they were there somewhere but no one thought of it!

The one left behind was to die at last; however, as death fell upon him, night approached. The barracks were not closed up with him inside, and the sick man could not remain in the courtyard. There they dropped him—"because" I will not say—so that he was carried into the hallway and placed on the bare floor next to two old buckets, one of which served as the chamber pot, and in the second is usually held drinking water. It is fitting for me to mention here that sometimes a mistake arises in the use of these two vessels, particularly when the nights are longer and the miserly officer gives too little light. Our sick man, abandoned in this way, moaned terribly for a long time in the night. I thought that one of his acquaintances, maybe some criminal accomplice, would approach him at least in the final hour of his life, but everyone ran away from there, and nobody even gave him water. Then taking over out of kindness and having nothing else at hand, we gave him hot tea—it is true that he didn't drink much of it—but with every drink he calmed down somewhat, and sometimes he pronounced the words, no longer clear, "Thank God." About midnight, the moaning ceased, because life also ceased; the prisoner was dead. You should have seen the next day when the doors of the barracks opened, how everyone leapt out of fear—it is difficult to describe. This circumstance raised for me repeatedly the thought (maybe in any case erroneously) that capital punishment in Russia should exist for crimes. In my further opinion, in my further research into causes and numerous offenses, I became still more convinced of this, and today I repeat that only the death penalty is immediate; in the short term,

36 This is about 300 kilometers to the west of the Novosibirsk region (V. A. Lamin, V. A. Il'inykh, and A. Kh. Elert, *Istoricheskaia entsiklopediia Sibiri* in 3 vols. [Novosibirsk: Istoricheskoe nasledie Sibiri, 2009], 1:167).

it could be that you prevent crime at least in part. For every prisoner, the knout is not as horrible as the bludgeon, but everyone trembles at the recollection of death.

Everyone knows well that it is necessary to bribe the executioner well, because the executioner, just like he, is a criminal and like he first received the knout (he became an executioner), and today beats others with the knout. At the office of executioner, they usually select people sentenced for crimes requiring physical labor. No qualification is needed for this; it is enough that either the chosen has physical strength greater than others or is built more athletically than the rest. The bludgeons are more awful than the knout, because there it is more difficult to bribe, although even there if one can succeed by oneself or through someone else to insert something in the paw of the officers, one can always be certain of mitigation, because the officer of the execution will go to the execution and will constantly repeat to the soldiers, "Easier guys." The criminals have their own technical expressions for the articulation of how they were punished and so, e.g., "to plow by two petty officers" means to take the bludgeons, because usually those petty officers accompany the culprit, having previously tied his hands to two crossed rifles. "To ride a mare" means to take the knout, because the plank to which they tie the culprit during the knouting operation is called a "mare." Later still, I was convinced many times that every prisoner trembles at his own recollection of death; going into many chats and telling them about how in places they punish crime, I almost always heard, "Oh there it is worse for our brother. What is all this to me, what is money to me, if it is gained after having killed someone when they will kill me and will not even let me atone.[37] It is better with us, because although it is rather hard that it often falls on you take the rap, the hope will always remain, after all, that a man, having survived everything, can sometimes live it up."

A month ended the travels; we had already gone through 500 versts and the first city, by the name of Tara, only now appeared before us. Some of our brothers came out to meet us, since they knew about our arrival; being notified from Tobolsk, they immediately notified those who followed. In Tara there were about 12 during this time; however, except for Karol Bogdaszewski (from the Aleksandr Wężyk affair),[38] Konstanty Drotkiewicz, Ciesicki, Skierski, Kłosowski, and Chomnicki, no one came to us, since all of them, having married Siberian women, had built themselves

37 There is a footnote marked at this place, at the bottom of folio 10: "The sentencing to penal servitude in their conviction cleanses one of the crime perpetrated."

38 He was arrested in 1840 and sentenced to hard labor at the same factory where Rufin Piotrowski was located (Śliwowska, *ZpIR*, 67–68).

their own partition, dividing themselves from us forever. Among the above-mentioned, two whose names I underlined, later did the same. The reception of us in Tara was sincere, genuinely brotherly, since it was not really a law that everyone fairly good help those in need, but the one who evaded this law was usually was paid for his indifference with indifference—such a one was always excluded from the fraternal circle.

We had already passed Kainsk, the first district city in Tomsk Gubernia, when the party was delayed on account of the coming winter. Twelve comrades who left before me from Tobolsk turned out to be detained only about 100 versts away in the village of Bolotnoe, while we were in Itkulu.[39] Then we stayed there in that place for two weeks, and such a detention is called "Fall Break," and the second occurs in the spring, "Spring Break." The time of our stay in Itkulu was far worse than that of our brothers detained in Bolotnoe. Imagine to yourself that a man is forced to lie through two weeks in cold, cramped, stinking barracks without anything to occupy his time. Since the books which we had taken with us from the library in Tobolsk had been already read long ago, what more was there to do in such an abnormal situation?[40] Our brothers, detained, as I said, in the village of Bolotnoe for a time similar to "Spring Break," more easily found their way than we did, since they found a managing officer there with the rank of a captain, Fedorov, who from the beginning dealt with them humanely; he even let them go hunting sometimes without a guard. He well knew that everyone should be put in chains but never said anything if he saw someone without them. One could see that he trusted them a lot, because after our arrival to Bolotnoe he immediately said at the introduction, "Oh, I know what kind of people you are!" And well may you ask to tell about those who stayed with him for two weeks? He told us how they baked bread, how they themselves rode to the forest for timber, how they tried to have something to eat, and in a word, he told us various entertaining details about which (mainly about baking bread) I need to recall here.

Usually it happens that when a party is detained somewhere on the road for the reason of an ensuing spring, or an approaching winter, that the inhabitants of this village immediately double the price of victuals so that in this manner they force the extraction of money from hunger. Each arrestee

39 This small village was known for its Orthodox church and for its bazaars that attracted merchants from such towns as Tomsk and Barnaul.

40 The printed version contains the following footnote:

> The library in Tobolsk was filled up by Moszyński, after whose liberation it passed to the ownership of everyone, under the main administration of Pietraszkiewicz. In those times, how fine was the library in Tobolsk!

receives, as was said, 6 groszy a day—too small a sum that one would not be hungry. If you do not have your own money, what can you buy for 6 groszy? A few pounds of whole wheat bread and at the most a glass of milk, but this is all bought at ordinary prices. Let the party get held back, and everything immediately gets more expensive. A three-pound bread roll costs 20 groszy or more. Seeing such a state of things, our brothers resolved to ask the officer for permission to set out for a neighboring little village by the name of Sizina and to get a supply of flour, for a rather accessible price; immediately the next morning they began to bake bread, for which a pound, by my reckoning, cost little more than 1½ groszy.[41] Moldovans, of whom there were some in the party, took over the baking of the bread, and the bread was excellent! The officer in Bolotnoe delivered the notification that the party was to move further down where the ice was on the river Tom and where for the most part the detained party was already standing. When this order came down, our brothers still had a couple of pounds of flour in reserve, and, not wanting to transport it in its raw state, it was necessary to process it into bread; since the Moldovans were busy baking their own remnants, for this reason we decided to try the activity so important for producing a result. By general agreement, Tokarzewski was chosen as the baker for the reason that in Tobolsk he made good dumplings and also, having been at one time a distiller, he knew about fermentation.

They fired up the stove, made the leaven, not having paid attention to the fact that there was no piece of old dough in their possession—which is the leavening; it did not ferment at all. They mixed up the dough again without fermenting it, after burning a certain quantity of timber in the stove, after digging out the coal, and after cleansing the stove of useless ashes. Since it was already rather late and the next day we had to be prepared for the road, they took up the dough for the final task. Everyone not already working is helping apparently with the great task. Tokarzewski is making the little loaves, Accord is drying up the flour a bit on the shovel, and others are chopping timber and placing it on the fire so that it is clear how and where to plant the bread; still others are handing warm water to the bakers for washing hands, and, in a word, nobody is idle. After a certain period of time, curiosity taught us to look into the oven—what is happening with the bread? Marvelous! Ruddy like a girl, it grew so beautifully that it almost reaches the firmament. Everyone is overjoyed; everyone is calling

41 The published version specifies that it was Tokarzewski's co-conspirator, Hipolit Raciborski, accompanied by a soldier and the *starosta* who purchased the flour; his testimony may be found in Djakow et al., ed., *Rewolucyjna konspiracja w Królestwie Polskim* (712–20).

out splendidly and excellently—honor and glory to the bakers! "Sirs, an hour has already passed," said the dear departed Grzegorzewski, "I know for certain that now the bread should be washed in cold water and moved from place to place."[42] Such a small thing—not difficult by comparison with all the work, but alas! Barely had the shovel touched the first loaf when immediately the glory of the bakers died away, since the outer crust fell and from the middle of it poured out something in the form of a thick kasha. The bread did not turn out at all, but for all that there was laughter enough, since the story of the baking of the bread in Bolotnoe was made known to all, and even now sometimes it is still recollected. I remembered for a moment the word *kulaga* (thick kasha)—"What is this?" No one asks is this the Siberian dish that the European will try once and certainly will never be seized with the desire to try it again a second time. I remember too well how a certain day, having gone off to the night's lodging rather early, we had just arrived in the late afternoon at the second night's lodging; the station was to have been 30 versts away, but versts in Siberia, as the saying goes, the devils measured by rope. Back then, two of them stood to measure; having pulled well on the rope, one broke it in the middle, and the devils with needless tension ran far away, far away from one another and only here and there, where having lost the strength of speed, did they stand, and did they order the verst posts be placed.

Well, having crossed through these 30 versts, hungry to the point of not talking, we glimpsed a little village. As all our lodgings are at the other end, at the sight of the approaching party, the Siberian women come out of the homes and bring us various delicacies for sale, for example, a white loaf, cheese danishes, sour milk, and sweets with cheese, sometimes prepared roasted fish, sometimes roasted meat, which very often is not sold by the approaching first party and the arrival of the second is awaited. Although it happens that it is already a little spoiled, it is really nothing, because a Siberian woman assures us, saying "although it smells a little, it is still tasty; take it, try it." When we stood in that place while the huckstresses spread out their supplies, at that time someone ran between them, ferreting around so to speak, and tried it or not—enough that he bought the thick kasha, and maybe with another he bragged about the prank. Each person rushes thus and buys briskly with a bowl, but no sooner does he try it than he makes a wry face and frowns; the Siberian delicacy is not similar to anything—hence what to do with this dish? It is a pity to fear throwing it out, but it costs money. "Will the horses eat it?" asked one of the brothers. We try it;

42 Aleksandr Grzegorzewski died in 1855, so this provides a date after which one can assume that the manuscript was written.

the first and second only snorted, and the third, not so finicky, drank it up, and for this reason we gave the thick kasha a new name, calling it horse tea—although the thick kasha is not from herbs but simply is fixed with flour in this way: boiling water is poured over a certain quantity of flour of rye meal and made into a not-too-thick dough, next the dough is cast into a powerfully burning stove, where it stays for close to two days, and then is extracted from there and retained for the making of the *kvass*, which is in every home. Finally, the thick kasha is prepared from these dark to tawny pieces of dough, called *kvasniki* for preparation, owing to its thickness, in separate dishes—well known in some provinces and in ours for rye soup. From that bread baked in Bolotnoe it was necessary to make thick kasha; I remember all the jokes and laughter which took place, but I will take you further.

When we arrived at Bolotnoe, the officer, just like our predecessor, treated us and recommended us well to the next officer (called Zuravlev) who prepared a separate barrack for our reception and presented us to his spouse with her lofty pretensions of an acquaintance with music and literature and with pretensions of tone, because she had a father who resigned as a colonel. Rather a funny girl—for example, she suggested that we could dance a little, because she so loves dancing, but here it is so difficult. "Oh no," she complained, that she must live such a miserable life! There remained for us still two days of traveling to Tomsk; the two stations after 25 versts were remote. In the final station, by the name of Kaltai, having spent the night—or not yet having spent the night, since we set off at precisely midnight—I remember the journey so well, since I preserved it so vibrantly in my memory as if it were only yesterday.[43] The frost was strong, the sky as though leaden, and the night almost dark; a bit of wind blew from the north and, playing with the dry snow, cast it here and there and impeded our journey a lot. They guided us not by the road but by the meadow; above the banks appeared the flowing river Tom. No doubt, the waters spilled in the spring and later froze over, covered by the snow we had underfoot. Often someone or other would fall, although he did not topple over in a harmful way; however, it was always unpleasant when the snow was propelled often into the mitts or anywhere at all where the cold became irritating. If I were a painter, I would try to transfer to the canvas at least this one image: picture to yourself around 100 people extremely badly and strangely clad (only in Tomsk were we given winter clothes and sheepskin coats). Picture to yourself such people put in chains, which clang with a subdued clatter. Each

43 This is a village in the gubernia of Tomsk.

one runs as much as his strength allows, because he wants at least a little to warm his limbs, ossified from the frost. Add to this the cursing, somewhat wild laughter, and joking flung without interruption, and add still the stories—present moments about this or that with one telling about the crime committed at the time of great frost a hundred times over. When from far away there is a stronger wind, he is saved by escape, and the hunt for him is really drawing near. Not being able to hide himself anywhere, he comes upon the place where there is even more snow, and there he wants to hide and lies for such a long time that he almost dies. Gather this all together for yourself, and you will have some idea about everything that you candidly wanted to depict.

We were still at those fields or meadows, when on the right side appeared three great fiery posts, which almost daily portend in Siberia the rising of the sun. Having come to the city, I saw only an enormous quantity of smoke hanging over it, and the thought came to me: "It is the smoke of 200,000 commissions," etc. The thought of the description of St. Petersburg came to me, although Tomsk cannot enter into comparison with it—however truly gripping the image there. A freezing, thickened air does not circulate and is not given the liberty to disperse; the smoke is not allowed to vanish into the air, as it does with us, but is kept as though under a bell. Finally, we are in Tomsk after upwards of 14 weeks on the journey! A two-storied edifice stands, rather elevated, on a mountain—this is the dungeon! This is our dwelling! Scarcely had we stood before it when a soldier came running; a drummer, speaking with Mazovian pronunciation, greeted us, "Ah, how are you? Are you in good health, and also did you wait very long?" He immediately let the town know, and brothers who were in the army or in the settlement not long later began to arrive. At first, the kind-hearted Ksyś (Ksawery Stobnicki)[44] and Tomaszek Kraśnicki—both soldiers—arrived. Both of them have returned and are in Warsaw; the first having left his wife and child in the grave,[45] returned alone to Warsaw and being twice paralyzed today is almost helpless and is found in the hospital, The Infant Jesus.[46] He was a respectable soul; everyone who saw him at least once could forget him only with difficulty. Who first ran to help the

44 Stobnicki was a Ściegienny conspirator, like Tokarzewski, who was sentenced to Tomsk (Blake, "Traumatic Mobility," 248–49).

45 The published version in chapter seven contains the note that "Bronisława Rsytar, from Lublin, set out with him to Tomsk and there died of consumption" (255:1).

46 The published version in chapter seven contains the note that "He died on April 8, 1861. After the burial was the massacre near the castle" (255:1). This is a reference to the massacre of unarmed Poles by Russian infantry on Castle Square in Warsaw.

newly arrived brothers? This is kind-hearted Ksyś, who brought lunch to the prison for them. He was also precisely the one who could never hold anything back from devoting himself to others. Looking at this poor martyr, I will say this—involuntarily a question comes to my mind, "Why does this kind-hearted man suffer so?" when his life flowed without blemish. Tomaszek, the ex-seminarian of the Marianist priests from Podlaski, was sent into the army for "terrifying with hell and eternal fire." How many priests vociferate from the pulpit that sinners, who do not want to mend their ways, will burn in hell for the ages. Someone reading these notes of mine will say, "aren't they sending them to Siberia—they are not exchanging the spiritual state for the military."

Having said that, certainly they do not believe the truth of my story, so it is necessary for their sake to clarify how things were. When the dear departed Pantaleon Potocki died on the scaffold, at that time was heard the conscience of a miller (by the name of Piesek) who formerly worked together with him, then apprehended the just one, and handed him over to the torturer.[47] This miller wanted to be purified of committing such a crime and set off to look for absolution in the confessional. The priest who heard his confession refused the absolution of the miller until such time as the crime committed did not efface the next kind-hearted life. Then he went around the confessional and in the monastery's corridor met Tomaszek waiting for him, "Well, what did you do?" The young seminarian asked, "Do you not know what awaits you after death for this?" And what if to him then in fine words it is pronounced how the devils will bake him in fire for the ages in hell! The worried miller returns home and tells his wife what happened in the church, but he heads for the forest, where after a couple of days he is found, hanged on a tree. Thus, the newly created nobleman perished (since Nicholas I ennobled the miller for such a service rendered to him). His wife, by contrast, carries her grievance against the Marianist priests; the gendarmes take the priest who did not want to grant the criminal absolution, and they take away our Tomaszek. What happened with the priest I do not know, but Tomaszek walked to Siberia in his white habit so that he could exchange it for the grey mantle of a soldier. Soon Colonel Serebrakov, the commandant of the battalion there, arrived in Tomsk and, having examined the sentence of Tomaszek, in which was written the expression "for suffering in hell and in the eternal fire," he ordered our Tomaszek to be taken to the battalion orchestra. A man who did not know the first note had to become a musician! From the beginning our

47 Agaton Giller depicts the encounter between Potocki and the miller Piesek in his *Podróż więźnia etapami do Syberyi w roku 1854* (Leipzig: F. A. Brockhaus, 1866), 1:24.

new soldier did not want to take the violin in hand, since that instrument was assigned to him, but the will of the colonel, like the will of the tsar, must be obeyed. Soon he was informed that the young Pole did not want to study, and he ordered him assigned to clean . . . .[48] In this way he was forced to go to the colonel and swear that he would learn to play, and he began to study. After several years, Tomaszek was already playing at the first balls in Tomsk, and he played in quartets at concerts, when an artist strayed through Tomsk; moreover, Tomaszek taught others and took half a ruble for an hour of lessons. Tomaszek is currently the steward of a home, even a palace, in Warsaw.

Others, such as Tomasz and Teresa Bułhakowie, came to us in the prison; he was sent to Siberia for a connection with the Szymon Konarski conspiracy.[49] She voluntarily shared the fate of her husband; their wedding took place in the hall of the Commission of Inquiry in Vilnius at a time when Tomasz had already been sentenced to Siberia. On the eve of his departure, she set out immediately after him and found her spouse only just in the village of Pisiul situated in the gubernia of Tomsk, where he had been assigned. Curious is the life of these two people, but I will not linger long over them, since I suspect that sometime they will tell you more about themselves separately from me. Mieczysław Wyrzykowski from the affair of the dear departed Aleksandr Wężyk—the present supervisor for the tribunal in Warsaw—in Siberia married the sister of this Bułhakowa, who arrived from Vilnius to visit her sister and, shortly after marrying, she died. Mieczysław for a long time kept himself to private service; at last in the year 1846 the tsar allowed him to enter the civil service, on whose authority, after his return, he became a supervisor. His home in Tomsk, during the entire time of his stay there, was the way station for all those having newly arrived, with the only difference that at a way station it is necessary to pay for everything, but there each arrival found that which he needed until such time as he was in a position to maintain a living. Józef Adamowski, a doctor or rather a medical student in Vilnius, was arrested in the fifth year of medical studies and assigned to be a soldier; despite the fact that he was not a doctor, everyone listened to his advice anyway, and no one who

48 The ellipses left here seem to indicate that the reader is to fill in the word "cesspool" for oneself, as the published version does.

49 The names of Tomaszek and Teresa Bułhakowie appear in several remembrances from this generation of exiles, partly because in 1849 in *Rocznik Literacki* her letters about their life in Siberia with a few sketches were published.

carried it out complained.[50] Well-known throughout the whole gubernia of Tomsk—since for a long time he had a lot of friends there, because he saved quite a few from death—this man was righteous, not a charlatan at all. Any other person in his place could collect more significant funds for himself; he never had almost anything, since he shared everything with those in need. All of them visited us every day in the prison, and then, having equipped us with everything we required, they took their leave on the road after our three-week stay. I do not remember on which day fell our departure to the Ust-Kamenogorsk fortress, situated on the bank of the Irtysh and a small tributary called Mordovka. During the course of our stay in Tomsk we read various newspapers and journals in order to have an idea of what was also going on in God's world.

The Road to Ust-Kamenogorsk

Next we were given a guard from the invalid soldiers, and we headed for the aforementioned fortress, to where our brothers had already been sent previously. The road to Ust-Kamenogorsk runs through Kaltai, which we already once had the fortune to see through the village itself from whence they led us after a night during a snowstorm, as I not so long ago recalled. Next through Varinkhin until Proskokovo from where we just turned left along the road through Barnaul and Zmeinogorsk.[51] Although I will conduct you to Barnaul, here I have to recall the soldier, who escorted us, since he is worthy of remembering. Born somewhere in the depths of the North on the banks of the Lena about 200 versts beyond the Yakutsk, he had purely Mongol features.[52] His eyes forever narrow as if frozen, his face equally flat as his nose and both broad beyond measure, of an average height, and rather stocky—here is the figure of the invalid soldier by the name of Shelagin, but it is not in recognition of this that I here remember him. I want to present to you the image of a man, for whom the Russian expression "complete scoundrel" is drafted perfectly. This Shelagin leav-

50 He is connected to the conspiracy of an exiled comrade, Jan Woźniakowski, whom both Piotrowski and Bogusławski mention meeting in Omsk (Śliwowska, *ZpIR*, 32).

51 Explorers and exiles, including Dostoevsky, visited the mining operations in Barnaul and Zmeinogorsk, and the latter may provide a model for his Schlangenberg in *The Gambler* (Blake, *Dostoevsky and the Catholic Underground*, 69).

52 The Lena is a great river in Eastern Siberia which flows northward through the town of Yakutsk, about which Cottrell writes that it "is not so deep as the stratum of soil found to be constantly frozen in its vicinity" (*Recollections of Siberia*, 99).

ing from Tomsk was then very drunk; I thought from the beginning that my comrades, wanting for us to earn his favor, treated him to this degree, and, sitting on the sled, I thought, "Certainly kind-hearted Ksyś treated my guard." Though, I was soon convinced that Shelagin was able to remember himself better, since at every village we reached our guard immediately ran to the tavern and laid in store a new bottle[53] for the road, which he almost emptied before he managed to reach a new station.

On the second night after Tomsk, we were appointed quarters in the community office or as they called it "Freedom." Shelagin ordered a guard from the peasants, not because they had to look after us but because they compensated him for it. Since Shelagin ordered the newly-arrived guards to go outside, he lined them up at intervals under the windows and doors, and had only just dismissed them from their post, when they proposed a redemption to him, which usually immediately followed before line-up, because it is not easy to find someone who had a mind to stand in some 30 degrees of frost, where there, beyond the window, each of them prefers to live in a warm hut.[54] For the first redemption, Shelagin dismissed them home from the guard, but he did not release them again until a repeat contribution. What's more, I remember that there was such a place at every station. On the next day, Shelagin again had a new means of extracting money, since he demanded an escort comprised of peasants, not on horseback as usual. Therefore, at the second night's lodging after Tomsk, after the rural guard had gathered in the office and after it had already offered a certain redemption, Shelagin laid down on the hay and thus lay for a rather long time, without even moving; maybe he fell asleep sooner, but he certainly dissembled. Having arisen, he took the bottle in his hand, drank up the vodka, repulsively contorted his face, and then reached for a little money from the pocket and a little red string with a small stick. He deftly rolled up the string so that it formed two oval circles (the ends of the string were tied), and having turned to the sitting guard, giving him the little stick, he said: "Hit the one you want." In this way began a game, which the Siberian seems to have already played. Shelagin plays and loses, and before long he lost everything; next he placed as a pledge his sheepskin coat and began to play further. Fortune, however, somehow is not in his favor, and then he wins, and then he loses again. Not long after he plays this, he beats everyone to the last penny. Standing on the side, I admired the skill of a

53 Here appears a Polish transliteration of an old Russian liquid measure of ~1.23 liters.

54 Presumably here Bogusławski is basing his units on the Réaumur scale, a scale that was common in Europe and Russia of the period; 30 degrees of frost would then correspond to approximately—35 degrees Farenheit.

swindler, since he rolled his string and arranged the circles in such a way that when he wanted to lose in some circle, the player placed the little stick so that the string always caught on it and then the opposite. In this way, our Shelagin did not play long and won at least 90 rubles. So, he is rich, has something to drink with, and he drank, too, until it was horrible to watch.

Often, my travel companion, Benedykt Kosiewicz, and I were very much afraid that Shelagin would burn up from drink, although in any case our fear was empty, because "the redeemers" do not give vodka that burns. But let's not go down another road, and let's return to Shelagin. Precisely after some days of travel, having reached the town of Ligostaevo, I was exceedingly surprised that someone came to our quarters and that everyone knew our hero Shelagin. When I asked why, I was told that earlier he used to come often, and once he even cured a priest of dropsy. Having heard of Shelagin's new talent I wanted to find out about how far he had gone down the road of Asclepius. Sometimes Shelagin loved to talk about his pranks, as he curiously called them, when he was in good humor, and to get in good humor required nothing more than a little vodka and a warm hut, and both happened at that moment. In the hut of the Siberian in which we stopped for the night, it was at least 25 degrees (Réaumur) and the vodka in the bottle was not yet running dry.[55] Shelagin treated the host and hostess, and for this they continuously offered him some soup, then various types of fish, then a turnip roasted in the oven, and then various similar Siberian delicacies. Wanting to learn about how Shelagin healed the priest, I did not ask him straight out about the cure, but I slightly drew the household into the conversation. Those, warmed by cordiality, began to tell me, but since they missed the truth, Shelagin then corrected them.

Then no one hindered him anymore, and this is what he said: "The priest in Ligostaevo had a daughter by the name of Seraphina." In the story of Shelagin she appears rather often on the scene in various forms. Her father was a widower, and she was a maiden. She governed the household and tended to the sick one and summoned various medicine men and women folk healers from God knows where. She did not spare work or expense, so long as her father was restored to health. The whole village, where a few years before Shelagin had come, knew about the efforts of Seraphina for her father, and he could have easily found out about the illness of the priest from the first good old woman with whom he had entered conversation, since at the first question, "What is new here with you?" from everywhere they answered, "Oh, it is going poorly—our spiritual father is

55 This translates to about 88 degrees Farenheit.

sick and very likely almost dying." Shelagin, in speaking with the inhabitants of the village Ligostaevo, let it be heard that he could cure the priest: "Already sometimes I have happened to bring people almost out of the coffin." News of the arrival of the medicine man in the village ran at the speed of lightning to the dwelling of the priest, and not long afterwards Shelagin himself went to the rectory, examined the sick person, assured him that his health would return, then drank up some vodka, had something to eat, and accepted a gift from the hands of Seraphina (which Shelagin often recalled with pleasure), with whom his relations became connected, supposedly, more nearly and dearly. Next, if Shelagin was telling the truth, he took a couple of rubles for medicine, which he fixed, as he admitted, with a little quantity of vodka and honey, and he overcooked it with a little bit of soap and powder common to bricks, etc. As he spoke rubbish, he prepared the medicine in a fair-sized flask and carried it to the rectory. Seraphina was waiting for the doctor with a reception, "what was not there," said Shelagin, "everything was in abundance (everything in abundance by the grace of God)." So Shelagin drank and ate without measure, and the priest drank that medicine from the prepared bottle in whose treatment was placed complete faith. Such a state of things lasted some days, but our medicine man came to his senses, certain that in a few days the illness would subside. He explained that he could not, as a man not free after all, want to remain any longer, and he ordered a peasant cart and left. On the road before Tomsk, however, he stopped by a market with traveling people, who told him that driving through Ligostaevo they were at the funeral of the local priest—thus, Seraphina lost her father!

I should quote here another incident about Shelagin. The village where it took place I do not remember, but I know that it was not far from Barnaul. I went out into the street from the lodgings where we had to spend the night in order to take a walk anywhere. The night was majestically beautiful; the moon gleamed in full. The frost was so great that it took one's breath away. But paying no heed, I went out into the street and had barely run through a dozen paces when I caught sight of something moving under the fence. It seemed to me like some man crawling on all fours. I drew closer and caught sight of Shelagin in a desperate state! I will say, in a few moments, there certainly would have been a corpse of our hero: his cheeks—flat, his hands white like snow, and drunk—he was in no state to support himself on his own legs. So I returned immediately to the lodgings and scarcely managed to persuade a second soldier that he had to come to render him assistance. He came out from the homeowner's house and that Yakut-Mongol was carried back and with well-known means was kept from becoming an invalid. After all that, we were supposedly to go no longer further with Shelagin, and we resolved to send again to Tomsk so that we did not immediately answer for ourselves when traveling. The voice of authority in the community gave evidence that on account of weakness he was not in a state to be traveling further. Several years later I found out that he was no longer alive!

Before I arrive in my story at Ust-Kamenogorsk, I owe you something to remember about the regional city Barnaul. By its broad expanse it cannot be considered a large city; however, it is rather decently built. It lies on the river Ob, has an office of Siberian zoological animals and ducks, contains a collection of minerals, and has a lot of factories. Here gold and silver, mined from some type of sand, are melted down, and the melted silver and gold are transported later to St. Petersburg. I saw on the road two such transports, the first of which came from Barnaul. It consisted of about a dozen sleds and was loaded full with gold, but the second with silver had been sent from Zmeinogorsk—that other city situated amid the mountain range of the lesser Altai. I am sorry that our journey turned out to be in winter and that it was not possible to examine the admittedly still wild but always majestic nature. I have seen the Urals, and I have seen the Tatra and the Carpathian Mountains, but such a severely and immensely magnificent situation I have never seen, since it is something that frightens and amazes the onlooker. The first time, you see ruins like high bare pyramids of various frightful forms of various eccentric shapes and sizes. The second time, it appears to you like a slanted column; it appears to threaten to crash and appears that any puff of wind piles up its tremendous rubble and strews everything about that is sitting at its foot. Farther and farther away, from beyond the mist, came into view something tremendous in a form similar to that of a sugar loaf, a sharp point, and to the top had been lifted a huge flat plane similar to a platter. It seems that someone so diffidently placed it there, and you watch and are surprised that unintentionally it lies peacefully, that it does not fall. On all these heights, you will not glimpse any sapling; rarely somewhere halfway up will flash a dwarf pine, nothing more. On one of these mountains we wanted to go on an excursion; it lay rather close to the village where we were spending the night. It was one of the less regularly rounded, and at its very apex, as if deliberately displayed, was a large square stone. The reason for making the excursion was the story of the residents there that some years ago on that mountain there had been some kind of traveler, that there on the rock he had carved out some kind of letter; the traveler was not (as is said in Russian) visible to you, as our Siberian residents told us. We wanted to go to the top, judging that we would find, perhaps, a trace of Humbolt's stay, but an enormous snowdrift caught our curiosity.[56]

In the environs of Barnaul and Zmeinogorsk are expansive villages; the most well-to-do residents make a living breeding cattle and farming; they have numerous apiaries from where there is also an abundance of honey, which sometimes cost 40 groszy for 2½ pounds. They call the residents "Poles" although none of them speaks Polish; they are all so-called Old Believers. They are always called Poles, because they are the descendants of those who, being persecuted for supposedly moving away from Orthodoxy in the first half of the past century, sought refuge in that part of Poland, which after the first partition of our country passed under the domination of Russia. At that time, Catherine II ordered that all these Old Believers (schismatics)[57] be transferred and settled on the banks of the Ob. They belong currently to the mining administration; they deliver ore, coal, timber, etc. to the factories and call themselves peasants registered to the factory. Still today, after so many years, you can encounter in them many things, slight in appearance, that give unquestionable evidence that they had closer relations with Poland. For example, nowhere except with them are you going to find wholegrain bread baked as it is with us, and no one aside from them will prepare fatback as it is prepared by us. In clothing one very often encounters something like those which recall certain people of our parts. These Poles by name received us almost always with great reluctance. When the rural authority leads you to some house and announces that here you must spend the night, then the homeowner shuts the door in your face and will barely open it at the order of the village elder. Whereas when he chats, when he familiarizes himself to the extent that for a short period of time he can acquaint himself with people having arrived from distant parts, then he will bid you farewell with a certain sign of friendship. It is not often fitting to wonder at the repulsion they display when receiving those passing through, because such a guest takes something out of the household possessions and also inflicts unpleasantness on him. All who do not belong to their sect are called heathen or unclean. Each person who smokes a pipe is considered by their beliefs to be a person thrice accursed.

56 The celebrated Baron Alexander von Humboldt was a traveler, who published accounts of his expeditions, including one he undertook to Russia in 1829 when he visited several cities to the east of Ekaterinburg, including Semipalatinsk, Ust-Kamenogorsk, Orsk, and Orenburg.

57 Here the manuscript uses a Russian word (translated in parentheses) that underscores the dissent of Old Believers whereas the Polish variant suggests a retention of old beliefs and rituals.

It is the greatest sin, one of the greatest obstacles to obtaining salvation. The girls here almost all, when one courts them, make a fuss over tobacco smoke in the most awful way. They immediately feign either the barking of the dog, the meowing of the cat, or the crowing of the rooster, or along with this something ridiculous—sometimes they weep, have spasms, laugh, get angry, and threaten the one smoking the pipe with a knife or with taking his life with a small ax. The place where this pagan sat they scrape down and wash out, and they fumigate the hut with a palmful of resin, which is used to excessively spread incense at the time of prayer. Sometimes I thought looking at a similar dusting of images that if you were to plant the living God in this place he would surely jump down and flee. I happened to bump into a girl on this journey—she is called ruined. This must be a disease, which I cannot believe was real; it was pretense or a habit out of necessity. Everyone who only just arrived in this part of Siberia knew about these comedies since everyone immediately upon entering the house received a warning from the homeowner that his wife was ruined, and each person was asked if he had used a pipe. I must recall here a certain event which happened to me in a village by the name of Sikisuvka, close to Ust-Kamenogorsk, by which I was shown again that this sickness is bogus. Just before evening, having arrived in Sikisuvka, I received lodging from a similar Old Believer, who, having asked me immediately upon entering whether or not I smoked, wanted to throw me out of the house. He made a tremendous amount of noise and ran off to the village elder. In the meantime, I, having deposited my things on the ground, sat down on the bench in the corner, precisely where icons are suspended. On this same bench in front of the stove was sitting a middle-aged woman; next to her cuddled what must have been her daughter of seven or eight years. They were both sincerely crying (and that had been a sign of the illness).

I do not know why, but I had a fancy to chat with the homeowner, and I asked in these words, "Tell me, mother, why do you weep so, do you feel poorly?" She was silent for a moment, and replied, "How should I not cry, when I am to be unfortunate. You are smoking a pipe, and I am ruined; I could kill you." "If that is so, kill me quickly, and I will tell you in advance 'God bless you,' but do you also as a mother know what murder is? Do you know what awaits you for this?" And then in a few words I presented to her how they put her in prison, pass judgment on her, and lash her with the knout; not only that, how she must be cast out of her husband's home and away from her daughter, who was so dolefully crying next to her, not knowing why, and she would have to scurry about long, long years somewhere in the mines of Nerchinsk. Every word uttered she heard with a certain impression, she stood up at last, wiped her eyes with her apron, and calmed down. At that moment, her husband arrived and led some sort of village writer by the name of Ikonnikov. Both of them began to shout terribly and berate in a nasty way, when I gave him to understand that I am not the type of person who would repay good with evil, that I am not in the custom of inflicting even the smallest unpleasantness when someone treats me even in the way he did, and that, sure, I had try to convince him that he has it so much better than I do. There is, in a word, a reversal with a short conversation and then an emphatic declaration that I would not leave his house until tomorrow morning, and they calmed the homeowner down, because shortly later he asked if I needed anything.

"My brother, I will not take anything from you without paying you for it," I responded, "Could you bring the samovar?" There was no samovar, because the Old Believers do not drink tea for the reason that this grass grows in the earth of people not baptized, that these non-baptized cultivate the grass, that the tap of the samovar has some resemblance to a snake, etc., and that all these were barriers to salvation. Nonetheless, he went out and brought back a samovar from the Russian priest, whom the government sent to them and about whom everyone is so concerned that he issues, in a time of need, certificates that they are Orthodox and, as such, are fulfilling all the Orthodox rites. Then my host, having chattered away, was entirely different, apologized for his impolite reception, asked for forgiveness, and often repeated to me, "Don't remember the offense!"—the hostess after his example did likewise. His spouse turned out to be nice and obliging, did not cry, forgot about the murder, and, moreover, in the morning went to the closet and brought out from there two fair-sized nelmas (a splendid type of fish caught in the rivers of Siberia). She prepared an excellent soup and was exceedingly surprised that I did not want to eat her soup gratis. She did not want to take anything and after a long bargaining instructed me to give something, as she expressed it, "To God for a candle."

It is surprising that someone could so rapidly give themselves over to hospitality and that, moreover, on the morning of the next day when the hostess lit the fire in the stove and I approached it to take a coal for the pipe, which I smoked on the porch, she herself gave the coal for the pipe to me with tongs and did not act out a comedy. I do not believe in the existence of this illness, as I said above, although some maintain that it is real and call it hysterics—maybe, besides I am not a doctor and thus will not get involved in an analysis; however, I will relate what I was given to hear about Siberian spoiling. When we trekked from Ust-Kamenogorsk to Omsk I met on the Cossack line in the settlement of Uvarovo a Cossack called Karpovich, who was born in the Duchy of Poznan. Already in the year 1812, having been taken prisoner, he came to these parts, settled here with his muse, became a Cossack, married a Siberian woman, and had two Cossack sons—his sons are already *Moskali*, since they do not know how to speak Polish and confess the Orthodox religion. As soon as he learned that some Poles had arrived, he immediately came and welcomed us, speaking in pure Polish. I will recall Karpovich again, but now I want to tell you what things I heard about Siberian spoiling, and beforehand I assure you that I do not believe in the reality of that which Karpovich maintained was true. He said that the illness is by no means a fiction, that he does not know from where every such illness is picked up, but since his woman was also spoiled he therefore was convinced that it is real. When the smell of tobacco reaches the pregnant woman, then she is already spoiled to such a degree that even a newly attached fetus will be turned into a certain pliable mass, which is a mass that will remain in her almost always until death, and such a woman is, at once, the most unhappy creature. "My old lady was in such a state for some years; I did not have any peace with her, and I had to very often run away from home." When this illness attacked her, however, someone (no doubt similar to Shelagin) advised Karpovich to give his wife a powder to drink, from the root of a certain herb growing in the mountains close to Uvarovo. Karpovich heard the advice, excavated a large amount of the root, made a lot of powder, and took it for treatment. He did not cease sweating in his desire to cure his wife, in spite of the most terrible pain she underwent while she was not completely well. With a description of the root that was similar to Chinese bark, but differing according to taste because it has a more bitter one, he then fed his wife this powder until she got rid of the hardened pliable mass and then gave him some healthy children. I believed that such food could not be pleasing to the woman, and she had to cease the acting. Today the tobacco smoke is completely harmful. It is too bad that one of the doctors there does not assign himself the work of examining this paresis and describe it precisely.

Arrival and Imprisonment in Ust-Kamenogorsk

We will return, however, to our journey. From Sikisuvka to Ust-Kamenogorsk, which was already very close, shortly after embarking thus and after an entire month of travel, I caught a glimpse of the promised land—the fortress of Ust-Kamenogorsk, in which we were to bury our most beautiful age, our dreams, our hope, in a word, everything, everything by which we had lived up to now. There was an early frost, but it was already possible to recognize the form of a settlement, which with each step stood out more prominently, and at last it appeared rather distinctly. My gaze swept around; I found the surroundings mountainous and looked for embankments, ramparts, redoubts, gates, and drawbridges, but all this I searched for in vain. I spied only a painted one-story building, a church, then a place surrounded by a palisade, and I thought at that time, "My God! Here I am supposed to survive ten years and maybe even die." Lost in thought, I passed by the wretched settlement, the so-called city, and then I stood before the wooden house in which was the chancellery of the commandant of the fortress. I was conducted to it. Shortly thereafter arrived the commandant; this was Major Macenko, a Little Russian commanding officer of the 9th Battalion. About the commandant, about those who surrounded him, I do not have a lot to tell; later I will indicate to you which of them behaved the best with us. I must remember each one who here distinguished himself in his position and who exactly had what kind of authority over us. Already, this commandant was the first; he answered for everything of ours. The major of the engineers, Gusev, was employed in the division of labor; he had as an assistant a Polish officer Jakublewicz, who was among those two or three officers of the fort's artillery, whose authority did not extend to us. Upon his arrival the commandant gave us some instructions or admonitions, which I no longer remember. Then, he ordered that we be led to the prison.

Bad, very bad did my future seem to me; often when traveling I thought, "What else awaits me here?" I did not expect to find anything good, and because of this I also painted myself a future as if it could only be in the most filthy of colors. Having arrived at the prison barrack and having cast an eye around, I was convinced that my imagination was far from reality. I involuntarily recoiled for a moment at the view of filth itself that reign there, and I will concede that it made me a little weak for a moment. Imagine to yourself a rather long hut with three filthy square windows—damp, smoky, and foul-smelling. Streams of water run along the walls; the air is stifling, heavy, and full of fumes of sweat, rot, and grease, which overflow from the iron pots with food standing on the stove. I ask you to imagine that though various rags are suspended in this hut, the floor is always strewn with hay (which is continuously trampled by wet feet)—long ago transformed into manure, which would be of excellent use on the improvement of a garden. I ask you to add to all this that the hut was filled with the outcasts of human society, almost every one of whom bore a stamp that indicated the crime that had been committed. Their eyes glowed with curiosity, but an ironic smile of satisfaction—somewhat mockery and somewhat wild joy—gleamed on their faces. I ask you to gather all this together and to tell me, is it any wonder that a man, even with the strongest character, flung into such a den will become weak for a moment, and is it any wonder that even his courage will abandon him? Only the one who did not see, only the one who did not taste this hell, only he could disavow something of the sort! So Brothers of mine, my courage fled me, my fancy for jokes and laughter fled me, fled not only me alone but fled almost everyone. Only the demeanor of the dearly departed Dominik Chodakowski was one of silent composure, only he alone managed to perpetually maintain a stoic countenance, and only he alone with indifference to everything that surrounded us approached this one and that one and laughingly asked, "So what? Does it seem to you that everything will be fine?" Seeing him with each of them, the thought occurred to me that he should despise laughing at adversity. A couple of days after our arrival, they gave us prison issue; however, seeing as we were to be so attired we did not care at all about the good quality of the attire but hunted for the worst. For example, I got a sheepskin coat without wool, some kind of bicolored jacket, pants, too, and a kind of hat. Everything was already in such a state that there was no way to touch it but with a recollection that clothes could be used by more than one criminal, as revulsion took possession of you. Here there exists a custom, completely similar to customs practiced in many families in which the cloth of the older brother often is remade for the younger. When someone comes out of prison and the term appointed for the wearing of prison issue has ended, he must give it back to the depot, which the newcomers receive next, regardless of the fact that the clothing is already so worn out that it will barely suffice for a few days. With this administration of prisoners' clothes, the officer distributing them augments his income even less by looking after security of the prisoner. Having obtained the prison issue, I was summoned to work; for the whole day with the others I cleared out snow, which lay in an enormous snowdrift in front of the residence of Major Gusev. This first test of penal servitude I admit wearied me a bit too powerfully. I returned to prison completely without strength but, in comparison with what came later, it was only child's play.

I must here recall and devote a few words to the memory of the woman who was a lone sweetheart I happened to meet in the distant and empty region. The daughter of the Cossack Colonel Ivanov, born in Siberia—and therefore a Siberian—but my God! Was she like those others? The name of this woman was Elizaveta Evgrafovna, and she was the widow of Bartoshevich. I do not know from where such lofty and such noble feelings and thoughts were awakened in this inhabitant of Siberia, from where came such contempt for everything sordid and low, and finally from where came such high respect for everything that is great, sacred, and beautiful. She did not love the *Moskali* and often repeated that maybe for her father's guilt God chastised her by having her born a Russian woman and moreover a Siberian. She was a Polish woman in the full sense of the word—a Polish woman of the type that we need for the rebirth of our country! She was without a doubt a singular flower that grew in the depth of the Northern soil, a singular star that shone in the cloudy Siberian sky! Honor to your memory, righteous Elizaveta! Peace to your ashes!! The dearly departed Napoleon Górski acquainted us with her—he, himself, was sent as a soldier in the 9th Battalion—was alone for a long time in Ust-Kamenogorsk. When for the first time the dearly departed Elizaveta came to see us at the prison, I admit that her visit was not nice for everyone, since everyone thought that the fancy of satisfying her curiosity brought her—and the fancy of seeing the people about whose arrival the entire settlement had spoken for rather a long time, expressing it in this way, "They are bringing great criminals." However, having become acquainted with her more closely, each person regretted his hasty judgment when each person had to become convinced shortly of how much she suffered over our situation and how sincerely she desired our liberation, when she then announced the project of escape through the steppe of Bukhara. Moreover, she made a promise to expedite things through the mediation of arriving merchants, and she actively helped us connect with relations in our country, with our family. She was not careful in anything and allowed letters to be addressed in her name, although through such a deed, she could have very easily exposed herself to great liability. Everyone in the city knew her from childhood; everyone knew that her relations and acquaintances did not extend beyond Siberia, and here suddenly, right away, after our arrival letters to her begin to arrive from Warsaw! What could be easier than to open those letters that belonged to us and what could be easier than to conduct then the affair and to tie us all together with her as being responsible? The dearly departed Elizaveta was not careful about anything by which she could sweeten our fate or situation. She subscribed to a newspaper only so that we would know what was happening in the world; immediately after picking up the newspaper from the post office she sent it to the prison without even having unsealed it, and only later did she read it herself. In a word, she was a respectable woman in every respect; honor to her memory!!

Several weeks after our arrival in Ust-Kamenogorsk arrived the dearly departed Father Jurgielewicz in order to celebrate liturgy for the scattered believers of the Roman Church. Then we had the opportunity to get acquainted with all the Poles living here. For the liturgy we gathered at a house not occupied by anyone; there a chapel was quickly arranged in which the mass was celebrated, and confession took place. After the liturgy was carried out, an officer of the artillery, Bazhanov, married to a Polish woman, invited us all to lunch. In the house of Bazhanov we had already come upon the dearly departed Elizaveta as well as Boiarska, the wife of the chamber clerk, and no less than the wife of the officer of the engineers, Jakublewicz, who was born a German—also a respectable woman. Then the Jakublewiczes often with the permission of the commandant invited us to their place on a Sunday or on a holy day in order to forget in their circle, if even for a moment, penal servitude! In this way, time flowed lazily; in the morning we left for work, or rather for a stroll (since in comparison to work performed afterwards in Omsk, the work in Ust-Kamenogorsk was only child's play). They made use of almost all of us covering pits caused by the flooding of the Irtysh; for all that it was futile work, continuing for rather a long time. Usually that which will be covered in summer, in autumn will be ruined, and the spring flood ruins the winter work; in a word, our work could be called the pouring of emptiness in vain, according to the Russian proverb: "From emptiness into the hollow he pours." It was only a source of larceny for the head of the engineers, remembered above as Major Gusev, since he took in a significant sum for improvements to the fortress, but he used not a grosz. Each pit remaining after the flood of water was usually filled with manure and covered with small gravel on top, and it must be a dam against the flooding of the Irtysh, a river two times larger than our Vistula! One would have to be a *Moskal* in order to manage to steal so brazenly, and in order to take advantage of every little thing. Besides the covering of the pits, we were employed additionally on some crafted bricks with the burning of lime and on improvement of the treasury buildings. Everything that was done, was done any old way. Nobody strove for the durability of the work, because what then would the convicts do and on what would all the engineers live? After all, each person must live, and this soldier who used to rush us to work had his own source of income. The totality of prisoners paid him always one silver copeck per month apiece for which, naturally, we were let off work earlier than was prescribed. So it was in my time at Ust-Kamenogorsk; later everything underwent such a transformation with the change in leaders that it was even worse than in Omsk.

Our association soon became larger, since notification in the chancellery of the commandant was received about the dispatch from Tobolsk of four tailors from Warsaw: Jan Marszand, Kazimierz Bazylski,

Konstanty Kalinowski, and Feliks Fijałkowski—arrested, forced under the rods, and sent to hard labor in Siberia for releasing a kite in the shape of a white eagle for amusement over the Vistula. The Commission of Inquiry made out of it a great political affair—that the four tailors had disarmed Warsaw guard stations in 1848. Very probably, then, came the notification about the arrival of the six new exiles among whom were Antoni Lewicki, Mikołaj and Hipolit Radzikowski, Łukasz Lachowicz, Chamiec, and Chęłmicki. The tailors from Warsaw arrived in May, but the others came after we had been sent to Omsk. Why Tokarzewski, Żochowski, and I were sent to Omsk I will tell you directly. Major Gusev made a report to Omsk with the following nonsensical contents: that the Poles who arrived in Ust-Kamenogorsk are conducting correspondence with Paris and even London (since he knew that the hearsay is that it is Paris and London) and that these Poles intend to arm 60,000 Kirgiz and then want to destroy the fortress! He did this in order to take revenge on Officer Jakublewicz, who, as his assistant, did not want to sign off on his account, finding it unfair, since the major gave in the account that during the blizzard at night he had to clear the fortress of snow and to do this he used a pound and a half of tallow candles per hour per month.

The misunderstanding between Gusev and Jakublewicz brought an investigation from Omsk, since as soon as the report arrived there the Governor General of Western Siberia, Prince Gorchakov, in greatest secrecy immediately sent the Cossack Colonel Kryvonogov, entrusting him with it so that he visited Ust-Kamenogorsk, made the inspection, conducted the investigation, and reported everything that could be found by special messenger. Kryvonogov then rushed down unexpectedly, drove up straight in front of the jail, ordered the commandant to be summoned, and immediately began the inspection, after which we were split up in the guard stations and forbidden to have any connection with each other. Czerwinski and Accord were put in one guard station; Korzeniowski and Chodawowski in the same one—only in a special room; Tokarzewski and Gruszecki in a second guard station; and the rest were left in the prison. During the inspection a small card written by Józef Malecki was found on me; and on Tokarzewski a letter of Ksawery Stobnicki, brought by a newly arrived tailor; but on Żochowski his own notes, written in the style of the apocalypse, nothing more. An inspection also took place in the house of the righteous Elizaveta and at the Jakublewiczes. Kryvonogov immediately sent back to Omsk, to the General Staff, everything that he could find for translation into Russian. Kryvonogov remained in Ust-Kamenogorsk and awaited the arrival of the papers, which we all awaited with uncertainty, not being able even to guess from where such a storm had befallen us. After ten days, papers arrived from Omsk and at that time Kryvonogov began the investigation, during which even when he wanted to he could not find anything to discover.

The affair lasted three weeks, and during the three weeks we were separated from our comrades, who endured far more than those of us who had remained in the prison, especially Gruszecki and Tokarzewski, since both of them were locked up in a little guard house with one barred window, in which were housed ten soldiers awaiting judgment. The guard house was so small that not everyone could be accommodated with a bunk, but a third of them lay under the bunks; there was no place to walk at all, thanks to which everyone had to lie literally like herring in a barrel. Lying on a wooden cot for three weeks, someone will say, is not a great misfortune; it is certainly better than going to work. Really to sit in a clean room, to lie down on a soft (although not too soft) bed in clean bedding, perhaps not just one lazybones could like it, although it would bore him in the end. But to lie on bare dirty planks, on planks along which slither and jump multitudes of white, black, and bronze maggots—and every one is bred and fattened to such a degree that it would be difficult to fatten them better or more! Oh!—such lying around is worse than the most burdensome work, worse than making bricks! In the guard station where Gruszecki was locked up with Tokarzewski sat ten under judgment among whom was one decommissioned Cossack without a leg who killed his wife—killed her by chopping off her head with an ax—so this Cossack all day hung around his corner with a book for church services in his hands and continuously read various prayers and continuously quarreled with everyone, but especially with a noncommissioned officer who fulfilled the duties of a custodian of a grain warehouse and who was judged for the shortage of 200 sacks (I do not know if they were empty or full of flour). Everyday these two people invented for each other the most hideous words—one did not want to give an inch to the other for anything. No Leg, as the righteous man (never mind that he sat in prison for murder) lay down at night, blessed his bed a few times, and each time repeated, "Lord God Jesus Christ, forgive me a sinner that I that berated that dog of a guard." If someone for a moment entered that cabin and took a look at that cripple without a leg with a book in his hand, with a long beard, with hair parted in the front, combed sleekly in the way in which Orthodox priests wear it, the person would without a doubt have taken him for a very decent man, for some persecuted victim of another's wrath;

but having sat with him for longer, before long he would have become convinced that such a beast, even among beasts, is a rarity.

After three weeks Kryvonogov left, and they moved everyone from the guard stations back to the prison, to those same dirty barracks, but which seemed to each person like a respectable salon. Once again life dragged us back to the former routine; once again, as before, we went to work in the morning, we returned for lunch, we went out in the afternoon, and we returned in the evening. On July 17, 1849 the death of Feliks Fijałkowski tore away at our circle of friends. At that time, I was lying in the hospital, and I saw his end—he died peacefully. On the second day after his death, it was a Sunday afternoon. His mates gathered together, carried the casket, and on their shoulders, while carrying the body of the dead, modestly and without any display they showed him this last service: a quiet, mournful singing of "Eternal Rest May God Deign to Give Him" emanated from the breast of each one. During that time Elizaveta was not in Ust-Kamenogorsk; Macenko had transferred Napoleon Górski to Bukhtarma, to a little fort lying on the Irtysh above Ust-Kamenogorsk; the Jakoblewiczes and the Boiarskis were transferred to Omsk and to Petropavlosk; and who else came?[58] Could death manage without some other convict there and moreover without still another Pole? After the burial of Fijałkowski, there were still 14 such candidates; we were awaiting, as I already recalled, new ones, when in the meantime the order arrived from Omsk to bring Szymon Tokarzewski, Józef Żochowski, and myself to Omsk. Why? What was the reason for such a transplantation? No one knew; everyone, though, easily guessed that it followed as a result of the recently conducted investigation, since everyone pulled into it was recognized for his guilt. However, the most guilty turned out to be the informant, because after all it is not for nothing that the *Moskali* have the proverb: "To the informant goes the first knout." Thus, Gusev paid in advance three-quarters of the cost of travel for Colonel Kryvonogov, which came out to 75 rubles. He further sat out a month in the guard stations, and next he had to hand in his resignation. They brought Jakublewicz to Omsk, for a week he was under arrest with leave for duty, and he bore a quarter of the cost of 26 rubles for just the few times he received us at his house and for the permission of the commandant, who received a severe reprimand for not following instructions and for arbitrary willfulness in conduct. Since we three had nothing with which we could pay, we ended up under the care of Vaska (about whom later I will relate more extensively); moreover, poor Ksawery Stobnicki

58 Vrangel describes Bukhtarma as being south of Ust-Kamenogorsk, right on the border with China (*Vospominaniia o F. M. Dostoevskom*, 99).

then a decent soldier of the 11th Battalion, for writing the letter, was sent a couple of thousand versts to the Kirgiz steppe, to Armul.

The Road to Omsk

On September 20, they put us in chains and we set off on our journey. At the time I was very weak and did not expect to catch sight of Omsk, and I did not even suppose that someday I would catch sight of my country or that, just as I am now, I would also be writing to you that I am looking to be saved from a new illness in Carlsbad. Every step of mine produced a cough, but with it I spewed great chunks of dried, black vomit. I looked every now and then as though the end would come, as though my comrades would bury me somewhere on the steppe. I asked them at least let a cart be ordered, which could convey me from station to station; my request, however, got no result. While leaving Ust-Kamenogorsk we saw our righteous Elizaveta again for the last time. She badly wanted to bid us farewell, but she could not come to us and so asked that we be allowed to drop by her house. She lay in a bed from which she never again arose afterward; her face, yellow and pale, did not divine a long life, and although she promised to see us again, we were certain that she was deceived by a vain hope! And at the beginning of 1850, she finished her pilgrimage to the sorrow of those who sometimes experienced her favor, who esteemed her for what she was worth. The commandant allowed everyone who remained in Ust-Kamenogorsk to escort her body to a place of eternal rest. The first night's lodging fell on us at the village of Uvarovo; we arrived late—they held us in what was called the "gathering point," which was a little house in every village serving as the living quarters for prisoners under transport and at the same time for gathering Cossacks when there was something important to say to them.

Such a "gathering point" usually stands empty, nobody lives there, and it is not heated except when someone is brought to spend the night. Karpovich, about whom I already reminisced, wanted to receive us at his house, but the old Cossack did not want to agree to it under any circumstances; Karpovich sat with us rather late into the night, constantly asking us questions, constantly asked to be told as much as possible about Poland, about that Poland, which he left in his prime and which he could no longer see. We satisfied his demand. One gladly glanced at the various expressions of his face, once you saw him straighten up; in his eyes a smile of satisfaction settled in. Then once again the face was encased in sadness, and sometimes even a tear glistened in his eye—it was the evident struggle of recollections of the past with his present position. He said that after the negotiation and signing at the Congress of Vienna, when everyone who had been sent there [Siberia] was returning, he had been let go, was traveling, and had already even reached Kiev, but having found out that the Kingdom of Poznan had been incorporated into Prussia, he returned to Siberia. On the second day, having arrived at the village second in order by the name of Krasnoyarsk, we were likewise held at the "gathering point," however, with the difference that the Cossacks did not care about us and did not look after us at all. It would have even been possible to flee, if the Irtysh were not the border of the Kirgiz steppe, but France, for example, or some other nation! Having made ourselves comfortable in our new residence (especially since here we fell into the daily routine), I went out into the street and noticed that a Cossack was distributing and selling fresh beef; I ordered him to weigh out a few pounds with the thought that on the next day I could prepare a hussar roast from the Cossack meat.

That day I looked for that which was necessary to prepare the roast. I chopped the onions finely, cut up a dry roll, and having added some salt, pepper, and butter rather copiously I smeared this into the scores made in the meat and looking at my culinary masterpiece, I was surprised at my talent, heretofore hidden! I still needed some sort of dish; I had to make a try for it, and with this goal once again it was necessary to make a trip to the little house, standing there closeby near the "gathering point." There they gave me a vessel, a type of oval platter molded simply from clay, and at least a quarter of it was coarse; it was so dirty, dusty, and smoked with grease that I sat at least an hour over it before I was able to use it. The next day I got up very early so as at the proper time to carry my roast to the house. The Siberians only once a day fire the ovens and cook once a day. In the house I made a small acquaintance and came to know to what degree Siberian women are naive, not less than the degree to which they are neglected in a moral direction. Two young women and two children—one of whom crawled around on the floor and the second slept in a cradle suspended on a pole at the ceiling (a kind of hammock)—were the residents of the house, and I did not see anyone else. They were looking at me rather curiously, they examined my roast, wondering excessively that I had used so much butter and maintaining that it was absolutely not necessary. Not long after I arrived, a conversation between myself and one of them was struck up, in which I asked where her husband was to be found at the present time. No doubt in service on the Kirgiz steppe, I added. "I am a maiden, not a married woman," she replied and said with a certain indignation, "O, he gravely deceived me to the devil." I thought that she was ready to shove me out the door and to chuck out the roast after me, like rubbish. I, too, was too ashamed to apologize and to request forgiveness of the maiden, who, with a better and most attentive scrutiny, somehow did not seem to me to be a maiden. Having consumed a fair-sized morsel of the roast—which was not at all, not at all, good—and having slept a few hours (not having anything better to do) I went out into the street in the evening.

Having sat down on a log of a tree lying there in front of the doors, I set my mind to wandering, which returned to Ust-Kamenogorsk among my comrades and ran to Omsk—there my future appeared to me, bothering me everywhere with its rather dark colors! Near me floated about a rather fair-sized lot of young little Cossacks. I was watching them leap and frolic, and then, not thinking at all about those who were encircling me, I turned my gaze to the right from where the cry of a small child had just reached me. Oh, what a strange thing! At the threshold of the door my familiar girl was sitting and was giving her breast to the crying child; I did not want to believe my eyes, and I wiped them once and then again. Each time I see her, still the same maiden, as she really was. From the beginning, I thought that maybe my gaze was deceiving me—that certainly that second one, whom I did not see, that she was the married woman or also a maiden, about whom I did not want to ask, no longer wanting to fall into one error after another. I had the intention of approaching, no matter what, the space dividing us and had cleared not more than five steps when the second one came out likewise holding a little child in her arm, and since it could already walk, set it on the ground, while she herself sat next to the nursing maiden. The event which I just narrated astonished me so much at that moment that later I became convinced that in Siberia commonly it works thus: every maiden can have beautiful healthy children by the half-dozen and always be a maiden if she does not have or did not have a husband. Never anywhere did I happen to see such moral neglect in people, such moral dissipation, and such an insult to familial relations. Do not look for love there, or in the family, or among spouses; do not look for mutual esteem, because you will not find it. There the mother, herself, sells the daughter, and the daughter also insults the mother. The husband does not trust his wife, and the wife does not trust her husband. It happens that the husband often beats his wife, and the wife poisons the husband! I am not saying this exclusively about the lower working class, because even in higher society you can find the same thing, and with the only difference that with the higher one, it is more possible to have more ways and means to conceal lechery and abomination with the appearance of integrity and virtue!

In the continuation of my tale, you will find passages that without a doubt[59] are not easy to trust, about those that, out of respect for the reader, would deserve, perhaps, to be kept secret and which more than one person, perhaps, regards as a work of my fantasy, as a malicious desire to lash out with mud at the society there. Someone will, perhaps, at last say that I collected only that which was dirty and black and about the rest, about the enlightened side I kept silent. I have none from my own studies, and I will say, after all, that I write about that which I saw with my own eyes and observed for too long. It is not my fault that I spent seven years in excrement and dirt, that after those seven years only dark criminal images spun before my sight. But let's return to the matter at hand, since first I should recall Semipalatinsk, a city situated on the bank of the Irtysh, where we arrived after eight days of travel. To see which of our brothers were located there, we proceeded to Józef Hirszfeld, a soldier who played a central role there. He lived in the house of the merchant Popov and had management over his property. Józef had a sincere desire to take us for a few days to his place, but despite his efforts, despite running about to the various sites, he could not do it. Everyone was afraid to issue permission, and we were forced to live during our stay in Semipalatinsk at the guard station. This is just one thing our good Józef did—having an acquaintance with Officer Tarasov who looked after the guard at that time, Tarasov let us quarter in the officer's room, when according to the law we were to be quartered in the general convicts' barrack. Anyone who wanted came to us, and we here got to know Zieliński, a clerk from the customs house, and Ordyński who together with his brother was exiled to work in 1825 and who now served in the provisions commission.[60] Also, he was formerly made a seminarian from the spiritual academy in Warsaw with the efforts of the rector of this academy, Father Rutkiewicz, and presently a soldier Jan Maj, and also a soldier Rokicki who having returned to his country, lives in Lithuania whereas Hirszfeld leases a good government house in Owczary on the Pilica in the vicinity of Sulejów.[61] Officer Tarasov served

59 A comparative examination of the manuscript with its published version in *Nowa Reforma* demonstrates that this folio 25.5 continues on folio 38.

60 Karol Ordyński could have been a source for the Omsk affair, since he was implicated (Śliwowska, *ZpIR*, 436).

61 Jan Rokicki was a student in the Vilnius Medical Surgery Academy, who was sent for having had contact with Jan Woźniakowski and served in the 7th Battalion in Semipalatinsk (Śliwowska, *ZpIR*, 306).

once in the [Congress] Kingdom when he was a junker, knew Poles, and trusted them with whatever arose so that everyone who wanted to visit us arrived freely, without asking anyone. And the time passed pleasantly (although in prison) talking with people about whose sympathies none of us had any reason to worry.

On the second day, when the guard was changed, Tarasov requested that the officer relieving him grant that we stay, and the officer agreed and would have certainly fulfilled his pledge, if not for another, who was the officer of the guards on duty by the name of Gilov. He, having learned that some convicts dared to spend the night in the officers' room and that these convicts are insulting this room with their presence, immediately set off running to hand over a report about this to the commander of the battalion, Major Belikov, and, having returned from there, he ordered us at that moment to be transported to the general convicts' barrack, while Tarasov and the officer on duty were arrested. There was nothing to do; having gathered our stuff, we suddenly saw ourselves surrounded with people of diverse sorts—those in heavy [chains], those in light, and those completely without shackles; those who are half-shaven, others only from the front, and others not shaven at all. In a word, there was such a hodgepodge of everything that one could want. If Józef Hirszfeld had been present in the town, such a change would certainly not have happened to us—he had departed for a few hours to Popov's garden. Having returned, he immediately mobilized everything, and in order to free us from that place, he brought Major Belikov and still several others. Belikov, having entered the barrack in which we were quartered, evidently was waiting for them to ask about the change of place, from which we were very far away. He left without saying anything, gave an order to free the arrested officers, and next arrived again and ordered that we be taken to a small room occupied by several Cossacks who were sitting under judgment. These Cossacks were all from the Semiyarsk settlement, and their affair was rather important, since they actively helped in the destruction of matrimonial ceremonies by Old Believers from the surrounding villages—those same whom they call Poles, although they are not really. A priest from Semiyarsk was bribed and issued testimony that the ceremonies were entered into in the Orthodox Church according to the Orthodox rite. Having such testimony, the Old Believers married, baptized children, and buried their dead according to the ritual of their sect—the priest took big money for each testimony, and it worked very well for him. The Old Believers were satisfied with the priest, the Cossacks had their income from trade, and in a word everyone was satisfied, but as it usually happens with every, even the best, affair, some devil sweeps in and alters the whole thing to his tastes. This is exactly what happened here. Someone informed about what was going on, and the priest was caught, driven off to Biisk and handed over to the criminal court. The Cossacks were sent to Semipalatinsk for military judgment, and the rest of those who shared the guilt were distributed around various places, and certainly each was deprived of his things. Having spent the night with the Cossacks, we wanted to set off farther down the road. However, they held us back, saying: "You do not have to hurry. Omsk will be a bother to you and, still more, the major of Omsk"—the aforementioned Vasia—"he will taunt you plenty. It would be better if you had never known that scoundrel." So, we agreed to stay another day in Semipalatinsk.

An incident happened when I was witness on that very day to an awful execution served to a certain writer at the rank of a noncommissioned officer. This writer, having spent a few days in some dive, drank himself so that he could only just walk under his own strength, and in this state met his officer performing duties as quartermaster for the battalion. This officer, as the writer remembered, was a confirmed drunk, who more than once had been found unconscious on the street, or who, when no one had found him and helped him get to his dwelling, more than once had spent the night under the fence. Then this officer, the quartermaster who had met the tipsy writer, began to reprimand him, to scream at him, in a word, like an older person speaking to a young one whom he liked. He became bored with seeing the drunk writer, who, knowing the good nature of the officer, replied: "What are you, Your Honor, throwing your weight around? You, yourself, not long ago had a *hangover*." *Hangover* is a technical expression for the designation of the state of a man on the second day after being drunk—it is also the same as fighting fire with fire. Every habitual drunk constantly drinks the hair of the dog that bit him—that is, he keeps drinking constantly until finally there is no longer anything to drink or when his strength fails him and then he is content. If an officer had been speaking to a similar officer, then he would have left, but the writer—a noncommissioned officer—was subordinate to his superior and such incredible impudence without parallel must also be exceptionally punished. They took the writer to the guard station, while on the second day the officer arrived to mete out justice to the guilty. The Cossacks calculated the number of times and then they said that he got "okay" which means that he got as many as a good 750 birchings and got it with "a sprinkling" (that is, from one side they beat him with the thin end and from the other side with the thick—this way is called "a sprinkling").[62] I involuntarily had to watch this entire scene, when it took place before my eyes, and I had to listen to the complaining and moaning of the one beaten until the moment when the voice, growing weaker and weaker, had almost already wasted away in his chest, when his face looked as though it were covered with a solution of soot, and he was all drenched with coagulated blood from the shoulder blades to the knees—until the moment when some paramedic approached the infuriated officer and dared to decide that the beaten writer by the name of Peremikin could withstand no more. At that time the officer, not from mercy certainly but from having come to his senses most rapidly, ordered them to cease the beating. Then the writer was placed on the blanket and began a second painful operation as well—removing the pieces of the twigs stuck on the beaten body, during which one could hear weak and still weaker moans. Next, they brought Peremikin to the field hospital, while the officer walked away satisfied with an uncertain wavering step. I am certain that he had from the beginning of the despicable business drunk at least a quart of vodka, because otherwise I doubt that his courage would suffice (if it is possible to call this courage) for carrying out such a murder.

In this way, I spent two days over in Semipalatinsk. It was time to move on. At the outskirts were gathered Hirszfeld, Rokicki, Maj, Zieliński, and others. A small breakfast had been prepared there, finally Tarasov arrived, and we apologized to him for the trouble that he had encountered, and he responded to us in these words: "I smile about what I did for you, and I did nothing great, but I did what I could, and I know that I did it well." After breakfast Józef escorted us again and showed us Popov's garden—all the trees were already stripped bare of leaves, because, although it was only the end of September, in Siberia winter begins far earlier. I saw the garden, I saw the orangery and staircases, and everything was rather neatly maintained. There were a summer house and several ponds into which water flowed in and flowed out through cast iron cannons—a mass of cannon balls lay scattered here and there; in a word, there was everything that could be anything in a similar garden in a region like Siberia. I even saw there one small apple tree, which Popov imported from Russia and planted; it blooms every year but never bears fruit. Farther down the road nothing in particular descended on us; every day we were in some station or other,

62 Because the quoted terminology is in Russian, it is evident the author is recording what he overheard.

and sometimes we were treated humanely while sometimes in the worst manner. There was a certain variety so absolutely necessary in the life of a human being! Otherwise it would be difficult to remember, and it would be difficult to differentiate between one state of life and another. It is even a kind of happiness when a human being unwittingly finds himself thrown in a place among such people, for example, as we found at the station Pesherana. It was the quarters of a regiment. Having entered this gathering point, we found a crowd of Cossacks who were waiting for something very important and were talking loudly while making various observations about the new arrivals. They were recalling the Hungarian war and their victories, but they were not so clear, and it was impossible to understand anything. Shortly thereafter, an officer with papers in his hand arrived and read out the tsar's manifest about the complete defeat of Hungary and about the submission of Görgey. Certainly not everyone understood what was read to them, but everyone kicked around the poor Hungarians, wished to have them in Siberia, and pointing at us said that those people certainly must be from that same band. It was necessary to arm oneself with patience, and for a moment necessary to muffle all one's organs, e.g., sight and hearing, etc.—retreat into oneself and be silent. The elder Cossack inspected us comparatively well, and some officer spoke to ask a lot of particulars about our affair and, having paid his respects with a bow, departed. Only then did a tall and grey-haired Cossack, already rather old, to whom the others presented a certain respect (they called him Mikita), approach. He began to look through the papers and to inspect things, and finally ordered that we be taken to torment and be put in shackles. They shackled me more tightly than ever before, and with still more than 300 versts to Omsk. To go on such a long road in such heavy chains or something similar . . . after two days my legs—scraped, reddened, and swollen by force—already renounced their obedience and happily requested freedom from one station to another. A Cossack was found who for a half ruble carried an ax and chisel and so could assist in taking off the weight to no purpose.

Only a few days remained to Omsk—the goal of our pilgrimage. They are treating us more and more harshly. The Cossacks tell us strange things about Krivtsov, such strange things that are even difficult to believe. They tell us, for example, that when a dog meets Krivtsov it runs away from him. Listening many times to these Cossack talks, I already impatiently desired to meet with this devil eye to eye, since in the form of a devil he was introduced to us. The travel itself finally bored me powerfully; I wanted already to take a rest, if only for a moment. The Cossacks, more and more wildly and more and more harshly, receive us with disdain and, with a craving for torment, abuse us most originally during the nights' lodgings—for example, at the station before Ochair (the name slipped my memory). Having been rather lately numbed from the cold, we had to fight the whole day with an opposing wind, and the wind from the steppe is not like our wind. Having arrived at the station where we were to spend the night with drenched legs, since the land was already covered with snow, each person was happy that he had arrived and that he would be able to take a rest in some warm hut, to drink some glasses of tea, and to warm numbed limbs. Meanwhile Cossacks were packing us off to an unheated, dirty gathering point and saying that we had to spend the night here; judging that such a verdict of a trial court may still be dismissed, I asked who here is the administrator of the station. They said to me that it is Officer A! Maybe with the officer the business would be easier than with the clerk I thought, and I asked the Cossack if he would be so good as to conduct me to him. The Cossack agreed, and I arrived at the officer's residence, in which I found two girls and with them advanced into a chat, saying who I am and what I need. Next the officer entered, struck the Cossack a few times in the face, shoved him at the door, and did not want to even listen to my request. He only ordered that we be locked in the lockup. There was no one to whom to appeal; it was necessary to submit to this destiny. I returned to the others and told them what had happened. We were housed, according to the order of the officer, in lockup, and it was neither more nor less than a box of 2.5 arshin per square; it did not have any window, and even any slit, with which daily light could burst through into the center; leading to it were doors that were so narrow that the smallest person entering had to bend well, and even scraped with his shoulders the outside doorframe.[63] On the floor in the lockup lay a little pallet meant for bedding for the prisoner and at the same time for the storage of small bicolored maggots about whom I can only tell the reader that they were usually hungry and that the friends reminded me of Lvov, Lublin, and Modlin long ago after judgment and of that hut with the babe in Ust-Kamenogorsk, where the legless sat. When we found ourselves in the center of the box, in spite of the anger that governed everyone, each person began to laugh with a loud and heartfelt laugh, since each person was for the first time in such a position.

About how we spent the night I have nothing to say, but I will say that everyone was exceedingly tired, not having slept; an absence of healthy air made it feel unbearable. It would have been possible to suffocate, having sat for still several hours, during which naturally the

63 An arshin is an old unit of measure equaling 71 centimeters.

Cossacks were not to have troubles with the guard and with justification they would find cause for an incident, and the thing would have been finished. However, no one thought of dying until we all reached Omsk. But first before I conduct my reader there I want for a moment still to stop at the station remembered above called Ochair. We found there a compatriot born in Podolia, serving formerly in the rows of defenders liberating the fatherland in 1831 and then driven like many others into Siberia, where at first, he served as a soldier in the 4th Battalion, and later, having been promoted to the rank of noncommissioned officer, he became assigned as a guardian of a cereal storehouse at Ochair. His name was Karol Krzyżanowski (he died in the military hospital in Omsk in 1850), and he had a Russian wife and two small daughters, Anna and Olga.[64] His wife was the daughter of a colonel, a duty officer at the general headquarters of the Siberian Corps. She was called Natalia Stefanovna Krivanko and was said to have been a beautiful woman in her day with very little intellectual education, as is usual for daughters of all officers who do not at all go for inculcating moral principles in their children (because from where will they take them, if they themselves do not have them). The officers do not strive to educate the heart of the soul of their daughters but care that the daughter knows how to be pleasing and to get married sooner so that her father no longer needs to lay out the cost for her maintenance and so that her husband already needed to be mindful of it. Among such women, although rarely do such occur after all, they feel the needs of another life instinctually and with a blind stroke of luck they arrive at some result that is not the worst, that does not descend down the worst path. The wife of the dearly departed Krzyżanowski was just one of these women, who made up in heart for the inadequacies of her upbringing, loved Krzyżanowski when he was a soldier, and, despite the opposition of her parents, especially her mother, married him, and it was necessary for her to recognize that she had to reconcile herself to a fate not absolutely wonderful. I do not know her past life, and I also cannot say anything about it; I knew her feelings for her husband only in later years, but only in passing at Ochair. Later she lived continuously in Omsk, and I saw her very often, since she always tried to meet with whomever-of-us and often she took up advice when she planned to undertake something with resolve. We left our funds in Ochair; otherwise it would have fallen into the hands of Krivtsov, and we wanted to leave our things, too, but the Cossack officer did not allow it.

---

64 His wife, who corresponded with Dostoevsky, is discussed in the introduction to Rufin Piotrowski that follows.

Navigating Various Strata of the Prison World in Omsk

It would be fitting for me now to lend a pen to a well-known artist so that he could properly sketch the events, which I will bring immediately to the stage—events that will become the most principal epoch in my life. But from where will I take it? How I feel at this time that I should have written you! Meanwhile, I will accompany my story as I have up to now simply, without raptures, and will tell you that after 52 days of travel on the evening of November 12 in the year 1849 at not less than 8 versts away I caught sight of the city of Omsk! The view, although terrible, had been already longed for in a certain sense. What kind of disorder reigned in my thoughts. . . . I looked only with strained vision, judging that as in Ust-Kamenogorsk I would discover a tomb where our name is to be buried alive, but in vain. It was a solemn moment! None of us said a word; walking through the entire city, everyone remained silent, and each without a doubt prepared himself for what he was to meet. The Cossacks finally came to a halt before the house of the commandant, and one of them headed for the chancellery. We remained in the street and waited for that Cossack to return and say something new. When the Cossack came out, he ordered us to head for the Administration Building and pronounced the name Krivtsov. "Ha, finally," I thought, "I see this terrible devil." (Krivtsov was called Vasilii Grigorevich. We called him Vasia and from now on when I come to speak about him I will always call him that.) In the Administration Building, we found only a clerk by the name of Ipatii Semenovich Diagelev; courteous and rushing about, he made a face with such mercy—that was so sorry for us, that so pitied us, that you would think he was a completely kind-hearted man—but he was a scoundrel among such scoundrels as you do not often meet. He was like a dog that fawns and hungers quietly. Again, he was supposed to lead us to Vasia, to father, to the guardian. Diagelev declared that they would take everything from us and that they would leave nothing behind so it would be far better to give it to someone (certainly to him, for example). He said then that we would put on a prison uniform, because Vasia harshly did not like them to wear other clothes. "Let's go," he said, "let's go to the Major's place."

We lined up at the courtyard of the house where the Major lived, and Diagelev went inside to report our arrival; before his departure he reminded us about taking off our hats. In a robe and glasses a man, already half grey and a little more than average height but not quite obese came out to us. His not-so-large mustache joined with his weighty sideburns, which ran in a line to the middle of considerable old-fashioned cheeks and the cheeks were reddened like the eyes, and it followed clearly that Vasia was already half-way down the road of complete drunkenness. And Vasia drank horribly and at the time was rabid! Such was more or less the appearance of Vasia. Scarcely had he noticed us when he immediately roared at the top of his voice "What is this? What is this? Are they supposed to be fortress prisoners, hard labor convicts, in civilian clothes, not shaven with beards and mustaches? What is with the rules, how can this be, and whom do they resemble?" and so on. I left all these questions here seasoned in the style with which Vasia lavished them, because why should he spare you? Would it bother him to move the ashes of someone's mother? Would it bother him to insult one to the last, not letting anyone else utter a word? I looked at Vasia with a certain pang of fear that a man would momentarily feel at a rabid dog running to him from whom he could not protect himself. At the moment when Vasia screamed and berated us, everyone stood in silence and no one responded to him, knowing him to be our future head. Everything certainly would have ended with that had Vasia, pointing out Żochowski, not said: "This one is a real tramp" or had Żochowski in a disdainful silence repulsed the insult. (They call each vagrant a tramp and fugitive, and every criminal, namely those who being sentenced to labor, who flees and does not know where to head.)[65]

At the moment when Vasia said this, Żochowski with a raising of his voice and with evident outrage said: "I am a prisoner of the state," nothing more. With such a response Vasia was led to the most furious rage. He ran to us like a hyena or jackal and in a voice no longer human threw everything at us without exception, particularly at Żochowski; so dearly are the expressions resounding in my ears—expressions that again, as previously, I did not allow myself to quote for they have no comparison. It is true that wanting to have such a supply of expressions—those such as Vasia still possessed and thus had them to use at these times—it was necessary to be either Vasia himself or finally the best first officer *Moskal*. I remember well that Vasia a few times stopped screaming, walked around a few times and returned to start again, as if he regretted it, as if he reminded himself that he had let something pass and left something unspoken. He ordered that the name of Żochowski be written down so that they could tomorrow give him 300 lashes. (The execution of such a sentence did not there perjure the judgment, but the will of a single person, to whose direct authority we had

65 Vagrants are, in fact, a particular category of prisoners among the common convicts.

been given, tomorrow was to be fulfilled!)[66] Since they had barely let us go to the prison, they escorted each of us to separate barracks so that they could examine us well, and Żochowski was dragged to the guard station in order that Vasia could fill out the order. It happened so suddenly and violently that only when he returned did we find out what had happened.

Vasia, having ordered them to write the name of Żochowski, returned again to us and responded with these words, "I will teach you, I will show you what service is." And having turned to Diagelev, gave him this errand, "Shave and clothe them as one is supposed to according to regulations, chain them in regulation shackles, and bring them to me tomorrow for examination."

Diagelev asked Vasia, saying, "Your Honor, what will you order be done with their personal things?"

"Take everything, describe it, and sell it for public auction, but take their money to use for the improvement of food for the convicts." A philanthropist for the common man?! He walked around again, raised his hoarse voice, and shouted, "Go to hell you sons of bitches!"

In the Administration Building where Diagelev had led us we stayed rather briefly, only as long as it was necessary to sign for our things and to change our clothes, after which they escorted us to spend the night in the guard station. It was already rather dark when we went to find the night's lodging and met Jan Wożniakowski, who was passing this way briefly for a few moments and only managed to stop (I will tell you about him later). At the guard station, the noncom departed, after having called us (I remember) "merchants." One must know the language well in order to know the traces of another meaning—"thieves"—for which he took us. We joined the inspection, but since Diagelev already scoured our pockets well and found nothing on me, the effort of the noncom was in vain. He let us go to the hut for those under sentence and locked it. Soon thereafter someone knocked on the door, the noncom opened it, and on the wooden cot the officer placed our dinner, sent from the prison: half a loaf of bread, weighing at least nine pounds, and a fair-sized wooden bowl of soup—the beloved *shchi*—a Russian-made dinner. I thought, it is good to see they think about our appetite. The night spent at the guard station was similar in many respects to that night before the settlement at Ochair, not on account of it having been so cramped as it was there, but on account that equally as

---

66 So svedeniiami o litsakh, otdannykh za politicheskie prestupleniia v voennuiu sluzhbu i arestantskie roty. Fond 312, opis' 2, delo 1484. RGVIA. A report by Commandant de Grave on Żochowski's death in December 1851 clarifies that he was spared corporal punishment when sent to Siberia.

many vermin crawled around, to be sure less hungry than there but equally irritating. We slept very little.

Early the next day, it had scarcely become light when they already had us in the guardhouse. The barber was waiting for us there—the one who was supposed to carry out Vaska's order and who was supposed to make real convicts of us (of our appearance, you understand). I came to the operation first and after a moment I was already ready; Żochowski came next and finally Tokarzewski, who, when he saw me entering, involuntarily covered his eyes and asked, "Jożka is it you? Oh? I swear to God that your own mother at this moment would thrice renounce you and would thrice proclaim that you are not her son." He was right; when he entered I thought the same thing after looking at his head. After everything, they led us to Vaska, and it was rather early. Vaska had to go with a report to the commandant and so was not drunk; it must be said that his cheeks were not as red as yesterday, he did not scream as powerfully, and of course he strove with his voice to broadcast muted restraint, compassion even! Always, however, with a sign of severity. He strove to convince us that the tsar knows what to do should we merit similar insults, that the punishment is proper and just. The words "tsar" and "law" escaped his mouth as many times as he needed to support his assertion with something. Finally, he instructed us how we should live so as to become deserving of his grace, regard, and indulgence. I thought, so what is to be our life? What will we be suited for doing? How should we behave? Will I respond to similar instruction, to imitate you or to remain an animal like you? I am the first one prepared to answer, "I don't want kasha and won't go for the water, either."

After listening to all the instructions and admonitions, Vaska led us to the smithy, we were chained in heavy shackles, and afterward again went to the Administration Building. They made a list of our things and took everything but he deigned to allow us to take only a few shirts— not Vaska but Diagelev—and how did they sell the rest? Who bought them? This is a secret about which no one knew; I know only that nothing later was in the dwelling. While working for Vaska, I saw our leather pillow on his bed, and the deerskin attire of Aleksander Mirecki protected him from the cold! Aleksander Mirecki arrived in Omsk in 1846, in August—he belonged to the Stefan Dobrycz affair and was sent to a particular person belonging to the association in Sandomierski with the letters of Kosowska and Dobrycz in his own hands.[67] He was arrested by the citizen Karczewski for whom he

67 Sudnoe: O politicheskom prestupnike Aleksandre Miretskom. Fond 16233, opis' 3, ed. khr. 2658. RGVIA. Through a school friend from his studies in Berlin, Mirecki met Dobrycz, who was involved in planning an uprising in Poznan; it was Dobrycz who gave him the letters and told him to meet up with Karczewski.

had the letters and at whose place he arrived, not expecting such a misfortune. Karczewski is still alive and after Aleksander's return even sent him a request that this very Aleksander give evidence for him that it is not true that Karczewski arrested him and gave him into the hands of his torturers; Karczewski wanted by this to set the record right as the event at that time weighed on him, but Aleksander could not make himself accomplish this task. He said that he could give evidence that for his deed Aleksander did not have any resentment for Karczewski and that he did not harbor hate in his heart, but nothing more. Aleksander (whom after this I will call Olech) until our arrival was the only one in the clutches of Vaska; oh, how the poor guy suffered from what he experienced—poor Olech did not have even a minute of peace. Vaska haunted him, hated him. He happened into Omsk just when Vaska, being the police chief, took the job of placmajor, began reforms in the prison, and drove the brigands (thus we called our fellow colleagues, and I will call them so further on) so that they arranged to murder him.

One of them by the name of Vlas even once cast his eye at Vaska, who had caught a brick to smash his noggin in Vlas's hand, but a guard who always surrounded Vasia smashed Vlas first and managed to bring him to the intended result. Vlas in 24 hours was sentenced to 3,000 bludgeonings and died in agony under them: he received two thousand while living and a thousand were counted on a body already dead. Everyone in the prison was present at the execution, because Vaska knew well that in such a way he was protected from similar events in the future. Despite that, however, there existed continuously a plan for murdering Vaska, but only apparently—it was far from any action. Once Vaska arrived at the prison, he was surrounded as usual by armed soldiers, and the brigands, saying nothing, allowed him to pass to the middle of the barracks. After the terrifying racket was initiated, certain ones encouraged others to act, saying: "Why are you looking there at him, let's shake him." Then others cried out: "Cowards, thugs!" Others cried out, "A thousand bludgeonings would not be awful; he did not find the whips and knouts!" It was all only shouting, wanting blood retribution, although no one could find a person with enough pluck to execute it, because fear of death mastered each of them. Despite that, however, Vaska shook, looked around, and even was in a state to track down the one here who shouted the most, the one inciting the most vengeance. He soothed them, responded to them; not wanting to listen to him, they finally settled down. Vaska vowed improvement, not in order to keep a promise, but in order to get out of a situation threatening him. They say, it was amusing to watch, how the all-powerful authority of the prison changed into a submissive lamb and with a faint-hearted trembling voice said: "What is up with you children? I will be a father to you, I will feed you kasha."

Our brigands settled down: an angry Vaska left and also kept his promise. He fed them barley kasha on Sundays and holidays but birch kasha on an everyday basis. There was not a day, not an hour, when someone was not dragged to the guardhouse, and there was almost never a day when someone was not flogged; 300 rods was the smallest dose of such medicine by which Vasia marked his beloved children! Sometimes he withdrew from the habit and had a shot or two tosses, but not always, because usually it depended on his mood or the measure of vodka that he downed. Sometimes, one must confess, Vasia punished his children properly, but for the most part he beat them just with pleasure, or it was enough to receive a cane, or let him find someone sleeping on his right side—yes, I am not joking. For this sin not just one was beaten. Vasia did not allow sleeping on one's right side. He maintained that Christ slept on his left side, and we must follow him in everything; and to such a man was given direct authority over the gangrenous part of the abscess of human society. A scoundrel, drunk, and debauched one was supposed to influence, to watch over the improvement of customs and morals of those who never thought (just like he, himself) about any of them anymore—only about the satisfaction of their animal desires, about the fulfillment of their ignoble intentions. In the further course of my story, I will tell you something more about him, and you will encounter him still another time; meanwhile I should remember those whose fate was united under one thatched roof and less about those who had authority over me. I am forced to place before your eyes a lot of evil, not much good; I am forced to lead you to a scene of the most sordid transgressions of moral turpitude by those on whom my life depended, with whom I was united equally with everything. So I start from the top.

At the time of my arrival the Army Governor General of all Western Siberia had been for 12 years Petr Dmitrevich, Prince Gorchakov—thug, executioner, tyrant of the unfortunate slaves of 1831—an old licentious and lecherous one, because who didn't know that he lived publicly with Shramova and who didn't see that she was his concubine? But we will leave this respectable couple for later and will charge forward with the murder of victims by Gorchakov, about his blood-thirsty judgment of the innocent. The fate of a murderer of the unfortunates, wherever you are, curse you for the blood of the innocents! God Almighty will demand an accounting from you, God will pay you for your crime! There is no way, brothers, that you have not heard of what is called the Omsk affair; maybe you even know more about it than me, although I was at the place, although I knew the one who ordered it, although I often visited the grave of the murdered, and although finally I tried earnestly to find out something decisively. It was the year 1835, and thus 14 years before my arrival [in Omsk]. Half of those who could provide me details were no longer living, and others were sent around to different places, while still others could not explain well and said various things. It seems that the Omsk affair had this sort of beginning: Taken into captivity by the *Moskali*, the soldiers of the Polish Army arrived in Siberia only in 1833. They were scattered about Cossack regiments, standing battalions in Siberia, and on the Orenburg line; in a short time all became convinced that hope for rescue had already perished for them, that here they must die or hurry about with a yoke on their necks. After being thus convinced, some of those bolder with more sturdy strides were determined to try to see if it were possible to free everyone, and on this account they worked out a plan of escape through the Kirgiz steppe with arms in hand to Bukharia and finally resolved through Persia to get to Europe. In order to attain this goal, they allowed into their association people on whom they could count. In this way the association expanded throughout all Western Siberia so that at the given time all were supposed to reach for weapons and come together one after another, heading as soon as possible for Omsk—the main gathering point from which they would initiate the pilgrimage to the steppe of Bukharia. The cannons had to be nailed shut and the weapons collected. The project was not able to be executed, and we will examine it more closely.

The Siberia Corps beyond this was composed of 15 battalions scattered in this way: in Tobolsk, the 1st Battalion, in Petropavlosk the 2nd and 3rd (from these two battalions always about half of the soldiers were on the Kirgiz steppe in the Akmulla district, in Kokhchetav and in other places, spread over a large space), in Omsk stood the 4th, 5th, and 6th Battalions, in Semipalatinsk the 7th and 8th (from the 8th one company is always located in Ust-Kamenogorsk). The 9th Battalion quartered in Ust-Kamenogorsk, apart from one company which continually stood in Bukhtarma. The 10th Battalion stood constantly in Barnaul, the 11th in Tomsk, the 12th and 13th in Krasnoyarsk, the 14th in Irkutsk, and the 15th in Nerchinsk. Thus, something like 15,000 of a regular army occupied living quarters on a space surpassing 4000 versts in length and as much width, and how does one here wage war? Is it the battalion of battalions, with important brave people attached—each of whom defends like a swordsman and could rush in with help? When the news about the attack on the uprising reached, for example, from Omsk to Tobolsk at an advance distance of 700 versts it was at a time when there was not a single soldier. Thus, the plan, although maybe some called it overly brave, was well thought out and even could have easily succeeded, could have made great trouble for the tsar, who naturally would have had to move against it with the interior guards, spread in the near provinces of Siberia. For them he would have had to lead a second army with food, because an army of 50,000 having stood on the border of Siberia for a month would starve the residents to such a degree that not only the army but the residents themselves would have died from hunger. The soldier during this time was not trained in anything like that, such as today's soldier. In a word, if the intended plan had not been discovered by betrayal beforehand, the Omsk affair would have been renowned throughout the whole world; then began the suppression. Almost no one didn't know about it at the time; today it is already difficult to learn about it, because it is difficult to meet someone who belonged to it. Being in Omsk, I tried to look at the act conducted by the investigation. If there were no lack of funds, it would have been easy for me to get it, if not completely then at least I could have made extensive excerpts. I lacked the 100 silver rubles by which it was possible to buy it from the clerk. At that time, none of ours was in freedom, so there was no one through whom in even this way to raise a loan, but later it was not like this.

But let's return to the affair itself. At the time when they were agitating, there were two scoundrels: a certain Grudzinski purporting to be the brother of Joanna and maintaining that there was a Prince in Łowicz (who had not been alive for a long time). For his betrayal, he received monetary compensation and the rank of officer and was transferred to Tomsk where shortly after his arrival, they found his body on the banks of the river Tom, but his death was covered in secrecy. The second scoundrel by the name of Adolf Knake is maybe still living today; he is a noncom in the headquarters of invalids in Omsk. I knew him personally and often was even forced to speak with him, since I lived in the house of the commandant, where we often went to work. About his sordid fratricidal deed I really do not know what I should say; the deed, besides being stupid, was done with some calculation. However, the latter arrived at the house of Aleksei Fedorovich de Grave. He was at that time the commander of the 4th Battalion and later colonel and commandant of the Omsk fortress; he was the first to tell him what was likely going on. At the beginning, de Grave did not want to believe it, but because Knake did not withdraw his testimony—since to support his opinion he had remembered Grudzinski above—he had naturally to take the report and communicate it to a higher authority. Then immediately followed the arrests, without exception, of everyone—both the guilty and those who had not gathered in Omsk—the investigation began at a time when two of these scoundrels with increasingly new accusations appeared; they entangled, without exception, everyone and even said about them things that had never been. In connection with this affair was also arrested the colonel of the artillery in the Russian service, of the name Markevich. After conducting the investigation, the military proceeding followed, and at least 40 people were sentenced to bludgeonings; the following six about whom I can prove only by name were beaten under bludgeons—namely, the priest and canon Sierociński,[68] Szokalski,[69] Drużyłowski,[70] Wróblewski,[71] Melodin,[72] and Biron.[73] All received 6,000 blows and were buried in one grave; wormwood and wild asparagus grew on their tomb.

Before the departure from Omsk there was a denial of prayers for the just. I tore off a little dried wormwood, and I attached it for you to this letter. I ought to mention something else about this execution. They showed me the place where it was performed beyond the city; by the road to Semipalatinsk leading to the steppe, barracks were built in which the army camps on summer holiday. Well, right by those barracks on the Irtysh, Gorchakov ordered that the 3rd Battalion of the army move out (meanwhile the artillery, Cossacks, and invalids took up the guard); they led out the unfortunate victims, and here they killed off every last one. The execution lasted from morning until evening, since the six remembered above were executed; still others were those who received 3,000, 2,000, 1,000, or 500. All left alive had to go rushing around for long years either in the ranks of convicts or in the

68 See Rufin Piotrowski's account of his martyrdom in the next part.

69 In the published version, "Recollections of a Siberian Exile," the following footnote appears in the sixteenth chapter (282:2):
Thanks to an acquaintance with the local doctor, Wiktor Szokalski, at the doctor's order during the execution, was carried to the hospital and after healing received the remaining blows. He was then sentenced to hard labor in Nerchinsk and tried to escape from there several times. Devastated by failure, he shot himself.

70 Władysław Drużyłowski, an 1830 insurgent, was sentenced to a battalion in Tobolsk in 1832, was arrested for his part as an organizer of the planned escape in 1833, received 6,000 blows at once, like Prior Sierociński, and died of his wounds in the field hospital (Śliwowska, *ZpIR*; Śliwowska, *UzS*, 60).

71 Jan Wróblewski, a participant in the 1830 uprising, served in a Cossack regiment as a gunner, was arrested in 1833 in connection with the Omsk affair, received 3,000 blows, and died in the Omsk hospital (Śliwowska, *ZpIR*, 685).

72 Włodzimierz Milidin as a "continuator" of the escape plan of Szokalski received 5,000 blows and died in the field hospital (Ibid., 338; Śliwowska, *UzS*, 61).

73 Aleksandr Biron had been sent to a battalion in Omsk for his participation in the 1830 uprising, and he did not die in Omsk but was sent to hard labor in Eastern Siberia in 1837 (Śliwowska, *ZpIR*, 64).

mines of Nerchinsk. The bludgeons at the place of execution, as they told me, were hauled in some boats up the Irtysh. Only this for certain more or less, it seems to me, can I write about this whole affair, which was renowned in its own time; today there is barely a time when someone recalls it, and for years some people recounted things that had never happened. A cross was stuck in over the tomb of the murdered who perished and fell; and for just a moment when I was there already for the last time with effort could I read the name Drużyłowski. The rest of it was destroyed, and without a doubt they would not permit a renovation of the monument, since the cemetery is already saturated with burials of the dead. Since 1850 there has been a new one, and the old is surrounded with many more residential homes; slowly, slowly other new people will enter on the scene of life, and the remembrance will perish. Let this be my remembrance, therefore, even though it is short and although the reference is preserved inexactly—for it I will call upon each person who could clarify it. Let them give us more details about what happened, and let them set my account right.

Let us return now to Gorchakov, to Shramova. Shram, the general director of the cadet corps, had a wife who as I remembered was more lofty; she was the concubine of Gorchakov and nothing else. She governed Siberia with an omnipotent right; she did what she wanted, and everyone who wanted to receive something knew well about this. First, he had to bow down to her and only then could he definitely succeed with "Princess" Shramova, who had three daughters and a son. The daughters were given in marriage, and immediately their husbands received profitable jobs; for example, Kleist was a leader of the Kirgiz and could flay these poor people as much as he liked, in which he never slacked off at all. Shakhovski was new in the Commission of Provisions, where even more was stolen. But the less-than-a prince gave balls, teas, dinners, various walks, and rides on the water and on land. Everything was done openly, and everyone was surprised at the tolerance of her spouse, for which he once more took away crosses, ranks, and stars. The one who did not want to befriend Shramova fell into disfavor with the prince and was harried, and there even happened to be occasions when they devised minor offenses, judged them, and drove them out of the service. Such abuses, for example, the commandant of the fortress Aleksei Fedorovich de Grave tolerated. He was descended from a French family which was certainly driven in this direction by the revolution a century ago. He was a man, who in comparison with others, was not mean. He did not do a lot of good, it is true, but also was not Krivtsov, not Vaska; he loved hunting, shot perfectly, loved revelry, got drunk even, and that was his thing. In the early years he served in Lithuania, about which the advice he always gave was that he repented not once those moments happily lived. In his house there was always a pair of young women; they were closer or more distant kinship and received there a rather careful upbringing by the window ledge of Mrs. Commandant about whom it is fitting to remember that she was kind-hearted; she was named Anna and was the daughter of Andrei Romanov. Seven years I survived Omsk, and I never heard even one thing mean about her. Sure, quite the contrary, she somehow or other understood life; she lifted up a human being when she saw him falling under the weight of destitution, and she needed to bring him the help quickly; she considered it her duty, and having done it, did not do it out of any pride—in a word, Anna Andreevna was not like any other. She has great power over men and of this power we availed ourselves more than once in the following manner: My colleagues like Szymek Tokarzewski were used to paint rooms, from which he became acquainted more closely with the wife of the commandant. As always, those, who had the closest influence over us, crossed the bounds of authority; he had rather a chat with Anna Andreevna about it, and she immediately put pressure on her husband so that they eased up on us. Then for a similar intercession we carried our request only to her, when our leaders, thinking that they were making order, made the greatest disarray.

Because there is, as if in the nature of the *Moskal*, the one who fawns before the elders, tramples those lower than himself, and reflects what is most evident in those who make officer after serving 12 years in the noncommissioned officers' ranks. I want you to imagine a man who can barely read and write after 12 years of service in the noncommissioned officers' ranks and as little as six years of service as a soldier—after 18 years, having assumed the uniform of an officer and having been raised to the dignity of an ensign—a man who was just beaten and now can, himself, beat those lower than he. Each of our officers, newly created in this way, solemnly treats himself at this first moment. He gets drunk in a few days, after which he learns the officer's tone and thus, for example, constantly obtains the service of a soldier and therefore calls to him, "Hey there, give the master a pipe—hey there, give the master a glass of vodka" and so on. In a word, that poor being constantly must be at the command of his master, constantly fulfills edicts, constantly bustles around him, for which he is dressed the worst and fed the worst. I could write you an entire jeremiad about these new officers, who are commonplace in Russia; they are called *bourbons*.[74]

74 A jeremiad is a lengthy lament that includes social criticism and is so named for its connection to the formal elements in the prophecies attributed to the biblical prophet Jeremiah.

They will advance in service and with their subordinates will be here for a long time.

So, I am returning to the interrupted story. I return to Anna Andreevna, who brought horrible persecution from Gorchakov on her husband because she did not want to befriend Shramova, did not want to frequent her place, and did not want to receive her. For her conduct, Gorchakov bothered her husband as only he could and never attracted the least attention to the fact that Vaska did what he pleased and that he did not listen to the commandant, although in Russia respect for order was very strictly observed. Anna Andreevna, when we were freed from work, out of decency went to thank the commandant (although maybe it was not for this that she thanked him). Having seen us with Szymek, she was sincerely delighted for us, freely and with true joy ran into our hall to our place, candidly squeezed our hands, and congratulated us on a new life. With this up until now I have told my certain knowledge of people standing more or less at the forefront of Omsk, and you doubtlessly recognized how much each person could do good or harm to us.

Now it falls to me to ask you into the prison, to the place where passed the most beautiful moments of my life. It falls to me to acquaint you with those with whom we had to live. Therefore, let's return to those moments when, after the inspection was performed and after we were shaved and chained in fetters, Vaska decided that everything was fulfilled as it should be and ordered us to be conducted to the prison. The soldiers escorted us as usual with arms in hand to the gate itself, and there awaited our arrival Aleksander Mirecki, who himself had finished three years in this grave of the living, not having had either a peaceful day or night, because Vaska himself singled him out for something, and only he could have invented such ways of insulting and bothering poor Olech. Once he did not know for what he ordered that Olech be led to the guard station and given 100 lashings. And for what? Vaska did not know; it pleased him, and it was enough: "You are a peasant," he said to Olech, "one can beat you." If there had not been an officer by the name of Kuplennikov, if there had not been any Lieutenant Colonel Novoselov, who knew Aleksander closely and stood up for him, and who at that time had sat under judgment because of a false accusation by Vaska, Olech would absolutely have been taken away and set for the most outrageous punishment. Vaska did not come to watch how they beat poor Olech, because he could not even imagine that he would find such a brave soul who dared not fulfill his order. At the time of our arrival in Omsk, Olech was used for the most onerous and disgusting work. He was a *parashnik* (as are called those who clean the cesspool). This cleaning always happened at night from ten to one and later. He had already spent two months there before our arrival and as much as two after it. Poor Olech completely lost his sense of smell and has not yet recovered it today. It is difficult to find out the reason for which poor Olech suffered such persecution; it may be that this miscreant regretted this course of action later, if he ever reflected on his course of action. I myself heard he regretted the affair with Żochowski when they had Vaska driven out of service, and he then said, "God will judge me for Żochowski. My conscience continually torments me." Did that vile one even have a conscience? Well, I again deviated from the subject.

I had to conduct you to the jail and scarcely had I stood before its gates, when I fell into another matter as if I feared to enter into the place where, as I already recollected, were left my youth, my youthful strength, my dreams, my health, my everything! So, let's go, let's go acquaint you with the hard labor camp—that is, with the people who lived there—acquaint you with the customs and with their way of thinking. I will lift for you the veil and will show you what happened behind it. I will share with you my prize, and you will learn about something that not one of you has thought; you will there encounter those whom you already know and many new ones besides. I only ask you to believe that everything that I will tell you is the sincere truth.

The gate was opened and by it stood poor Olech with some kind of melancholy smile; pale and emaciated he rushed to hug us, and together with him, however, a group of scoundrels greeted us with another sentiment. O my God, how I here beheld those figures! And they all come to us and give us their hands, hands that so many times were stained with blood so that not one effaced their transgression or crime! And although a man is concerned with the horror, he must give them his hand. I will confess sincerely that I ran short of courage, repelled each of them, and none of them has loved me, too; they called me as they wished: either devil or Satan. They persecuted me and insulted me, as they wanted; they abused me as they knew how, and the *Moskali* know how to abuse. There was a time when I could not pass through the courtyard, because from everywhere a volley of verbal abuse and curse words flew; there was a time when moments were so difficult, when it was as if the earth opened beneath my feet and as if I leapt into it without a moment's thought in the hope that under it I could find something better, but there was not much land—our world is only 333 paces in circumference! The world is so small that to be alone, if only for a minute, if only for a moment, would be difficult—it would be for an hour, for a moment. Oh, thank God that there was only one such moment, when despair on the one hand and madness on the other assaulted me, when I was close to a downfall—I will never forget that moment! With a clenching of the heart in the breast, with a head full of the oddest thoughts I ran out into the courtyard and shortly began to take measure quickly in different directions. I know nothing of what was happening next to me, I remember nothing, I only felt that I was somehow in delirium, that my entire order of thoughts was suddenly mixed up, that my convictions shredded my principles, everything spun around me, and everyone before my eyes went almost dark. Oh, I suffered! I suffered a lot in that awful moment! The good God rescued me from my downfall and examined me at that moment with an eye of compassion, because I do not know in any case from where came the idea, but I will call to mind the passage and declare it rather loudly:

> Let us learn to conceal joy and anger.
> And to be as in an abyss, thoughts unattainable.
> We have to be quietly destructive like effluvia
> And wait unassumingly like a cool snake![75]

Then I repeated the entire verse of Adam to the Polish Mother and felt for one moment a passing doubt, for one moment despair approached me, and for this one moment I was immediately punished, since common sense returned, the blush of shame warmed my cheeks, and I remembered that God bestowed on each human being volition, his own shield, his own power before which everything should be humbled, before which everything should repent. I calmed myself and resolved from then on to regard everything with cold blood, to hold in contempt all adversity, and to repeat these verses about difficult moments of doubt like a prayer.

The Arrival of the Petrashevtsy

In 1850, in the month of January two Russian prisoners of the state arrived at our prison from St. Petersburg: Sergiusz, son of Fedor Durov, and Fedor, son of Mikhail Dostoevsky.[76] They were extraordinarily weak, irritable, and overloaded with iodine and mercury like a pharmacist's cupping glass; they were sentenced to four years of labor and then the army. This Durov, at least he reconciled his past position with his current one, knew the world, and had enough learning that helped him make accurate observations concerning the predispositions and character of some people. And although

75 This is from Adam Mickiewicz's "To the Polish Mother" (*my translation*).

76 Here folio 49.5 is joined to folio 26 to continue the logical order of the published text.

sometimes he fatally bored us by repeating several times stories from his life or from the life of his acquaintances in St. Petersburg, although all of these scenes took their starting point if not in restaurants then in bars or, finally, in offices, although from this it was easy to infer something about his past life, although one could think that nothing important occupied his time like collecting bits of news, and although Durov was sometimes rather ridiculous, he was however not a bad *Moskal*. I heard at least 20 times how he repeated that his uncle was governor somewhere supposedly in Smolensk, that his mother was descended in a straight line from Khmelnitsky, etc.[77] Often it was possible to talk pleasantly with him (we understand one another without spilling too much). But the other, the renowned novelist, the author of *Poor Folk* and several other greater or lesser stories, that glory of the North, that tremendous talent, that renown greatness, how he in my eyes appeared ambitious and insipid. In no way am I speaking to his talent in writing stories—he could have it, and he could even have a lot of it, but this is not about his talent—here we are talking about his character. As a graduate of the cadet corps, he absorbed every evil, which is nestled in such establishments, and he effaced in himself all nuclei of good, which were, or even could have been in childhood. He was a *Moskal* in the entire sense of the word—he hated Poles; about himself he said (since from the features of his face and from his name, unfortunately, it was possible to recognize his Polish descent) that if he knew that in his veins there were even a drop of Polish blood, he would order that it be removed immediately—and this was supposed to be a man of progress? This very one was supposed to be a representative of a new principle, new ideas? Judging from his opinions, I would have said he was an advocate of rule by the knout, since many times he expressed himself in the following manner: "I will be happy only at that time when I see all neighboring people under the dominion of the tsar, because what are these French, English, Germans, and Spaniards—in other words, are they a nation? These are caricatures, a parody of a nation!" Dostoevsky never said of Ukraine, Volhynia, Podolia, Lithuania, and all Poland, that this is a nation plundered by force. He always maintained that it was their age-old property and that the hand of God's justice handed it all over to the authority of the tsar, only so that the people were enlightened

77 Bogdan Khmelnitsky was a Cossack hetman who led a revolt against Polish rule to establish regional autonomy in Ukrainian lands, but he eventually was forced to sign the Treaty of Pereiaslavl with Moscow in order to protect the liberated region from the Poles; Durov wrote an article on a descendant, the playwright, Nikolai Khmelnitsky.

and were enlightened by the paternal blessed reign of the tsar; otherwise, he said, if it were left to itself, the nation would be indigent, ignorant, and barbaric. The Baltic provinces and likewise Siberia and the Caucasus are also Rus proper. Listening not just once to such absurdities from a man from whom one ought to demand something more, I thought to myself, is he not by any chance a lunatic?

At the beginning of the Eastern campaign when the Russian army passed beyond the Danube, Dostoevsky, although in jail, walked around with a glowing face, ironically smiled while looking at us, dreamt of a new annexation of Turkey, loudly said that Constantinople, that all of European Turkey should have long ago belonged to Russia, and that it will be the flower of the Russian empire! But what was his expression when he found out that Gorchakov was returning from beyond the Danube, and it meant a road of retreat with corpses. I remember well how much it disturbed him, how wildly he looked all around him, how walking around the barrack he sat down at last near the stove and poked his finger in a gap, not saying anything about anything. For a long time, we had been at odds with each other, since it was difficult to maintain even an ostensible agreement with a man, who always remembered that he had been an officer and as an officer had always wanted to proceed forward. As an author, he loved to talk about literature of every nation, which he could not know aside from his own and some French. According to him everything in comparison with Russian literature was not of any worth. Once we said something about *The Wandering Jew*; I recalled when in 1844 a subscription for a translation of *The Jew* was announced in Warsaw. I wanted to say something more—it seems that I wanted to continue with something further . . . that only in '45 after my return from Tambov could I read it—but Dostoevsky did not let me finish, did not want to believe it, and even brutally accused me of lying. Durov reminded him that there was no need for any spitefulness; however, he did not retreat from his principle. His principle was (speaking no longer about his hateful Poles) to strip every nation of everything that only it could have as beautiful, great, and noble and to degrade and starve it of all national keepsakes—to use honest or dishonest means, to elevate only oneself while pushing others down to the bottom, when possible. These are the results of a pernicious upbringing in the cadet corps. In my opinion, upbringing in the corps is as pernicious for humanity as it is advantageous and necessary for the currently existing government. The upbringing is incompetent, narrow-minded, and neglectful; let's look at what they do with a young one, who enters into similar establishments. In advance, they order him to forget about father and mother; they tell him that the tsar is his father and mother, his everything. The young one must not have his own will, but they impress upon him from the beginning that will is foreign, and they order him to listen and perform blindly that which is his duty. In this way, slowly the habit of servility becomes automatic in the execution of orders; about his father, mother, and familial relations he has already long ago forgotten, and he knows only the hand that feeds and clothes him, which beats strong emotions and a moral essence into him. And in exchange for this, did it give him not a wretched means of life for a battered morality, for ruined emotions, for a debased character? That same hand that feeds and clothes him, shows him and gives him trinkets and baubles but calls them honors and says as Satan tempted Christ: "I would render you all this if you bowed before me." After several years spent by the young one in such an atmosphere, he grows into a young man, and he already reaches the rank of a uniformed officer. Never mind that he was healthy and hearty, and today he grows pale in the face of licentiousness; never mind that after several years he learned nothing—he is an officer and has means to live. As long as he fulfills orders blindly, as long as he is enterprising, as long as he takes advantage of everything that passed through only his hands, he never lacks bread and after several, some dozen years he can rise high, very high. A young officer assigned somewhere far away for service succeeds there, knocks about there for the rest of his life, and there wretchedly perishes, because rarely does one leave victoriously from this precipice. These cadet corps are houses of public breeding. I would call these public houses the corruption of youth! About what goes on there, I cannot even say; I knew a lot about what they thought from these establishments. What's more, once I read a letter written by one of the graduates released from the Siberian cadet corps to his young colleague, still in the corps, and from its contents I have the complete right to judge how the relations that existed between them were in no way the relations of collegiality or friendship, but simply the relations of two differently-sexed beings, both ruined by licentiousness! Someone can impute something, but not being oneself in a similar institution, I cannot know everything that takes place there, so with this I write only that it seems to me that the allegations are completely correct; however, this in no way weakens the truthfulness of my statement. It is enough to speak only once with graduates of the cadet corps, and it is enough to listen to their conversation in order to be convinced of the principles inculcated in them in childhood—each one wanting and not wanting to declare to you everything that happened with him from the moment of stepping across the threshold of the edifice of the cadet corps until his departure. One's decency should not be offended, and maybe not one thing is filthy. Admittedly it is not always authentic (but pronounced for the stage) and everyone who got an upbringing in the corps must admit that it is no different than this.

Someone contradict me that a young officer, having been released from the corps, without any moral principles, not knowing and not conceiving any duties of a man or any goal in life, gives up and perishes in the throes of dissipation. His recollections and his thoughts hang on the edifice where he passed his adolescent years, where he so often (as in St. Petersburg) saw the deity of his nation—the tsar, whom he was accustomed to venerate like God, because he constantly saw only an Orthodox priest dressed in vestments, which must signify the attire of Christ with a chalice in hand, walking before his people, and he heard him enumerate the names of all the members of the tsar's family! Someone asks again in what manner, by what way could a man such as Dostoevsky, who similarly received his upbringing, descend to labor in a fortress? Is this the proper question? The thing is, however, too simple; some works of progressive French writers fell into his hands, such a truth as he read there forced its way through to the abode of his reason. He could not fail to understand it; it roused his senses and showed him the falsity of his conduct and life, and he desired improvement. Given favorable circumstances, he could still become a man who could rehabilitate his life, but once disappointed he was not able to persevere, set out down the old path, and once released into freedom became destined for service in Semipalatinsk. He earned restitution to the rank of officer, married a widow, and even before he obtained an officer's rank he wrote a laudatory poem for Tsar Nicholas, in which he extolled his greatness and the power of his reason—and for what? For the Crimean War! When these two people were in Omsk and lived under one roof with us, it seemed to me that I was looking at two little lights of rebirth that glittered in the gloomy sky of the North! Alas, with sorrow I come to admit that I was most strongly disappointed, because not only near the end of the imprisonment had we all severed our relations, especially with the second one, but moreover we had to hold him in contempt; he threatened us with the reporting and publication of our former conversations—and, in a word, he said that if he had a mind to manage it, we would perish in the prison. From word to deed, everyone concedes, remains only one step! But as if that were not enough, I had later the cleverness to find out about others acting in this affair, the so-called Petrashevsky affair. All were, with small exception, similar to each other, and none was lacking in education, but each one was of very weak character, and each one was fond of drinking or also of playing cards. I am not enumerating their names, and I could do this, if I had not strayed too far from our topic, to which it is time to return at last.

Hard Labor

Maybe not exactly did I portray for you, however I could, a couple of images of people with whom either I was connected or also on whom I depended. Besides, I should give images of some convicts, for whose sake I will return to the moments when they opened and shut the gate of the prison. Vaska ordered us to be separated and that each of us be held in a separate barrack. For a few days we were not used for any work because of a shortage of sheepskin coats, which weren't worth anything, but without wool they ordered us in Ust-Kamenogorsk to remake our large loose sheepskin coats into smaller, shorter ones so that they would agree with the prescribed form; next they used us for various small services—there where someone was to chop a tree, to remove snow from a yard, or for the various building materials, which lay in large quantities on the banks of the river, or we performed similar activities. Until spring approached, we were used to make brick, this was the hardest work. Every day, with a dry chunk of bread in our pocket, we left early for the brick factory built about 5 versts from the fortress; we returned from there only at nighttime. From the beginning, work was limited to cleaning the shed and stoves from snow driven by the wind during wintertime; it was still nothing by comparison to our subsequent work. Several times I had to clear the stove of rubble and ashes; these stoves were long and it was necessary to drag oneself to the corner, to throw the ashes and rubble continually in front of oneself in order to clean it completely. Because of these two considerations, it was very burdensome work—one for which it is absolutely necessary to be in a kneeling position, and then the wind carried back the ashes that had been cleaned away. When a man comes back from there, then his caprice forces him to look in the mirror, and he often regrets that he does not have something at hand, since each of us was so similar after such work that it was difficult to distinguish one from another. I cannot say that similar work was not burdensome, but since I was given still lighter work in comparison to brickmaking, maybe there is not such barbarity in the world.

One must dig farther beforehand to bring clay to the pit, to bring water farther, but I can no longer tell you in what wheelbarrows or wooden pail, and it was necessary to bring water from below, not less than 100 cubits deep.[78] Next it was necessary to smooth out the clay with legs chained in shackles and to bring to the shed again clay from the pit, which had already been kneaded, and there someone was responsible for making 500 bricks (it was apportioned into thirds). Such work was too burdensome, although I thought slowly, slowly perhaps I will steel myself and become accustomed to this occupation, and maybe in time it will not be so very heavy. Meanwhile, however, my physical strength seemed too weak. I remember sometime in June 1850, having been as usual in the brick factory in the morning, I was assigned to the removal of the finished brick, already fired from the stove, at 1,000 bricks per person. Wanting to make use of the cold morning, we immediately took up our work so that before noon when the sun started strongly to beat down on us we would have finished maybe half of our work, and then would relax for a moment, thereby gathering enough strength to finish the rest. I had not yet removed 200 bricks, and I was already very tired, I felt very thirsty, and having eaten nothing that day I drank a little water. Soon I was not feeling well, and I remember that I sat on a loaded wheelbarrow, although what happen then to me I no longer know. Then, having regained consciousness, I felt horribly cold, I glanced at my white uniform, and I saw that it was soaked in blood.

"What is it?" asked Olech who stood next to me.

"Tell me, Aleksander, what is going on with me?"

"You passed out again. You fell and injured your face and forehead, and you are weak. You should leave here for the prison now, and from there they will take you to the hospital; you need help."

Soon thereafter I left the brick factory, not being able to abandon the impression that my weakness had come on so violently. In the prison, having drunk something warm already, I saw that I was remarkably better. Besides, it was necessary to head for the hospital, where, I know, after having arrived, I slept without a break—as if dead—for at least 15 hours. Twice the doctor came and twice he found me sleeping; I woke up after his arrival, and they let him know about it. He came immediately, and decided that it was a fever, he prescribed medicine, and the paroxysm did not return. I left the hospital and returned back to the prison. For several days, they no longer sent me to the brick factory, and I went with the bricklayers as an assistant handing them gypsum, bricks, and lime.

On July 16 of that year, our group became larger with the arrival of four new ones: Józef Anczykowski, Karol Bem, Ludwik Korczyński, and

78 A cubit is the length of the tip of one's middle finger to one's elbow.

Jan Musiałowicz.[79] The first two were sentenced to two years and the last for four years. It was easy to predict that from the enlargement of our circle things would be far from worse. After all, in going from one to two it is easier to walk far to work, when the work is less burdensome. After all, the engineers themselves after the accident with me in the brick factory were rather considerate with us, and they did not always send us there, but when there were ten of us, then it was already more difficult to assign everyone to lighter work, especially since our colleagues (usually prisoners sentenced for crimes) demanded loudly that we should work on equal terms with them! Such a cry arose because of this in the prison that it reached Vaska. He therefore came himself in the morning for so-called distribution of labor (work allocation). He called us all line by line and ordered that we be used to make bricks. He attacked Olech, as usual, and even struck him for the reason that he did not have a neck scarf on his neck. Perhaps, some will say that one should kill, murder Vaska at such a moment when he raised his hand at one of us and no differently did this thought certainly move like lightening through my head, but each person thought at the same time that he, himself, does not have, could not have anything at hand with which he could accomplish the just revenge. Everything was taken away from us, and, in addition, Vaska never walked without a guard, who not sympathetically but only fearfully and attentively guarded him. From that moment, one can say, by our highest authority we were assigned to make bricks, and we had to make them until winter. Oh, the year 1850 was perhaps the most burdensome for us. Vaska walked around the new arrivals, no longer so severe or so tyrannical as with us, and certainly he drank less vodka and therefore was a little more gentle. Perhaps anyway, it is true that his conscience tormented him for the deplorable behavior with Żochowski, and Vaska did not order him to remove things, but they had him lie in the magazine and be excused until the hour of freedom. He simply ordered the prisoners shaved, chained in shackles, and dressed according to the rules, and with this Vaska still explained himself to them, saying: "If my own father were sent into penal servitude, maybe I would cry over him and I would say: 'What is there to do, father dear? It is necessary to shave your head and chain you in shackles.'"

Of the new arrivals, only Karol Bem had a trade, since he was an interior painter, and the remaining three, just like all of us, became numbered among the unskilled laborers. With any trade, a man will never perish—the obvious proof that even in penal servitude the good and

79 For more on this group of exiles, see Blake, *Dostoevsky and the Catholic Underground*, 27–28.

even the not-so-good craftsman exercises certain prerogatives; somehow day after day passes more easily for him. Sometimes even a grosz can be earned sooner so that at least for a moment when having grown tired of the throne of Caesar a certain change is made and, by this, physical strength is maintained. As much as possible, a trade is necessary for each person, and young people should be instilled with this thought from the moment they already begin to comprehend life and when they begin to ponder over that which is life and when each person can most easily be convinced that they, like us, after arriving in a fortress, can be placed in a line and can be asked like us: "What can you do?" You say, for example, "I was at the university in the mathematics department, and I know mathematics," but to this they respond to you or they ask: "And do you know arithmetic?" A second replies, "I was in law courses," and another says, "I finished the gymnasium," to which they reply, "What is your gymasium to me? What are your law courses to me? Here we need good shoemakers, locksmiths, blacksmiths, carpenters, etc." Fathers to whom God gave children and who have sons, believe these words, listen to my advice acquired with difficult experience. When your son finishes university, give him plane or a trowel, an awl or needle, and finally an ax or a sledgehammer, and you may be sure that at some time your son will bless you for it!

Sons! Young Poland, desire to dedicate a few years to learning a trade, because in time it may be very, very necessary for you! Who knows, who will assure us that persecution in our unhappy country has already come to an end today? Who knows whether tomorrow they will return to the times of Nicholas's terrorism? Who knows whether you will not be abducted from the family circle, whether they will transport you, too, like us, at some time to this very place, to this very fortress in which we were? Will it be the same, will not you have to suffer as we suffered, will you not, like us, say at some time, "Oh, how my father did poorly that in training the mind he forgot to train the hands!"? Who knows what awaits you—you who step out onto that road which we have already trod. You step out with that same hope for life, and it seems to you that such obstacles as you encounter on the road, prove to be easily removed. So we thought when we were twenty years of age, and we looked at the world through rose-colored lenses—life seemed a game to us and we had only, ourselves, to gather the flowers—unfortunately! It was otherwise! Youth! Do not despise a trade, and certainly respect work! Unite with your impoverished brothers, warm them with the warmth of your wisdom, strive if not on account of intellect then at least on account of feelings and heart to make people of them, and sometime, sometime, when the appropriate moment draws near, the material will be ready for you to rebuild the country, which today moans from the violence—the same as it did of old, and which perhaps during Alexander is not as unhappy as under Nicholas. It is time to return to a continuation of the story.

Bem was a painter and immediately took to work; everyone admired his work, and everyone also demanded to have rooms painted, but the first was our Vaska. They assigned me, as his assistant, to mixing the paints, and, although fearfully, I began to go to Vaska's home for work. It lasted rather a long time, and in this way Vaska had the astuteness to become acquainted with us more closely, and soon even began to have a better impression of us. He was exceedingly satisfied both with the progress of the work and with the work itself, and it flattered his vanity that no one had such a pretty room. After all, we progressed with it very cautiously, striving, however, to attain some benefit from his good inclination toward us. We absolutely had to unite together with each other in one barrack. Cautiously we stepped up with the request for this subject, and he agreed to our proposal and moreover allowed us to make the choice from among all the prisoners—he allowed us to have more peaceful comrades. From his angle, it was exceptionally great. We asked him about the Kabardians and the Circassians who numbered ten and with whom from the time of our arrival we had been on very good terms; although it was difficult to converse with them, a particular sympathy, after all, governed us. You see, they sensed by instinct and made out that we were from a nation oppressed just like they. For a long time, no one was surprised when he saw that sometimes a Circassian walked together with a Pole, and that sometimes a Circassian will help a Pole finish assigned work and will finish it not for compensation but only out of sympathy. It is necessary to acquaint the reader with the Circassians, because more than once will it fall to me to say something about them. These people are called savages, why? I do not know—maybe for the reason that for so long they resisted violence and did not allow that a yoke be placed on their neck. If I had to generalize, I would have to recognize from several such individuals that I could admit that I in no way discerned ferocity in them. Indeed, I found that delicacy in manners, which one sees only among highly developed people. The Circassians trusted us in everything, were ready always to avenge injustice inflicted on us, and otherwise never said anything to us. Only *Kardash*, which means comrade in their language—by this name the Circassians call only those people whom they love, whom the *Moskali* called "*urus*."[80] In a word, the Circassians were our friends and defenders. Here are their names:

80 Bogusławski may here be referring to Urus Khan—a descendent of Genghis Khan who was a fourteenth-century ancestor of the khans of the Kazakh Khanate.

1. Ali-Bek Ali Ferdy Ogla, 2. Weli Ismakhan Ogla, 3. Ali Ismakhan Ogla, 4. Mamed Khan Mukhamed Khan Oglu, 5. Nuru Shakhmurlu Oglu, 6. Kierim Nijas Oglu, 7. Redzheba Kanbalai Khassan Gussein Ogłu, 8. Makhmed Mustafa Oglu, 9. Abdul Arstambek, 10. Molla Mukhamed Chadzy Khassan Gussein Oglu (surnames and first names of the Circassians—I wrote them according to how they were written in Russian).

When Vaska was placated a little, when he had already begun to become better convinced about us, when he at last agreed to place us together in one barrack, when he consented to the choice of the Circassians as people characterized by tranquility, and when finally he performed the transfer, the whole prison at that time became enflamed with great hatred toward us and still is today. Often one even managed to hear threats and so, on the one hand, our position improved by which we could enjoy some kind of peace in the evening, and then again, on the other hand, during the day was worse, because the convicts were advised to bother us in every place and everywhere it was possible, and they did not forget about it. We were already used to threats and to harassment; we did not fear them at all, counting always on the Circassians to defend us in case of an incident. In our barrack, we also resided with one Jew, who unintentionally remained with us, since all the others beat him with fists, as if for a joke but always for real. This Jew was a singular specimen—the single son of Israel in the prison, who was called Isai Bemstein—and he was a Jew in every meaning of the word. He was an ardent Hasid, a superstitious Talmudist, and he had his own books, because on Friday he went through Sabbath with the entire ear-piercing ceremony and at that time our barrack was transformed into a synagogue; on a little table he burned tallow candles, put a prayer shawl on himself, spread out his books, and in an ear-piercing voice continuously repeated: "Blessed are you, Lord our God Rabbah [abundant love]!"

The figure of our little Jew, thin like a skeleton and always dirty except for Saturday, was amusing. He took tobacco snuff to revulsion, he had too much learning, he himself was not utterly stupid, and he even lacked the usual Jewish artfulness. He was accepted by us into our Polish-Kabardian comradeship as more a curiosity, and what is more out of kindness to shield him from the inventions and jabs of the entire prison. Isai was, for this reason, at least seemingly obliging. I recall him only because he almost certainly played a role in this incident that took place in our barrack about which I will now recount. There was a fight, a terrible fight about which, up until now, I did not have a notion and which gained the name of a fight of the Russians with the Kabardians—Oh, this is a drawing of the barracks.[81] In such an order as I presented here we all slept, and each had his assigned square arshin, and this was his entire home. A man does not need a lot, right? It occurs to me to tell about the fight that arose on Christmas Eve, itself, in 1850—maybe at the same moment when our families, breaking the wafer, remembered us and when each of the members sent after us most sincere wishes. It was the second Christmas Eve in Siberia, which we decided to celebrate as formally as possible. Vaska, satisfied with the progress of our work, as evidence of his invaluable kindness, ordered us freed that day from work and moreover even put in to buy us half-a-pound of fish (a pound of fish in Siberia costs at the most 40 groszy). He ordered that meat, butter, kasha, etc. be added, and he announced that he permitted us to celebrate the holy day in our own way. Benefiting from this and having still a few groszy, we contributed a little to the Christmas Eve dinner and compiled the dinner in Vaska's kitchen with the help of his cook. Bem, who was painting rooms at that time, prepared everything, and in the evening with the help of his waggoneer from the hallway and the cook Fedka, he brought it to the prison. The soldier who let this entire transport through the gate, seeing that Vaska's people were bringing it, did not dare take a look at what they were carrying, although he had the right to do it, and in this way everything passed through without a search. Here, I am not talking at all about dishes but about forks and knives, which the cook took from Vaska and wished us to use together with plates, spoons, a tureen, and platters. Vaska knew nothing about it.

We hastily organized a table that would serve as our sideboard; it was removed from a bunk with its ends resting on boxes made impromptu. At the moment when we should already have sat down to the dinner, having called all prisoners of the Catholic faith—without exception—to it and at the moment when the soup had already been poured into the bowls, at the doors of our barrack appeared a thin figure, emaciated, a walking corpse. One of the most heinous creatures, one of the most despicable figures who were in the prison, was a prisoner by the name of Kuzma Gromov (I know well as a result of something). I cannot say for certain whether Gromov was really drunk or he just resembled a drunk at the moment when he entered the barrack. Being busy with the dinner, none of us paid attention to him until such time as he approached one of the Circassians by the name of Ali-Bek Ali Ferdy Ogla, when not knowing why and not knowing from where he started a quarrel with him. Finally, Ali-Bek—although old and

81 In the right-hand corner of folio 31.5 Bogusławski has sketched the layout of the bunk, discussed in the introduction.

gray, a tremendously strong man—not waiting long, seized Gromov with his sinewy hands, and in one moment threw him out the doors (which Gromov himself had opened) and into the corridor until he fell flat on his face. At that point, as if at a given signal, an entire mass of convicts flung themselves at the center of the barrack, and when a terrible cry went up at this, at that moment, having raised our heads, we saw the commotion—the beginnings of the fight. Everything happened so suddenly, so violently, that it took hardly a minute. If not for the Circassians, I do not know what would have come of the beating; they did not lose their presence of mind, because at the first push of the brigands, they let only six or seven pass to the center and at once two stood at the doors. They spread out and thus bravely defended the access; not only could none of the prisoners defend it, but even an officer with a guard, who came running at once and pushed in, could defend it. Standing next to our improvised table, we watched what was taking place; the door to the barrack, parted with the entire force of the crowd of convicts, seemed to break or fall from the hinge.

The prison was eaten up, I will say, from fury, but everything was to no avail, so from the middle it was nice to see what was going on. The Circassians in the blink of an eye took off their shirts and like gladiators stood ready at the fight, and they were not standing idle; their strong fists were raised up and dropped down like a flail threshing wet rye in a barn. They beat, as if smashing pots, into the shaved heads, which had passed through to the center; one after another they deftly gave it to them, and, as though throwing balls, showered them with a hail of fists. In a word, they were beating madly, and they were beating well! One could hear only deafening moans of the vanquished, vain screams, and vain straining of those standing behind the door. No one could reach the place where our table stood; the table stood unmoved. The entire scene lasted no more than three minutes, after which at the door appeared an officer with soldiers and weapons. The Circassians had already stopped beating, and they threw out only those who passed to the center. Beyond the door it was quiet and peaceful as if no one were there. Everything that had happened in those few minutes was difficult to describe, and the scene was horrible, but altogether rather amusing. Our Jew, whom I recalled above, however, laughed the most. Since he, seeing what they were bringing, did not wait until the brave fists felled him to the ground, but immediately having grasped the tallow candle, he scrutinized the entire scene and in a stifled voice—"Ah, ah!"—he admired the blows of the Circassians that were poured like hail on the menacing hell-raisers for a moment, who presently fell to the ground.

When the officer entered the center of the barrack, our Isai already calmly slid off the stove; the officer, having been persuaded that none of us was drunk and that the fight arose only out of the attack, ordered everything, aside from our barrack, to close up at once and left, having allowed us to finish the dinner. Only then did our Isai approach us with a triumphant expression that with complete satisfaction asked, "And what sort are we?" He said this as if he himself actively had belonged to the fight. I must now here explain the reasons for the fight depicted. We already had the least sympathy among the *Moskali*, as I already several times recalled. The better we got to know them, the more we became convinced that although one could speak in a supposedly polite way with them, it was always contemptuous in the soul; our convictions, our faith, and everything that I will relate to you divided us from them forever. It could never be otherwise. It outraged everyone that, although made equal with them on account of the clothes, the maintenance of the division of work, and, in a word, made equal by every superficial physical account that I hereby express, our moral might at every step seemed better. Each of those outcasts thought that a man, as long as he placed a bi-colored jacket on himself, should forget about his dignity and that under his clothes of dishonor, he is already free to do everything that he always does; generally, they were often heard to say: "And what do you think, that you're God?" There are thousands of such convicts—*varnaks* (a technical expression to signify a man deprived of his rights and exiled to hard labor) just like the rest of us. For this reason, namely *he* gave the catchword at the beginning of a fight; it was the agitation of brother convicts by the one exiled from Petersburg for ten years for spying by the name of Paul, the son of Peter Aristov. "A spy in the works!" someone shouts with astonishment.

Savage Villainies

So, Aristov was a spy, and I will tell you his story—it is rather amusing. Our hero found himself in Petersburg in the year 1848; he was expelled from service for villainies of various kinds and did not have anything on which to live (since his mother had completely disowned him, and he badly needed something to live on). He thought up this means of support: he goes to Orlov or to Dubelt and says that he knows about a certain political connection that threatens to fell the existing government. The year 1848 was the year of revolution throughout all Europe, as you know. Why in Petersburg—the atrium of Europe (according the words of a travel writer)—why, I would say, in Petersburg as well did someone not find a reason to think about a disturbance? Orlov and Dubelt both easily believed in this—Aristov says that the main hotbed of the conspiracy is in Moscow, that its main drivers are there, that here in St. Petersburg he knows only some subordinates, who do not even understand the entire affair, and says that in order to discover everything he needs to go to Moscow. There he will be convinced of everything and, having returned to Petersburg, he will just hand over the list of the rebels so that they can immediately be taken to prison so that none of them is in a position to save himself by escaping.

The plan, deftly wrought, enlisted the complete faith of Count Orlov, who ordered that Aristov be supplied immediately with money for the journey to Moscow. He also gave him various instructions and notified the tsar about everything. Aristov roamed around Moscow, engaged in his own villainy, and having spent through all the money, returned to Petersburg at the time of carnival—this was already in 1849.

Orlov spotted Aristov drunk in the theater, called him over, and asked: "What did you do?" Aristov did not lose his presence of mind at all and said that he was close to his goal but had no money.

"You are drunk," said the Count (who is already like a prince now).

"I am getting to know those with the association who constantly drink, and I must drink with them. Otherwise, I would fall under suspicion," replied Aristov.

Whether Orlov believed Aristov or not, it is difficult to say; however, he gave 300 rubles to Aristov, who promised to hand over to him a complete list of those who were connected, after a few days. In order to fulfill his promise or to find even the appearance of an association he ran on to the next stratagem; he went to the first nice patisserie, sat down at a table, and intently looked around at those assembled there. Some he knew by name, since for the most part they were officers of the guard, officials from various departments, and people who thought of nothing more than if only they could eat something good or drink a tasty wine—gluttons as they were called, or, as I know them, the devotees of Bacchus and Venus. Aristov noted them himself on a list and in a moment made them prisoners of the state! The next day, the fortress of Peter and Paul claimed a dozen or so frightened people, surprised at the inexplicable notice of the Commission of the Military Court, which tracked, examined, and could not discover anything, but it is difficult to fear spilling something out of nothing. The smallest shadow of suspicion did not fall on them, and everyone was the most loyally and the most favorably disposed to the throne.

The compromised Orlov cursed and swore and planted Aristov in prison, and everyone believed to have been with the association was immediately released into freedom. If that is not enough, one, supposedly the officer of the guard, went straight from being turned out of the prison to being conducted again to the Imperial room, and took back the command of the trifold kissing of the tsar! The tsar said that he was not misled in the truthfulness of his guard, unfastened some order from his chest, fastened it onto the chest of the officer, raised his rank, and ordered him to return to his place and to further fulfill his duty. The officer, having departed from the tsar's palace could not comprehend for a long time what was happening about him—progressing from the Commission of the Military Court, to the fortress, and next the tsar's room. He continuously walked around and repeated: "It's a miracle. The Tsar himself, the Tsar-Father, the kiss, the order and rank—is this a dream? Is it real?" Aristov was handed over to judgment and sentenced for ten years to Siberia, and, finally, before his departure from St. Petersburg was whipped by the power of the highest order. Aristov traveled to Siberia, arrived in Nizhny Novgorod, and there hatched new plots, because he summoned the colonel of the gendarmes who commanded the division there and who did not divine his rubbish from these plots. The colonel believed in the importance of Orlov, as the chief of the gendarmes, and was surprised when Aristov expected rewards; the chief took him away for a lengthy reprimand and sent an order to Omsk not to believe any of Aristov's reports following his arrival. Moreover, for the least of these measures he should have been immediately handed over to judgment and judged according to the full severity of the law. After such catastrophes, I do not know who would not conceal his spying, and I do not know who would not think to grasp a more honest means of living. This was not at all so with Aristov (whom hereafter I will call Krapo).

He, having just arrived in Omsk, immediately began to look for a point of support from which he could act freely. Krapo presented himself to Vaska as a portrait painter; however he presented himself in the following manner: One of the prisoners by the name of Susin went every day to Vaska's to work at the house, and Krapo used him for an intermediary. He, himself, through a servant informed Vaska about his artistic painter who had freshly arrived at the prison. Vaska wished him to come to his place and asked if he could take his portrait. It was an easy thing to think, since Krapo only desired that about which he could only dream, so he pushed into Vaska's home in order to win his favor. He undertook everything, and obviously when they had to use his painting, he had to try some lectures, because he knew that painting the face one could not use either black or even pure white for color. Krapo painted a portrait of Vaska; it was his favorite, and it flatters Vaska as only Krapo knew how. Besides this, Krapo informed Vaska about everything that was going on and about that which no one had even thought in the prison. He did not spare anyone but for the most part ended up with poor Olech, since he experienced more of these new affronts—now again there was new verbal abuse—and more deplorably sounding platitudes. It was difficult to have a notion of this persecution for those who have not had a look at Vaska. (This all happened over the course of a month, immediately after our arrival under the authority of Vaska.) In a word, Vaska loved Krapo like his own child, because how could he not love him when every morning he arrived with news at his place, bringing: this or that one was drunk, this one played cards with that one, those two beat each other up, etc. Mirecki blurted out such and such things, Tokarzewski did such and such, Bogusławski said this and that. In a word, Vaska knew everything, and for this reason, when he called on the prison, he immediately called to someone, "And you were drunk—from where did you get the vodka? And how did you get the cards?" Krapo also obtained vodka and cards, since the soldier who searched by the gate did not dare even to touch those who were returning from work at Vaska's. Krapo used this and always returned to the prison with a wooden container full of vodka, which on the outside lid was thoughtfully splashed milk for us. For this he took money, even drank the vodka himself and got drunk like a beast, but Krapo did not tell Vaska about this—it was a secret. If only in this manner Krapo had annoyed us—it was still less than he wanted—it was in part to protect himself and, on the other hand, to ingratiate himself with the greatest scoundrels and to drink with them. They were constantly saying that we Poles were guilty of that and that Vaska inspected everyone that strictly, and that he punished everyone that much. "They," they said, "have their own attitudes, and here there are a lot of Poles, and they complain. Those go to the Prince, and they ask and gab about what Vaska is doing in the prison." The Prince naturally shouts several times, becomes angry at everyone, and somehow believes and somehow does not pass judgment on that which Krapo says—the holy truth? "He," the brigands say, "was also at some time a nobleman and ended up in prison and does not disdain us—indeed he's like brother to brother, just like a pal! And all those [that is we] are walking around like tramps, who never have a word to say to anyone," etc. Krapo approached them just so and was afraid of no one—certainly everyone was afraid of him—because he went to Vaska and, well, complained, and what would come of this?

For some months Krapo, because until August 1850 he was painting Vaska's portrait with a paintbrush or rather the hand of a spy, had to retain for posterity the characteristics of a great man!! After this happened, that which I here briefly related, no one doubtlessly is astonished that it could sometimes shake one's convictions, which could be close to collapse. Finally, the measure changed, and Krapo fell from grace, because Vaska became convinced that everything that he had easily told him was the most impudent lie. He drove Krapo from his home and for a few days planted him in the guard station for some quarrel with Bem; since that time Vaska looked on us with a benevolent eye, and only Olech could he not endure to the last moment of his command. Whether Vaska was wanting to assuage his former conduct or whether perhaps he really wanted to block us from the attacks of the brigands, Vaska summoned the sergeant major a certain time to his house and ordered him to announce that whichever of the Poles arrived at his home and complained, providing that someone had harmed him, let him be certain that he would not pass through 500 blows, and the sergeant major promised this very portion—you can imagine yourself what could follow from such an announcement by the sergeant major, and the hatred rose against us to more than the highest degree. By this order of Vaska, Krapo became completely justified in the opinion of prison, so he therefore knew what flowed between us. He himself had submitted the plan of the previously described attack, the plan, which he was to finish by stuffing himself on our plates and by taking our spoons, knives, and forks, and everything that belonged to Vaska—that is, everything that was taken without his knowledge. The plan, as you know, did not succeed, and the Kabardians protected us from the attack; thanks to their presence of mind and their bravery we escaped those dangers, which were possible for us to meet.

The Kabardians are a courageous people. Take, for example, Nuru Shakhmurlu Oglu—on his face and on his body you would certainly not find a piece of skin that was not broken in various ways and did not announced that sometime in his youth the bayonet was not a stranger to him. I ask you to take a look at another—Weli Ismakhan Ogla—at his appearance, which seemed to be that of a bear who is barely in a position to turn. But let him move himself, our Weli—he had already several times fallen on his arm. And the others? And the old Ali-Bek, it was nice to watch how he not very patiently looked on when somewhere a quarrel began. He did not move from his spot, but waited until those arguing got into a fight, and then he fell between them and reconciling the two, soundly, who would both remember it for a long time. But we return to Krapo. It is known already how he began his life of hard labor—listen to how it ended after his being driven away by Vaska. Krapo cast himself about in various places and anywhere he had just exited the house, he immediately cheated and stole from every person. Slowly, however, when everyone knew him and when he no longer had admission anywhere, he undertook a new idea and launched down the road of forgery; he forged passports and money, and his comrades helped him as much as they could. Krapo finally intended to escape and arranged this plan: There was a General Major Vorobev, the commanding ataman of the Cossack Army in Siberia, who had a coachman (some tramp). When this coachman was accepted into service at Vorobev's, he showed him a passport as though it were really issued by one of the districts in Tambov Gubernia; meanwhile this passport was not his, and the coachman was a former soldier, next a deserter, then a hard labor convict, and finally a tramp. Vorobev did not get involved with viewing the special passport; he was even satisfied with the driver, but when the time limit of the passport had already ended, at that time the coachman knew that he had to reckon how to try to renew it.

To renew the passport it was necessary to write to the district, and there immediately it would be noticed—the poor coachman would be imprisoned again and again would be sent for judgment. Again he would the get the bludgeon, and again prison and hard labor awaited him! And how to address this? How to get a new passport? The coachman knew some prisoners among whom the most open friend was Aleksander Kuleshov of gypsy descent; inordinately cunning, clever, and remarkably devious, he immediately upon arrival at Omsk served as a horse doctor, because somewhere he found a gypsy, who could not work a swindle with horses. Every gypsy has a horse for some period of exchange; for each gypsy it is something to do, and one lives in this manner. Kuleshov was at some time in a splendid position and worked for a long time in the industry or business of horses; often he stole them for which he was sentenced to a company of convicts made up exclusively of gypsies. And being in Sevastopol, he stayed there a few years, and since it was very bad for him there, he decided, come what may, to exchange Sevastopol for another fortress. So, he killed a young girl who came every day to sell cakes in the fortress, and he killed her without any guilt. He killed her only so that he could again be judged and so that according to the pronouncement of his sentence be transferred to another place. In Sevastopol he got 1,000 bludgeonings and was assigned to Omsk in the so-called division of special persons with an unrestricted number of years.

In Omsk, as I recalled, he served as a horse doctor and through this he struck up relations with all the coachmen in the fortress and in the town. For a long time, he treated every horse that never thought of getting sick, and in this way he was graced with a certain fame no longer as a horse doctor but as a veterinarian. The coachman had enough experience, for example, and reported to his gentleman that the horse was lame in order to summon Kuleshov. Kuleshov beforehand knew that he would be called, because the day before he had beat a nail into the hoof. He was summoned to take a look at the horse and needed money for medicine; having received it, he removed the nail. He provided the leg with dust from the hay, and in honor of the money turned to vodka, which he drank up together with the driver and the soldier guarding him. The horse got glanders, and the driver told his gentleman to call Kuleshov. Kuleshov examined the horse, again took the money, removed from the nostril that which he had placed the day before yesterday, and that was the reason that stuff came from the nostril. The horse was healthy, because he had never been weak. In this way Kuleshov had many acquaintances, and in this way he recognized the coachman recollected above from Vorobev's, who confided to Kuleshov what kind of trouble he had with the passport; he was exceedingly happy that with the mediation of Kuleshov he could receive his passport. Krapo had to forge and really forge it, and not only for him alone did he forge. Having such good relations, Kuleshov persuaded Vorobev's coachman to escape; they had to steal the general's horse with the carriage. Krapo played the role of gentleman, Kuleshov his lackey, and the coachman was to stay the coachman. Only one knew of the plan, beside the interested parties; Krapo went with Kuleshov to work at the hospital, and from there they were to escape. I do not know by what means, but someone notified Vorobev about everything. Suffice it to say that Vorobev immediately let it be known to the commandant of the fortress, an inspection was conducted in the place where Krapo worked, and indeed the stamped forms were found along with the pair of prepared passports, the stamped paper for certificates, even the forms for money, and some pieces of prepared false coins. Krapo was placed in the guard station and handed over to military judgment. After several months the verdict sentencing him to 300 birchings was handed down but really Krapo received only 70, because the executioner could not get into his head how it was possible to insult noble skin to such a degree as to exercise birches on it. The emboldened Krapo with mildness at the verdict hatched a new idea, a new idea of escape. Sitting in the guard station he had gotten to know the soldier, some Pole, who fought in the national affair in 1831 and then became ignoble; he renounced not only the dignity of the defenders of Poland, but even disavowed the dignity of man. His name was Kotlar, and he sat as a defendant for the escape of two criminal defendants while under his guard, whom he let go in exchange for money. There was no good in him—he was a completely fallen human being.

Krapo concluded a close friendship with him and hoped that sometime he could make use of it. He calculated very well and did not wait long. Since Kotlar, having received his 500 bludgeonings, returned to service in the 4th Battalion, and they had even exempted him already, as if good conduct was capable of partially erasing the mark weighing down on him. A certain time in the year 1853, Krapo with Kuleshov, having spoken with Kotlar, arranged for an escape when leaving from work. No one noticed that Krapo, Kuleshov, and Gromov (whom I will recall in a later story) walked off to a single work assignment. Behind them went Kotlar and one soldier recruit who had to guard them. At work Krapo walked off with Kuleshov, having taken Kotlar with them, and Gromov remained with the recruit, as if he were at work. As they set out and then did not return—they had fled. Krapo had already long ago prepared the passports; it had been necessary to find a point of support and, after all, a place where they could spend time until their hair grew in (since we were shaved by the half-head every week). Either they could not find such a place, or they did not want to wait but to abandon Omsk more rapidly. Suffice it to say that they immediately set out farther until after seventeen days of passage they were captured in a village situated on the road from Kolyvan, and again our pilgrims were placed under judgment in Omsk. Kuleshov received 500 bludgeonings, Krapo 1000, and Kotlar 2000. The first two returned back to the barrack, and the last was sent to Ust-Kamenogorsk for ten years. And what happened in the prison after the escape of those two scoundrels, oh! It is difficult to say this—there was plunder on the public road. They did an inspection, searched, shook, and rummaged through everything, turning it upside-down as they say—what were they searching for? It is difficult to answer this; they took away whatever they found, as though it had to be a means of pulling off a second similar escape!

I remember well those moments they drove all of us out into the courtyard—no one dared move from his place, and in the barracks, the soldiers were searching and stealing all the best stuff! A few days before the escape, Commandant de Grave, recalled above, had departed together with his wife to the waters for six weeks on the Chinese borders, one-and-a-half thousand versts from Omsk, where they built a new fortress, Kopal. Meanwhile the replacement for the commandant of the fortress was a friend of de Grave's,

Colonel Shulgin, but I had no close acquaintance with him. However, sensing that they could rob us, I approached him and told him that everything we had, we had with the permission of Aleksei Fedorovich, and I asked that he allow us to peel off from the rest, since we had no part in the escape of Krapo. I could see that my speech convinced him—perhaps the former had said something about us at his departure—because Shulgin, although he had ordered the search, did not allow anything to be taken away. It was even done more pleasantly that it had been previously. Krapo, after having collected his assigned sentence of 1000 lashes, thought up a new means of getting out of the prison—he decided to lie in the hospital until they admitted him. They did not recognize him as unfit to work in the fortress and did not release him. Wanting to wrap up the new plan, he entered into relations with the paramedics. The latter provided him with various medical means, since they did not allow for wounds remaining after the bludgeonings to heal up; the shoulders constantly were rotting, and savaged flesh swelled. Furthermore, he used something else that caused his head to tremble, no less than his legs and arms. Maybe it could have upset his intentions, but the doctors noticed, and particularly the corps doctor Ivan Ivanovich Troitsky turned his attention to it. The pallet was searched and plenty of various salves and powders were found, and they even found poison. Certainly, the poison was to serve for something in the future for him, because for what other reason was he holding it? Driven from the hospital he again arranged plans; he had something to arrange, since I saw him constantly walking with his friend, Kuleshov remembered above. The man is capable of everything—a spoiled child of Petersburg and a junker of the guard; I am certain that he is prepared to kill a person for a ruble, even if it were his mother or father.

Next it occurs to me now to recall Gromov, who was universally called a priest, since he was supposed to come from priestly stock. I do not know if this sort of person anywhere else in the entire earthly sphere would turn into something more foul, something more atrocious, or if he would turn into a similar monster! I do not know the beginnings of his life, and I know only that he was born in Moscow, that he was the son of a priest, and that for debauched villainies of various sorts, or as he himself expressed, for mischief, he earned himself the army, from which several times he had escaped.[82] At the time he was escaping he committed more than one plunder combined with murder and for this he was sentenced to a military unit of convicts in Sevastopol. Thus, Sevastopol must have been a

82 Here folio 37.5 is followed by folio 50 to complete the manuscript.

school of debauchery for him—there without a doubt he learned every kind of wickedness with more criminal thought than he can summon. Gromov cut someone's throat in Sevastopol and for this was sentenced to Siberia and sent to the same unit as Kuleshov. I regret powerfully that I never entered a conversation with him, because I would have been able to tell you so many things from his past; today I will mention only that which I saw with my own eyes, but also I will tell that which Gromov himself told his comrades. He was an inhuman creature, spoiled, base, and despicable, as I know too well. I cannot all the same imagine that Gromov was capable of murder, because for this he would need more courage, and he did not have this, because he was too base! Everything that Gromov did in order not to express decency, I cannot tell you; however, it will be necessary for you to learn at least an accurate reference, and the rest you can think up. Gromov, going from Sevastopol to Omsk under the appearance of weakness, stopped in Tiumen in the county seat of Tobolsk Gubernia.[83]

Having gotten to know more closely the prison watchman, one Reimers, in this prison he collected a gang of scoundrels, and they began to plunder. Reimers, their accomplice, did not combine the decent ones together with them in a single barrack so much as he delivered or at least knew that knives were delivered to them. Every week to Tiumen came a party of prisoners sentenced to labor in various places in Siberia or also the general population, usually a mixed bunch from various tribes, various faiths, various dispositions and states that one curiously finds there: Moldovans and Greeks, Jews and gypsies, Finns and Germans, Georgians and Circassians, Kabardians and Chechens, Shamakhians and Lezgins, Latvians and *Moskali*—one can even find Poles. And among these peoples you have thieves and brigands, arsonists and predators, swindlers and cheats, vagabonds and scoundrels. Moreover, you have their so-called courtiers and peasants, merchants and burghers, and sometimes some monk is wandering around and very often a priest—sometimes but not others! Often, very often a clerk—in a word, every state and every age, every vocation, every trade, and every religious denomination year in, year out sent tribute to Siberia. They come naked and become gaunt without bread, without a grosz, and without a shirt; others ride in a carriage and are supplied with everything—sometimes, they

83 Capt. John Dundas Cochrane finds Tiumen to be a city "of some consideration" owing to Yermak, its fine pastures, its trade in timber, tallow, and hides, its chancellery of the "Russian American Company," and its location on the steep banks of the Tura (*Narrative of a Pedestrian Journey through Russia, Siberia, and Tatary, from the Frontiers of China to the Frozen Sea and Kamtchatka* [Philadelphia: H. C. Carey, & I. Lea, and A. Small, 1824], 83).

even have big money. Such parties by the few or by the dozen make their way from various countries and from various roads to the main road so that rivers from the lesser to the greater merge on the main road and progress together until Tiumen. Only there do they sort the deportees into separate categories: the shackled separately, the men separately, the women separately, and from that point when you meet your party you are immediately one of them.

To every such party or another, when it arrived in Tiumen, immediately a supervisor (NB: that is a clerk from the ranks), such as Reimers, issued the order that each person should hand over the things and money they had to the depot—mentioning at the same time that in the event of plunder not only would he, Reimers, not look for the thief but furthermore he would punish severely everyone aggrieved and complaining. Certainly, no one ever handed over anything; each person hid most meticulously his last grosz that he might have, because everyone, taught by experience, knew better than to hand it over for concealment. The supervisor no longer looked after it; in this manner, Mr. Reimers, made certain of what was to happen the next night in the prison whose confines he did not quit; he handed over the entire party to the care of Gromov, who with his gang hit the barrack and, having struck upon those from whom he expected to find something, collected it all—in a word, plundered the prison! The next day nobody complained, because to whom is there to complain? To the supervisor? And after all he warned everyone; he had ordered everyone to hand over their things to the depot so as in this manner to protect them from plunder. After the robbery, Gromov presented the entire haul to Mr. Reimers, progressed to distribution of the spoils again, and calmly waited in anticipation of the next party in order to rob again. Mr. Reimers grew his plumage, Gromov was satisfied with his gang, and more than once regretfully remembered this moment of the blessed life, and regretted that these moments passed and maybe would no longer return! More than once he repeated, "At least then I had something solid for myself, and it was at least for something!" Reimers, when everything came out into the open, not wanting to exonerate himself, was dismissed from service and in 1855 lived in Omsk. Gromov often prepared to visit him, and perhaps he was at some point at his house, although he did not recollect it.

From that which I have told you about Gromov up to now—and there are no longer anymore statements—it would be possible only to come to the conclusion that Gromov was a very boorish scoundrel such as one can find in almost every prison, but this was not all. Gromov had still other means of leading people to crimes, and Gromov very skillfully made money. I saw a certain time, while lying in the hospital, how Gromov in the stove melted some mixture on a metal spoon and poured it into a swage block, from which he brought out not-bad-at-all imitation *chetvertak* (25 silver kopecks). He smiled at it as at the dearest of his children, because how much in them lay his hopes? Everyone aside from me was sleeping. Gromov cast a few pieces and then all day under a quilt completed his work to complete perfection, despite oftentimes disastrous results for those on whom the police discover such money. Still I could not condemn Gromov for this too much, because at least in my belief, scoundrels or murderers ought to always get more than a counterfeiter of money; however, this offense is less than many other of Gromov's activities! People in Siberia believe exceedingly in enchantments, omens, and in all things extraordinary. Everyone sent, from wherever they are, is called experienced and knowledgeable; therefore, it is nothing strange that they believed blindly everything that Gromov said and carried out everything that he ordered. What is a *farmazon*?[84] It is money, which forever returns to its owner, which it is never possible to hand over, which by this protects the owner from indigence, and even gives him the possibility of the fulfillment of every desire, every sexual urge, and gives him the possibility of fulfilling everything for which he feels a desire—only he wants such a morsel for everyone, especially for the poor soldier, among whom Gromov often found the most willing. The one, who only once entered relations with Gromov, was already lost forever; he already became his servant and already had to do everything that Gromov demanded. Every soldier as soon as he revealed a desire to get a *farmazon* had to strive to be sent in a work convoy with Gromov and absolutely had to have on himself one half-imperial, because only from the half-imperial were the *farmazons* made. He must be dressed in one of his best shirts, he must get several rubles for secret materials and moreover a bottle of vodka. Then, when everything was already ready, Gromov had to proceed to exchange the half-imperial for the *farmazon*. The poor soldier—from where can he have similar funds? He absolutely had to have stolen them, because he would not find anyone to lend it to him.

I have to mention here that Gromov went most often to work alone by himself with only one convoy soldier, and during the wintertime he usually ended up with work like going around to all the treasury houses in the fortress and looking at what condition the stoves and chimneys were in to see if they didn't need repairs or if they weren't a fire threat.

---

84 Bogusławski may not have known that *farmazon* derived from "Freemason" also signifies "freethinker" in a perjorative sense and has been cited as a common bandit's alias.

For such employment, Gromov did his best according to his own personal expectations and in the expectations for making *farmazon*s and *przysuszki*. For when he found such a soldier for the *farmazon* and when the soldier reached Gromov in the end, then the latter, having conducted the soldier to some kind of attic of any old house and proceeded to make the *farmazon*. The first condition of this operation is the exchange of shirts—a trivial thing for appearances but how terrible for the soldier since in order for him to exchange the shirt, which he has on he must undress, take off his uniform, and put his arms somewhere on record. Only if the soldier agreed to these steps already is he taken in by Gromov; then he must already agree to everything, because Gromov recalls slightly for him what kind of punishment awaits him for similar offenses. One step is not a lesson learned, and he leads himself to another far worse. The soldier exchanges his shirt, and disarmed for a moment, willy-nilly must already go farther on that road and thus hands over the half-imperial to Gromov. This one wraps it skillfully in a piece of paper, takes out a second such piece of paper from its hiding place in which a kopeck was wrapped and hands over the kopeck to the soldier and stows the half-imperial in his pocket. Wanting finally to be assured that such a misdeed will never come out into the open, that the soldier will not dare to say a word to anyone, Gromov convinces him that as a final service for the transformed *farmazon* copulation is absolutely necessary, and that very soldier, that poor being whom the tsar's hand attired in uniform, becomes the concubine of such a scoundrel as Gromov!!

Then Gromov instructs each one to carry the wrapped kopeck in a boot under the heel for nine days, having forbidden him to look even one time at what is happening to it, and, what is more, for the best successfully transformed half-imperial into *farmazon*, the soldier should not even remove his boot from his foot for nine days. It is now necessary for me to say that Gromov was the most intemperate creature, and he was already spoiled for life, because the syphilitic illness for many years niggled at his heavy frame. This is not the end. Gromov instructs the defiled soldier, the poor victim, to dress himself forthwith, next to lower his head and having hit him several times with a fist in the nape of the neck with every blow pronounces: "Be happy." Now there is no longer anything to do: the soldier has been robbed, defiled, and screwed for a trip to petty crime, and will certainly descend to crime—if some special twist of fate or providence does not sustain him, what lies ahead? Here, after nine days the soldier finds the copper kopeck in place of the half-imperial, guesses that he was vilely deceived and when he begins to reproach his torturer, the latter abuses again him. In a word, he assures him that he did not know to persevere in his undertaking, and, induced by curiosity, he took a first look at the imperial, marked by him, and by this the half-imperial, which was supposed to make all his happiness, was tranformed into a kopeck. He assures the soldier that it is exactly his fault, that the operation must be repeated, because he (Gromov) does not want to be regarded as a swindler! He actually threatens the soldier with publishing his secret, he forces him to do everything that only he demands, and the poor soldier, the stupid unhappy creature, asks immediately that this scoundrel not say anything to anyone and hands over anything and everything to him. He promises to get everything that Gromov desires, and in a word agrees with everything and to anything. He becomes a transgressor by transgression and a criminal by crime, and he arrives at the prison.

Omsk Affairs

An Introduction to Rufin Piotrowski

Following the publication of accused Carbonaro Silvio Pellico's witness to incarceration, *Memoirs of My Imprisonments*, Rufin Piotrowski captured the imagination of the European reading public with his escape narrative, *Memoirs from a Stay in Siberia*, which was translated into French, German, and English in quick succession in the early 1860s.[1] In August of 1844 Piotrowski, shackled and in the company of two gendarmes, had arrived in Omsk from the fortress in Kiev, where he had been confined and sentenced for participating in unrest, concealing himself abroad, belonging to a Democratic society in France, living within the empire under an assumed name as well as a false passport, and ill-intentioned activities.[2] According to the report from the administration in Tara to the governor general of Western Siberia, Piotrowski escaped from the Ekaterininsky distillery in February 1846, and his file in the historical archive in Omsk shows that he completely evaded attempts to locate and apprehend him, despite various sightings and even a false identification.[3] His brief depiction of Omsk from *Memoirs from a Stay in Siberia* included here has provided Dostoevsky scholars with additional portraits of several influential officials, like Commandant Aleksei de Grave and State Councilor Iakov Kapustin (later Head of the Third Section of the Main Administration of Western Siberia), who attempted to alleviate the living conditions of political prisoners, including those of the famous Russian novelist. Piotrowski's account further attests to Bogusławski's assessment of the governor general of Western Siberia, Prince Petr Gorchakov, as a "true despot of Siberia" and

1 For more on Piotrowski's remembrances, see Blake "Traumatic Mobility," 240–42.

2 Po vysochaishemu poveleniiu o soslannom v Sibir' na katorzhnuiu rabotu Iosafate Rufine Petrovskom. Fond 3, opis' 13, delo 18203. Istoricheskii Arkhiv Omskoi oblasti.

3 Ibid.

a "thug, executioner, and tyrant of the unfortunate slaves of 1831." The second selection also complements Bogusławski's autobiographical account by providing greater detail about the infamous Omsk affair in order to show the international reputation for capital punishment earned by the Siberian town in Polish and émigré circles, owing in part to translations by Julian Klaczko and Aleksandr Herzen.

Already in the first pages of *Memoirs from a Stay in Siberia*, Piotrowski sets the parameters of the narrative by outlining the abortive conspiracy necessitating his journey from France to Poland, his capture by Russian officials, his escape from Siberia, and his arrival in Paris. To accentuate the perils and triumphs of his own flight, not only does he include many admonitions against escape, but he also invokes similar attempts by his compatriots—the failed conspiracies of Abbé Jan Sierociński and Piotr Wysocki as well as the success of Count de Benyovszki, who fled from Kamchatka in 1771. From the Omsk scenes, one can surmise how frequently the thought of escape is on Piotrowski's mind as he examines a map and attempts to understand the geographical layout of Siberia. As is evident from Figure 2 (dated about a decade after Piotrowski's stay), which shows a sketch of the fortress as one enters through the Tara Gates, the building dedicated to the topographers is prominent in the fortress. Piotrowski repeatedly attributes to divine providence his survival of captivity and his ability to evade detection on the part of the Russian authorities, but he does not display a personal devotion to God with the same intensity as other authors who wrote Polish accounts of Omsk. By comparison, Piotrowski, although traveling in shackles in the discomfort of a *kibitka*, clearly enjoys more privileges than his compatriots who shared Dostoevsky's imprisonment in the fortress, since he is not on foot, has money to reward his gendarmes, stays with the officers, and does not suffer the same deprivation of food described in other narratives. The fact that he is incautious about his conversations, even those with Russian officials, and does not fear denunciation as much as Bogusławski or Zaleski also attests to his being more protected than the other writers in this collection. At times, this privilege is revealed in the physical portrayals of his interlocutors that expose his essentialisms—for example, the courtesy of de Grave with "a Swedish background" as opposed to "the hawkish, wild, and pitiless" Cossack-Kirgiz-Tatar police chief of Omsk.

Piotrowski frequently recollects dialogues with individuals from his journey to Russia, in which he shares his personal sentiments about the Polish question. A comparison between Bogusławski's depiction of the distant de Grave and Piotrowski's more personal encounter with this sympathetic elderly colonel suggests that de Grave was attentive to the difference between a political prisoner in the fortress, as opposed to an offender assigned to labor in a factory. This variance in treatment reflects what Viktor Vainerman defines as de Grave's strict official responsibility for observing the rules regarding the supervision of the fortress's convicts.[4] Yet, Piotrowski's brief depiction of the silent Prince Gorchakov as a haughty despot with a powerful but shapely form corresponds to Bogusławski's assessment of the governor general as both sexually-driven but also cruel in his official capacity, especially since he encouraged the likes of the petty tyrant Major Krivtsov. Piotrowski's observations regarding his own sentencing in Omsk display the interaction between these government officials, which is absent from the political prisoners' memoirs. His portrayal of the consultation between the benevolent Kapustin and Prince Gorchakov reveals a layer of Omsk bureaucracy not appreciated by the convict-writers in the fortress. It shows that Kapustin—whose household was known to Mirecki, as a French tutor, and to Dostoevsky and Durov, as friends of Kapustin's wife—had influence in Prince Gorchakov's Siberia, as indicated by his decision to send Piotrowski to work in Tobolsk Gubernia rather than in the depths of Siberia.[5]

A comparative reading of the memoirs of Tokarzewski, Bogusławski, and Piotrowski demonstrates how the wives of Russian officials participated in the care of prisoners and exiles and further accounts for Dostoevsky's correspondence with such prominent charitable women in Tobolsk and Omsk—for example, Natalia Fonvizina or Anna de Grave—as well as his idealization of the Decembrists' wives who inform his characterization of Sonya Marmeladova (*Pss*, 28:175–77).[6] Piotrowski attributes the hospitality in Omsk to the commandant, but the memoirs of Tokarzewski and Bogusławski clarify that this type of generosity is more characteristic of his wife. Indeed, Tokarzewski speaks about how Anna de Grave established the daughters of the widow Natalia Krzyżanowska in the "House of Care" in Omsk and how de Grave passed books to the Polish inmates through Krzyżanowska: "Natalia Karpovichova had something to win over (certainly to pay) the cooks who smuggled books and newspapers for us,

4 Vainerman, *"Poruchaiu sebia vashei dobroi pamiati...": F. M. Dostoevskii i Sibir'* (Omsk: Izdatel'stvo Nasledie, 2001), 123.

5 V. S. Vainerman, "Omskoe okruzhenie Dostoevskogo," *Dostoevskii: Materialy i issledovaniia* 6 (1985): 188–89.

6 Budanova and Fridlender, eds., *Letopis' zhizni i tvorchestva F. M. Dostoevskogo*, 229; A. V. Dulov, *Petrashevtsy v Sibiri* (Irkutsk: Izdatel'stvo Irkutskogo universiteta, 1996), 102–3; Elizabeth Blake, "Sonya, Silent No More: A Response to the Woman Question in Dostoevsky's *Crime and Punishment*," *Slavic and East European Journal* 50:2 (2006): 268.

concealed in baskets of foodstuffs brought from the city."[7] Dostoevsky's Polish comrades seem to receive special privileges from the kitchen, since they not only received books through the cooks, but were able to have the Christmas feast in their own barrack and to hide out in the kitchen during the prison protest against food in the Dead House (*Pss*, 4:203–4). Furthermore, Piotrowski's passage on Omsk indicates that there were Poles sympathetic to the exiles in town, and he specifically mentions encountering an acquaintance, Jan Woźniakowski, who was still in shackles, near the guardhouse and administration building in 1844, just where Tokarzewski and Bogusławski met him in 1849.[8] Hence, the well-known history of Durov and Dostoevsky benefiting from the generosity of the residents of Omsk is not limited to the experience of Russian political prisoners, because the Polish memoirs indicate that the Poles, too, enjoyed such privileges.

Yet, the association of Omsk with the brutality of Nicholas's regime and its severe repression of the November uprising, which sent the Romantic generation into Parisian and Siberian exile, was a specifically Polish tragedy often attributed to the desperation of deportees who could no longer tolerate the harsh conditions of their limitless sentences or the endless separation from their homeland. In comparison to the account of the Omsk affair included in *A Description of the Zabaikalsk Region in Siberia* by the exile Agaton Giller—a former member of the National Central Committee (which helped organize the 1863 uprising)—Piotrowski's manuscript centers on the exceptional nature of Prior Sierociński's beating. Giller, on the other hand, focuses on how the doctor at the execution saved the only surviving leader of the conspiracy, Ksawery Szokalski, who was then relocated to Eastern Siberia to complete his sentence in the mines of Nerchinsk. Both Giller and Piotrowski fail to appreciate that the number of those sentenced numbered in the '30s and '40s (about which Bogusławski is more accurate) even though they emphasized the severity of the measures taken by General Apollon Galafeev on the day the soldiers so brutally bludgeoned the organizers that "the place of execution

7 Tokarzewski, *Siedem lat katorgi*, 183.

8 Śliwowska, *ZpIR*, 683–84; Tokarzewski, *Siedem lat katorgi*, 140. While Piotrowski knows Woźniakowski's background as an engineer sentenced for political crimes who was released from hard labor to serve in a Siberian battalion, Tokarzewski supplements this with the additional information that this Lithuanian deportee, sent to Omsk in 1842, was released from hard labor "as a reward for some scientific work in the field of mathematics and for work that drew the attention of Petersburg."

was purple from blood."[9] Bogusławski appears to find the nature of the legendary conspiracy, itself, more interesting than Giller and Piotrowski, even though Bogusławski admits that as an inmate in Omsk in the early 1850s, he was too far removed from the events to obtain an accurately detailed oral history. Piotrowski, by contrast, emphasizes how he draws on independent eyewitness accounts from multiple ethnicities that corroborate each other as he progresses to his martyr narrative that emphasizes the indignities visited upon Sierociński, who was thrown in a dungeon, defrocked, and forced to take up arms by imperial order for the subjugation of the tribes on the steppe, before his final legendary execution and the mutilation of his corpse.

Piotrowski, like Zaleski, was positioned better than the inmates of Omsk fortress to understand the hierarchical and rigid power structures defining professional relationships that impacted the regulation of the prisons, regiments, and administrative headquarters overseeing the exiles. Although Zaleski, Bogusławski, and Dostoevsky understand the capricious nature of the Siberian authorities, only Piotrowski fully comprehends that they are harmful precisely, because they represent "a power as suspicious as it is cruel." Such cruelty is evident in the psychological torture of the delicate Prior Sierociński, weakened by years of imprisonment and by a three-year investigation, who was forced to watch his comrades die of their own beatings before his own sentence was carried out "so as to exhaust his strength by the cries of pain from his companions and the view of the execution that awaited him." With the overtly Christological imagery of refusing a last drink that could alleviate the pangs of his execution and a last utterance from the Psalms that enraged General Galafeev, Piotrowski proceeded to depict a savage butchery that shocked the soldiers with its barbarity. Piotrowski's chapter on Omsk from *Memoirs from a Stay in Siberia* clearly indicates that such ferocity was designed not only as retribution for escape attempts but also as a deterrent for those who aspired to flee, so that, as Zaleski explains, escape came to be condemned, since the Poles were punished as a group for its failure.

9 Agaton Giller, *Opisanie zabajkalskiej krainy w Syberyi*, 1:196; Śliwowska, *UzS*, 60–61; Śliwowska, *ZpIR*, 64, 143–44, 388, 685–66, 695.

Fig. 2. Omsk Fortress: Part of the General Plan with Evidence for the Place Proposed for the Construction of the Lodgings for the Archpriest of Resurrection Cathedral and the Spiritual Authority (December 2, 1854)

Existing Buildings: a. Staff and Chief Officers' Houses; b. Soldiers' Barracks; v. Engineering Arsenal; g. Guardhouse; d. House of the Spiritual Authority; e. Building for Topographers; *Proposed Buildings*: a. Stone House for the Archpriest and the Spiritual Authority; b. Wooden Service Sheds

"Arrival in Omsk" from *Memoirs from a Stay in Siberia*[1]

Chapter XX

Arrival in Omsk. The guardhouse. A visit to it. The main administration. My final destiny. Departure from Omsk to the Ekaterininsky factory. Travel to it. A description of the parts of Siberia to which I arrived. Arrival at the factory and reception by the convict ranks.

Krakow 1849

Having driven a little bit further into town, along the right side of the road an embankment built of soil appeared, and this had to be the Omsk fortress, about whose power and importance I could not actually judge—at first because of the darkness of night, and the second time I did not have the chance to see and examine it during the day. But those who were in the fortress and lived for a long time in Omsk told me that there is no fortress—maybe only against the Kirgiz—who usually wage war on horseback, and they do not have any cannons. Having gone then a little into the town, soon then we turned to the right from the road to the fortress, before whose gate a guard stopped us, asking who was coming. The driver responded, "an unfortunate!" So usually in Siberia they call those who are sent to them from Russia, whether to the settlement or to hard labor. At that watchword, the guard let us into the fortress. Not far from the gate, going straight along

1 This is a selection taken from the twentieth chapter of the second volume of Rufin Piotrowski's *Pamiętniki z pobytu na Syberii* (Poznan: Nakładem Księgarni Jana Konstantego Żupańskiego, 1861), 178–99.

the left-hand side is the residence of Prince Gorchakov as the governor general of Western Siberia and the commander of the only entire lead Siberian Corps, by no means magnificent. As much as the darkness of the night could allow me to see, the house in which Gorchakov lived was longish, certainly painted because it was entirely white, and it seemed that it was one level. Riding a little further in the same direction, we stopped in front of a house with its front turned to us, also white; this was the residence of the commandant of the fortress, Colonel de Grave. A continuation of the line on which stands the house of the governor general up to the point of the extension of the line on which lies the home of the commandant of the fortress would be at a right angle to the latter; therefore both at the point of intersection form a simple angle, at which is found a rather spacious courtyard or a square. One of the gendarmes set out immediately for the commandant of the fortress, who was already sleeping, and a second gendarme remained with me in the *kibitka*. After a dozen or so minutes further the commandant together with the other gendarme immediately went to the residence of Prince Gorchakov, who was also already in bed. I awaited everything in the *kibitka*—at the most for twenty minutes—so quickly and sharply service goes in Russia. After that the commandant, who came to me from Prince Gorchakov with some officer and my gendarme and greeted me courteously, ordered the officer to lead me for the night to the guardhouse or the garrison, which was located there on the courtyard and not far from the residence of the governor general and the commandant. From the *kibitka* I went to the guardhouse, but in it were no separate lodgings; they led me to the lodgings where they usually place officers arrested for small military offenses.

Just at that moment I found one of the officers. He was young—this nice, tall, thin, and handsome man having completed barely 22 years—and rather a youth at the rank of a lieutenant or something similar. He received me with great courtesy and to show that he was content that he would have a comrade in solitude. Yet, having proven that I was a Pole and for what reason I was imprisoned and what fate awaited me, the youth was terribly upset, but not for long. The inexperienced youth does not know a great misfortune; full of hope and the future, full of life and his delights, it seems to him that it is possible to manage everything easily. It is enough to desire to stand on one's own, so you do not have a misfortune, with which it could not be possible to struggle over time and would not be appealing to bear courageously. Then, in good order he began to cheer me up and to advise me in his own way, but with such a joke, with such courtesy, and above all with such merry humor, that I immediately remembered my position. He frankly laughed, and from his solace and from his joy, which he imparted to me freely and cheerfully, I also fell into humor. Since in the guardhouse there was no bedding, the hospitable youth began to care that in some way it could be possible for me to work out bedding as soon as it was convenient; here he lavished an amusing compliment on the comforts and pleasantries of the imprisoned life, with praises for those people assigned a similar life, and as well as he could, he prepared bedding for me. Then the commandant of the fortress, and maybe Colonel de Grave, sent me from his home a decent dinner, which being in cheerful temper, I ate with great relish. This humane courtesy, which a prisoner always accepts with gratitude, was from the direction of the commandant; I, at least, accepted it thus. My young co-prisoner, incomparably happier than me, put the samovar on and, drinking tea, we spoke with each other about various subjects: about people, about things, about Poland, about Russia, and so on. While speaking the officer noticed that from time to time I was suffering and asked what was bothering me. I responded that it was the tight-fitting fetters on my legs for twenty days and because of which it was not possible to take off my boots, even to refresh my legs. With the sliding during travel, my more calloused legs caused unpleasant pain. "Then I will order someone to unshackled you," and he was immediately off to find the tools and the man for the unshackling. Though I stopped him from this thoughtless but noble intention, presenting to him what kind of responsibility could fall on him and on myself for this, if someone were to find out about it—this was doubtlessly so. As in the prison in Kiev, the turnkey every day, as long as I was in fetters, immediately examined them, just as the gendarmes favored me—as if often looking at the fetters—although I was always with them and right in front of their eyes. Besides unshackling me from the fetters at that moment and in those surroundings—this would be for nothing! "You speak the truth," he said, "I did not think about it at all," and he abandoned his intention, only regretting that he could not give me relief by another means. He was native to Simbirsk or Saratov Gubernia, the son of nobility, and, wealthy, as far as it was possible to judge. He spoke French well, but that which caused the greatest pleasure was that he had a very good, although not large, atlas on him. I pounced on it greedily, and I opened the map of Siberia in order to orientate myself as to where I was on it. I paid attention above all to the course of the rivers and the direction of the roads, because while still in Kiev, once having adopted the intention, it stuck powerfully in my memory, and I urgently wanted it to bring about results. This means I could not neglect such friendly surroundings for an acquaintance with the map of Siberia. Therefore, while looking at the map of Siberia, I began to ask him about towns, about the background of residents of Siberia and their customs, about passages and roads to Asia, with which Siberia conducts business, and about similar things, and pinned the map anew. Seeing with what great intensity of attention I was browsing the map and how through approximation I was calculating the distance of various places from myself, he said to me with a smile, "If I were suspicious, I would suspect you of some intentions. But all joking aside, I will tell you the truth, sir. There are those here who wanted to run for their lives from Siberia, but they did not succeed at all, and I would not wish anyone to suffer their fate. Who were these unfortunates and what did they encounter? They were Poles; all Siberia knows about what fate met them, and you, sir, will be shown it. Now then I do not want to poison your heart with pain, with a sad story, sir." Speaking so, didn't he have in mind then Colonel Piotr Wysocki, Father Sierociński, and their comrades, whose terrible fate and tortures I later accurately discovered and which a little further in these memoirs I will recall.

I was afraid, however, lest he had worked out the matter itself, lest he had drawn a conclusion on the strength of my preoccupation with the map, although he did not appear to be an insincere, nor a duplicitous man. But already I, having experience with people, answered him with indifference, "Siberia before this, when I beheld and got to know her, was always for me a region of ices and snows, of tears and misery—then, having arrived in Siberia I begin to gather different notions and convictions about her. Natural curiosity got me to get to know her carefully and completely, here in this place, at least from the map, and not anticipating the opportunity of getting to know her through travel, since certainly I will be tied somewhere to a single permanent place in Siberia, from which I will not be free to move. From now on, Siberia will be certainly my only homeland for my whole future, for my whole life—not a homeland of heart and soul but of torment and suffering—so the only intentions that I could have in Siberia then would be these: so that if I could at some time (about this I have doubts) quit hard labor for the settlement, it would be possible there in seclusion, among those deserts, to settle peacefully and so to complete an unfortunate life."

"As you will come to know, sir, Siberia better and more thoroughly, I am certain that you will gather a better notion of her, and here are people . . . here are noble hearts."

So as to interrupt the matter, I asked him for what reason he sat under judgment. "I myself do not know for what. It is not the first time I am sitting here; this pleasure awaits me at least once or twice a month. We have with us a colonel, an old-timer and harsh martinet, who does not forgive the least oversight in service. I, as you know, am fortunate or unfortunate to be always in a cheerful humor. For one so serious, often on the most stupid point of presentation or recommendation, I respond with something oblivious, involuntary as if jokingly, that he does not like at all; so enough is enough, he put me for a few days under arrest. And just what is there to say about my frontline service? Often my gait, my attitude, and even my command and rotation are still not pleasing to him; so again I go into custody. But that which offends him more is this: that I never ask for anything; for that he calls me out for impudence and freethinking and God knows what. For this reason, I am trying to transfer to another regiment, since, in a word, my colonel has taken a sudden dislike to me."

Later I asked him about the Kirgiz and about other inhabitants on the steppes and deserts extending to the north of Siberia proper, into which for some time now it had been incorporated both by a civilian and military name and administration. He related to me many curious details about those dwellers, about their way of life and fighting. But all of this—after asking for more precise information—I will also place in these memoirs a little later. I studied Kirgiz like an amateur, but there was an opportunity for this, since in the prisons of the guardhouse then several Kirgiz—suspected of active participation in the uprising of their leader, the famous Kancar—had already been sitting for a long time. The doors of their prisons were open during the day, so they could see each other and my young officer could make much of their conversation about the science of language or also about the news of the Kirgiz regions, or rather the desert. The Kirgiz sitting in the guardhouse were the outstanding of their stock and, aside from the guilt weighing on them, considered themselves hostages of the peace and service of their countrymen for Russia. The officer, wanting to give me pleasure, the morning of the next day invited one of our prison mates from these Kirgiz—a minor prince (khan). I had this opportunity of seeing a Kirgiz; he was dressed in a brownish grey overcoat, woven from sheep's and camel's wool and made in the shape of a wide Russian coat without a collar and waist. He had a Tatar hat—high and round in the shape of one for the Jewish Sabbath—with a beard and whiskers (however the facial hair was not thick) and with an oval face, a dark complexion, black eyes, and a pleasant expression; later I saw more Kirgiz. We chatted therefore almost all night, which was already so short at this time of the year in Siberia. We did not sleep longer than an hour or two, and we did not fall asleep until day was upon us.

The next day around eight the commandant of the fortress Colonel de Grave visited me. Now I could look at him well, as in from close-up; of an average height but unusually overweight or obese, of a pleasant and kind physiognomy, he was about seventy and of Swedish background, as much as I could judge from his face. Having asked me about my health and while conversing with me about nothing at all significant, he often repeated, "What a misfortune that you, sir, returned from abroad to Russia!" Then, before long I arrived at the garrison, at my district prison, or rather at the location of the police chief of the town of Omsk, Nalabardin by name—tall, thin, wizened, straight as an arrow, and arched like a bowstring with an oval face—he had sunken but piercing little eyes, lively and restless movements, and narrowly set lips. He was certainly of mixed race—Cossack-Kirgiz-Tatar—and in his entire physiognomy, movements, and look there was something hawkish, wild, and pitiless. And as to the matter at hand, he is an inhumane and pitiless man; as a police chief of the great, he allowed the abuse and merciless handling of those who have the misfortune to fall into his hands. However, this man appeared to feel and to understand one's homeland, because among other things he asked me in a voice with an unpleasant expression: why had I returned from France to Poland without the permission of the tsar? And when I responded to him that I did it only out of yearning for my homeland, which I had not seen for a long time, he shouted three times: "Oh, homeland, homeland, homeland how dear you are!" Later a major from the Engineers also came to me, certainly only out of curiosity, since on no account of mine could he bear a responsibility. He was a man highly formed mentally. He was returning at that time to Russia from an expedition, voluntarily or by government order—I no longer remember—to the mountains of Altai and Baikal; he spoke to me with great familiarity of the matter and subject, about their beauty, about the rich minerals, about the residents located on them, etc. In the end, the conversation was directed toward politics—to Russia and Poland. He maintained that all the efforts of Poles today on account of regaining independence for their country led without a doubt to the noble and emotional attachment to their homeland, but by no means led to reason or clear vision about the matter. Everyone seems convinced that the epoch is approaching in which Poland must merge with Russia and be dispersed in it, since in the close connection of these two nations—which met with disapproval by many until now—is their shared strength and past happiness. He said something further about the government, the tsar, and similar matters. I established things otherwise for him, from another point of things, since I was attentive and emboldened by the condition in which I found myself, that is in a position that could no longer get worse. He looked at me with a certain kind of astonishment and maybe even pity and said: "May God fulfill your premonitions, but I cannot have a good augury about them. I see only that suffering and Polish misfortune still has not ended, if it has still more Poles like you, sir." And we parted with each other; I do not know whether he was content with this conversation and why he got involved in it with me.

Around noon, already after breakfast, which Colonel de Grave sent me, a commissar of police (a private police officer) arrived and announced to me that I had to proceed immediately to the Main Administration. Having parted therefore with the young officer, I left the guardhouse and, dragging myself as I could in unbearable and bothersome fetters to the company of the commissar and my gendarmes from Kiev, I came to the Main Administration building, being rather near to the guardhouse. Upon arrival I had the opportunity of seeing and recognizing one of my compatriots with family from Warsaw, a certain Woźniakowski, still young and fit, and as I was told, an engineer but sentenced for some political crime, like many others of our compatriots, to the convict divisions in the Omsk fortress. He was also shackled in fetters on his legs. A year later I found out with certainty that Woźniakowski was taken from the convict units to be a simple soldier in the army in the Siberian battalions—after several years of convict labor, it was considered a great favor. Thus, Tsar Nicholas is generous in his compassion and nobility. May God measure out with such a tape measure. Going out after a while by the spacious square, I cast a glance at that part of the city, which I could see; it appears to me not very solidly built—however after Ekaterinburg it was the most solid of all of those cities and villages, which I had seen up to now in Siberia. The city of Omsk must number up to thirty thousand residents and lies at the mouth of the rivers Om and Irtysh. But since there was only part of it and since I saw the edge of the city rather than its entirety, I cannot, therefore, give an opinion. In Omsk among the other up to three hundred Poles who were there at the time, as in the army so too in the convict ranks, there had been also handed over to the settlement the exile Januszkiewicz, taken into captivity on the field of battle at the time of the uprising. The Main Administration lies on the spacious square; it is a rather large, painted building with multiple levels. Moving closer to it as the commissar escorted me, some good-natured man, in the course of his sad and varied walk, devised questions for me, concerning my position; he finally added: "If you stay in your place, that is how they will allot it to you; be obedient to the local authority and bear perhaps the greatest trouble with patience, because ahead of the smallest recommendation or disobedience is severe and corporal punishment, and in the second place, for acting like this for ten or fifteen years, they may release you, sir, from hard labor and appoint you to the settlement, where you will be freer and happier." I thought to myself, *This is a beautiful hope for my future.* "Only, sir, may you not try to escape, because the political prisoners never can succeed. Here were those, who wanted to escape from Siberia, and what of it? Some because of this are already resting in the grave, and others who withstood the bludgeons were thrown for the rest of their lives into hard labor. They are giving you, sir, this warning out of a feeling of humanity and so that a similar thought never comes into your head."

"So these were the Poles, who were killed to the last one with bludgeons for the reason that they wanted to escape from Siberia? Poles. I am not thinking of escaping for many reasons, but having imagined that I wanted to escape, would such a punishment meet me, if I were captured in flight?"

"And why not, when it is evidently the law for this, and because of this precisely I will caution you."

I was thankful for this good-natured man, who, as you see, frankly and from the heart advised me, but the heart did not stain me with blood—listening to how my brothers were murdered with a martyr's cruel death for a small offense. How to find here the courage to escape out of necessity, when there are so many difficulties in defeating and awaiting so relentless and cruel a punishment?

After conducting me to the Main Administration, we entered on the first floor and from the corridor to the right into a spacious and beautiful hall, in the center of which stood a long table, around which up to twenty people—for the most part all young—dressed in an upright and decent manner as a civilian or in uniforms, were sitting and writing. The gendarmes stopped at the door of the hall, whereas I was led to the other end of the hall near the window, where having sat in an armchair which was given out of politeness, I scrutinized the people and the place in quietude and sad silence for a while. At both sides of this hall and close to the windows were doors to the left and to the right for communication with secondary halls, in which certainly sat people from the administrative department. For the most part calm and quiet governed in this hall. In it several of those writing, having cast an eye at me, began to become disturbed and to bustle about the hall under various pretexts; they began to enter and to exit from the secondary halls around me as though for some business, but I saw, however, that they were doing nothing and conjectured that they must be Poles, who were only looking for a pretext to approach me and have a word with me. In this matter I was not disappointed in my belief—they really were Poles placed in that office from various causes and from various Polish provinces.

After the Poles, the Russians were emboldened partly and approached me to have a talk in a quiet voice as though furtively. I knew what and to whom it was possible and necessary to speak. The poor Poles—I was glad that I saw them here and not glad that they found themselves there. I waited for close to an hour and maybe more, so I had the time and opportunity to find out many things, especially which of the Poles came from where. My beloved compatriots would have advised me with all means to assist and bring relief to my position, but this was not in their power. With this we were given to know that Governor General Prince Gorchakov was coming. Each person, as quickly as he could, sat in his place, as if he were diligently working, and when the prince entered the hall, everyone at once, as if on command stood up at attention with deep respect, and I arose from my armchair. Since I was opposite the door at the other end of the hall and therefore straight in front of the entering Prince Gorchakov, Gorchakov fixed his gaze on me at his entrance. Almost having approached me for a moment, he urgently had to pass through that way, turned his gaze from me, and with foolishly proud behavior entered the secondary hall, being on his left-hand side. Everyone sat down and I did the same, but this time I did not cast my eyes around the hall; I sat down and reflected. Since I had been sent under the directive of Prince Gorchakov, where, therefore, he wanted to send me depended on his good will: to Tomsk, to the gubernia of Irkutsk, to Nerchinsk itself, or to somewhere else. This uncertainty was tormenting. The conference of the governor general with his advisor Kapustin and with other higher officials lasted a long time—no doubt pondering over my type of offense and over the place to which they had to send me. Advisor Kapustin had the most influence on this matter after the governor general. The advisor was a good man—as was the universal rumor about him—so that I was not sent by him to the depths of Siberia but remained in the gubernia of Tobolsk, and he insisted on account that my offense appeared to him of little significance. If this was so, then he was very obliging. So it was decided that I was to be sent to the Ekaterininsky factory (the Ekaterininsky plant) lying in the gubernia of Tobolsk, in the Tara district—where one finds the Treasury distillery and the factory of convicts, that is those sentenced to hard labor. I had found out earlier than the official communication about this consideration of a resolution for me, and it lightened the weight of my soul a lot, because, first, I was still closer to Poland and, second, better to work in the distillery than in the mines. After the conclusion of the meeting, which had lasted rather a long time, and after taking care of current administrative interests, Prince Gorchakov finally came out and approaching me, like the former, did not say a word to me. Prince Gorchakov is of a fair height, relatively thin although powerfully and shapely built, and remains a dark-haired, upright, and vigorous man with a fresh complexion—white but ruddy—he appeared to be about forty and a proud and haughty figure. In a word, he was a handsome, comely man and a real despot of Siberia; he was in the Vice dark green uniform with a red collar. Shortly after he left, Advisor Kapustin himself, politely and courteously, announced to me that I would set out for the Ekaterininsky plant, situated only twelve versts (closer than two Polish miles) from the district city of Tara in the gubernia of Tobolsk. The city of Tara lies to the north of Omsk and is removed from it by some three hundred versts (47 Polish miles). Only here I changed my former gendarmes; I wanted to reward them with money for their good treatment of me, but I do not know why they did not let me do this. Then I politely took leave of them, thanking them for their courtesy with me during the progression of the journey. These good-natured but simple people, parting with me, were visibly moved, and wishing me a better fate, they departed. I was sorry to part with them. They immediately gave me two other gendarmes from Omsk, of whom one had already advanced to the age of noncommissioned officer, for whom my money was taken from the first gendarmes by me and given to him to put away. None of the Poles working in the Main Administration had the opportunity to part with me.

About two in the afternoon, I sat in the *kibitka* with new gendarmes and, through the same gate in which I entered Omsk, I exited it. From the beginning, I was deep in thought and did not say anything; I even paid little notice to the villages and surroundings through which we drove. Later, I began to speak with the new gendarmes; they were also good people. One of these, the noncom among them, said, "This is not the first time that I will be riding with the likes of you, sir; I have already taken a good look at much misfortune and suffering of many other of your compatriots. It has not yet been a year since I transported a young Pole Rybczyński from Omsk to Tomsk to hand him over there to the army, to the Siberian battalion to which he was sentenced as a common soldier; he, also, as he told me, sat in prison in Kiev." Since, as I said elsewhere, in the prison in Kiev carved into the wall I found the name of Rybczyński, as I had surmised already in Kiev, he had been sitting for a long time in the prison (but before me). On this account, the suspicion was that he was some Polish nobleman, and was sentenced, as Bibikov told me, to the Caucasus, and the noncom said that he transported him to Tomsk; and I asked the noncom about the details of the person and the attributes of Rybczyński, and he spoke a lot to his commendations: he was young, thin, and tall, with a pale and rigid face, and long brown hair. He was sad and melancholy, and constantly, as the noncom said, pitied only himself that the condition of his health would never permit him to return sometime to his homeland of Poland. As to the matter itself, being already a soldier in a battalion in Tomsk, a year after my arrival in Siberia, I learned that he had died there—so sad that his presentiment was fulfilled; he did not have the happiness to look anew upon his homeland.

How many thousands of Poles of similar fortune were deprived, and in reward for so many decades of our torments and agonies, in reward for the superhuman efforts of Poland, and in defense of the freedoms of all Europe, today all Europe is affronted by and jeers at our Polish wretchedness. The selfish, greedy, and debauched heart of the peoples of Europe not only does not want to feel the injustices harming us and to help us in the reclaiming of our rights and our independence, but even shuts us out in our poverty. The Pole today has become lively, a walking reproach of conscience for them; wanting, thus, to drown their conscience, it is necessary even to get rid of the sight and recollection of a Pole and Poland, and it is necessary to enact criminal measures against them, even down to the remnants. Have we been watching, maybe not for a long time, how long Europe with a similar nature has been ascending to its desired goal? And whether in the final moments of a horrible end to its freedoms and independence, it will not remember painfully—unfortunately and too late—about Poland? The old noncom and well-traveled soldier remained for a long time in Poland and was for a long time in the regiment of Prince Württemberg, about whom he spent a lot of time telling me amorous adventures.

"The Martyrdom of the Prior Sierociński": An Extract from the Memoirs of Mr. Rufin Piotrowski Published in Poznan in the Journal *Polish Messenger*

Here is the fate of the Prior Sierociński and that of his companions in misfortune. I know so very well this story that took place in Omsk (Siberia), which is close to the warehouse, in which I did my part. Everyone in the region knew the story.[1] I took my information from different sources—from Polish, Russian, and Siberian eyewitnesses of this catastrophe, many of whom had even taken part in the confinement of the priest Sierociński, and all were unanimous in their account. It is on the uniformity of these various testimonies on which rests the appalling truth that I will recount.

Before the Polish insurrection of 1831, Prior Sierociński was the religious superior at St. Basil's at Owrucz in Volhynia. The schools of this town were run by these religious. After the insurrection erupted, Sierociński then took a very active part, but unfortunately he was taken prisoner and thrown in a dungeon, and soon a military judgment and the will of the autocrat condemned him to lose his priesthood and to become, not a priest, but a Cossack. He was then incorporated into a regiment of Siberian Cossacks and then forced like the others with lance and sabre in hand to pursue the

1 This is manuscript 5660 in the Archiwum Hotelu Lambert located in Biblioteka Czartoryskich w Krakowie.

Kirgiz on their steppe. But in waiting in Omsk, where I said above that there was a school of Cossacks, he sensed there was a need for a professor. Thus, Sierociński reminded them that he had directed schools; consequently, he would be capable of teaching. Moreover, the employees themselves in talking sometimes with Sierociński had recognized in him a man strong in superior instruction. In effect, a good Pole, a bright professor, a zealous priest, Sierociński, outside of the knowledge necessary for every professor, also knew German and French. He decided, thus, to transform by order from a Cossack to a professor of the school in Omsk. But this professor did not have the right nor the possibility to go up in the ranks, because with the title of professor he would only have the rank of a Cossack for life, one always counting on his regiment. These absurdities—as inept as they are ridiculously savage—are encountered only in Russia.

Abbé Sierociński of a weak and delicate constitution, of ruined health and an almost nervous sensibility, had a force of soul and the inflexibility of an extraordinary character. The love of liberty and the sentiment of a man's dignity made him vividly appreciate the glaring oppression exerted on Poland; these sentiments filled his soul with love and compassion for all his companions of misfortune and exile. Also, Sierociński, inspired by all these misfortunes, was taken by the thought of the immense steppes of Siberia and took into account the unfortunates that populated them. He supported the reserves and the forces that contained them and, feeling the presence of the spirit of Benyovszki's good fortune, he believed that he would see fortune smile on him, and he believed in the hope of the deliverance of its victims.[2]

Profiting from his position as a professor, Sierociński maintained relations with the Poles who were numerous in Omsk and even with the Russians who in heart or spirit were just as discontented. The latter penetrated the sentiment of Sierociński and, sharing his views and his plan, passionately dreamt of spreading the idea of an uprising. The task was easy, because the adept could not miss every interest ruined among the crowd showered with injustices in which every sentiment was wounded. All the Poles, Russians, Tatars, and soldiers, like the settlers, dreamt of the undertaking.

It was necessary to take part in the conspiracy and to be profoundly initiated in its secrets in order to be able to give a detailed account of what

2 This reference to Móric Benyovszki is part of the escape motif of Piotrowski's *Memoirs from a Stay in Siberia*, because, having been sent to Siberia for his participation in the conspiracy known as the Confederacy of Bar (*Konfederacja Barska*, 1768–72), he fled from Kamchatka.

were the means by which they wished to aid the conspirators to arrive at their purpose. Elsewhere, knowing even these details one could commit greater than thoughtlessness in having concealed them, since even today one could supply new victims to a power as suspicious as it is cruel. Suffice it to say that Sierociński wanted to detach Siberia from Russia and to thereby arrive at the liberation of all the condemned to hard labor or deportation. In case he did not succeed, it was necessary, arms in hand, to open up a passage to pass through the Kirgiz steppes, through the Khanate of Tashkent (where one could find many Christians) or even through Bukhara, so that under the proper circumstances, one could arrive at the English possessions in India.

The thought of Prior Sierociński found an immense echo in noble hearts and was heard throughout Siberia. Soon the preparations were finished, and nothing more than the signal was awaited. It was in Omsk that it was to begin, since it was there that existed the largest group of conspirators and the unique depot of artillery in Siberia of war munitions, rations, and treasure—and everything was ready. In twenty-four hours the movement had to begin, but here, as everywhere, cowards were found. And what men were these? The shame covers my brow, and the spirit would like not to believe in so much reprobation and infamy. What would I give to be able to hide from the world the stain of infamy that cost my noble nation? But the demand of equity obliges me to tell the truth, in all its purity and all its simplicity. The traitors were not Russian, not Siberian, and not Tatar, but Poles—the Poles who a little beforehand had been fighting and spilling their blood for the independence of their country and condemned by their oppressor to serve the remainder of their life in Siberian battalions. There were three of them; all three of them from the national war for independence of 1831. I forgot the name of one of them, but the others were called Gaiwski, born in the Kingdom of Poland, and Kanak, born in Warsaw itself. These three infamous ones—unworthy of their Polish names—the very day before the plot broke out, seizing an opportune occasion, went to the house of Colonel de Grave, commandant of the Omsk fortress, and disclosed everything. Unfortunately, these traitors, initiated profoundly in the secrets of the conspiracy, gave the most damning details. They revealed that Sierociński was the soul of the movement; they knew those who were the leaders following him and finally when and how the movement was to break out. The Russian authorities immediately took energetic measures and made it impossible to even attempt it. Since Sierociński and the principal leaders who were denounced were in Omsk, they were arrested immediately. Harsh orders were dispatched in all directions enjoining the arrest of all who could appear suspect, all who could exert influence: Poles as well as Russians, Siberians as well as Tatars, soldiers as well as settlers. It is not possible to know the numbers of those arrested in this way, but one would not exaggerate in putting it at 1,000 at a start. Later this number grew, even by a lot. Those arrested were brought to Tobolsk, Tomsk, and above all Omsk, where the leaders of the conspiracy were to be found. The arrests took place in 1834 and 1835.

Once the accused were gathered, an inquiry was opened to report the fact to St. Petersburg. Two commissions of inquiry did not arrive at any results. It seems that the members of these commissions, afraid of knowing about the conspiracy, its numbers, and the positions of the people compromised—just as they were not wanting to deliver so many unfortunate victims to the inexorable condemnation of the Tsar—preferred to disperse without conducting it. It was only the third commission composed of individuals sent from St. Petersburg, which ended the affair, which had lasted three years. Some of the accused were released before the inquiry, others during it, and others were finally condemned as the guilty ones.

Prior Sierociński with all the force of his soul and his unshakeable character was kept in captivity during the three years that the process lasted. His responses were always dignified and firm; never did he change anything about what he confessed. Despite the exterior of a soul of iron, Sierociński possessed delicate sentiments and a good and sensible heart. These qualities seem mutually exclusive and nevertheless, on the contrary, are very often found in the same fortunate organism of superior men. Moreover, no one who knows the noble children of Ukraine will be surprised at this joining of force of character and tenderness of sentiment. Their blood is not in a stagnant position, and their heart is not an inert mass; they want what they want, because their courage is not vain, and they are inclined more toward events than words. All who are born must die—that is their motto. I had the occasion to read different fragments of poetry that Sierociński wrote during his long captivity. One could say that the soul of the entire poet was reflected in these verses, a veritable inspiration of a superior being. One finds there at the same time all the humility of a Christian, all the dignity of man, the patriotism of a Pole, and the reverie of a poet.

Finally, Prior Sierociński, Drużyłowski, Jablonski, Gorski or Zagorski,[3] and Szokalski (sixty years of age and an officer from the time of the

3 Antoni Zagorski, a participant in the 1830 uprising, was serving in a division of invalids in an Omsk Siberian Corps when he was arrested for leading the conspiracy after the arrest of Prior Sierociński. He died after having received 5,000 blows (Śliwowska, *ZpIR*, 695).

Napoleonic wars)—all for having taken part in the war of independence of 1831—had been condemned to serve as common soldiers for the rest of their lives in Siberia battalions in Russia. Mieledun found those identified guilty. The judgment brought from St. Petersburg said explicitly for each of the condemned to receive seven thousand blows of a baton without mercy. If by accident one of those condemned survived this punishment, he had to be in a garrison afterward, employed at hard labor in perpetuity in the mines in Nerchinsk. The rest of the condemned had to submit to a punishment of 500, 2,000, or 3,000 blows of the batons plus hard labor in perpetuity or for a certain number of years, whereas others became settlers, and others were sent to garrisons in remote parts of Siberia.

The day set for this terrible execution arrived: it was held in the month of March in 1837 in Omsk. Never before had it been used against so many individuals and with such cruelty. General Galaficien[4] known for his ferocity was sent expressly from St. Petersburg to watch the faithful execution of the judgment. But the cruelty of Galaficien repulsed the Russians themselves. At the appointed time of day, two battalions of 1,000 men each assembled on a plain outside the town of Omsk. One of the battalions was to execute Sierociński and his companions condemned to seven thousand blows, and the second was for those who had the lesser sentences. The two battalions with a certain distant between them were aligned forming rows of two ranks at a distance. Galaficien inspected and surveyed everything; he placed himself next to the battalion intended for the grand execution. When one is made to pass the soldiers through the rods, the Russian regulations want the row to be formed by close ranks so that the soldier does not separate his arm too much from his body, so that he does not advance his foot but maintains the attitude of a man at arms, and finally so that the thickness of the batons may be placed in the barrel of a rifle. Here everything was changed: Galaficien ordered that the soldiers be placed at arm's length, for the arms to be raised to hit with all their length, and for them to advance a step so that the blow would be stronger; finally, the thickness of baton was such that it could not enter a single barrel of a rifle.

The prisoners were brought to the place of execution and the judgment was read out to them. Without taking an interest in the battalion charged with executing the largest number of condemned, I will give you details regarding capital punishment. I do not remember which of the condemned opened this bloody march, but I know that all submitted to their punishment and were hit literally without mercy. Also, no one, with the exception

4 Here, he means General Apollon Galafeev, who screamed at the soldiers to beat the offenders harder.

of Szokalski for whom the doctor of the regiment actively interceded and who because of it was saved, no one reached the conclusion of his punishment. Bathed in blood, each one fell in the snow and then breathed his last or a few moments afterward. Sierociński, as the leader of the plot, was reserved for last so as to exhaust his strength by the cries of pain from his companions and the view of the execution that awaited him. Sierociński was thus prepared for martyrdom by the torments and the heinous end of his companions. His turn came at last. They seized his arms, attached them to a long rifle held by two soldiers so as to keep the march in order, and uncovered his shoulders. The doctor looking at the weakness of Sierociński, who weak by nature and exhausted by captivity had the air of a specter rather than that of a living being, wanted to give him a stimulating drink. Sierociński, for whom morality had lost none of its heroic energy, pushed away the drink saying: "Drench yourselves in my blood, drench yourselves in our blood, but I do not want your drink." When the signal was given for Sierociński's funeral march, he broke out into a hymn: "Miserere mei Deus secundum magnam miseri cordiam tuam, etc."[5] At these words Galaficien like one possessed cried full of rage with three reprisals: "Hit him harder, still harder, still harder." In effect, he was hit so hard that when he arrived at the end of the battalion he, all bloodied and unconscious, fell in the snow. It was in vain that they wanted to place him on his feet—they gave way. But they had prepared in advance a sled with a kind of scaffold. Sierociński was placed on his knees, his head and his neck inclined, his arms tied up behind his back, and his entire body attached in a manner so that he could not move. Then he began the march through the ranks of soldiers who hit him again and again and whom Galaficien excited by crying again, harder, still harder. Dragged thus Sierociński from the beginning uttered some moans that became more and more rare; he was still breathing at 4,000 blows but finally he rendered his soul to God. The other three thousand blows fell on his cadaver or rather on his naked skeleton on which the uncovered bones were broken. The above affirmations by the Russian and Polish eyewitnesses were unanimous that all, but Sierociński especially, were hit with such ferocity that the flesh of their bodies—slashed in tatters and stuck to the batons—came off, so far off as to allow the terrible whiteness of the bones to appear.

Such a barbarous execution, uncommon even in Russia, filled all the Russian and Polish witnesses with horror. The soldiers ordered for this butchery were speaking of it only with horror and saying that they had

5 This is from the penitential Psalm 51, "Have mercy on me, Lord, according to your great merciful heart."

never seen anyone assassinated in a manner so cruel, with such ferocity and with such savagery, as these unfortunates had been. All of Western Siberia still speaks with horror of this execution, since until then no one had seen such an example. Those who breathed in the middle of these most cruel sufferings, like those killed on the spot, were transported pell-mell to the hospital. The deceased, reported as four Poles and a Russian, were reunited in the same grave outside of the town. At the fervent demand of the Poles, they were allowed to raise a sign of the Redemption over the tomb of their unfortunate compatriots. Until today (1846) there remains erected on the tomb a large black cross in isolated woods in the wilderness, appearing to protect them in its two powerful arms. Such was the end of Sierociński and his companions in misfortune; Szokalski—the lone one protected by the pity of the military doctor—escaped from this fatal departure the end of the martyrs. Being restored after a treatment of several months, in conformity with his judgment, he was sentenced to hard labor in perpetuity in the mines of Nerchinsk. But following the torture to which he had submitted, he suffered a derangement of spirit, and he ended his life by suicide a little time after his arrival at the place of his new sojourn.

Beyond Omsk

Notes on the Lives of Bronisław Zaleski and Edward Żeligowski

These final documents attempt to provide some historical context for Dostoevsky's Siberian experience beyond *House of the Dead*, since, owing to the novelist's own writings, Dostoevsky scholarship and reminiscences of him (with the notable exception of those written by Baron Vrangel) focus on his connections to Omsk more than on his service in Semipalatinsk. As a journal article, "Polish Exiles in Orenburg" differs from the personal testimonies of Bogusławski and Piotrowski, which do not aspire to present a multigenerational witness to a region synonymous with Polish exile. The article reflects Zaleski's interests as a librarian, historian, and journalist who thoroughly explored, described, and sketched images from the region where he spent his exile. At the same time, like Dostoevsky's *House of the Dead*, the article displays the author's nationalist sentiments, since it appeared after the suppression of the failed 1863 uprising in Warsaw and in a journal with links to the community in exile—that is, a journal that he edited for the Historical-Literary Association in Paris. Zaleski's support for the uprising is suggested by the opening and closing frames to his article "Polish Exiles in Orenburg," especially with its reference to the "tens of thousands" sent to Siberia after 1863, who filled the shoes of the former exiles. Yet, the document describing the Petrashevtsy found in Żeligowski's file reminds the reader that political offenders were not divided only by nation but by conspiratorial group, region of origin, and conditions of exile. Such correspondence, now preserved in multiple historical archives, was frequently exchanged among departments of state after Alexander II indicated his desire to provide clemency for some exiles, especially for those having served in the tsar's army. As a result, Shevchenko's name can be found alongside Dostoevsky's in letters about Western Siberia, and there is much discussion about how to address many of the Petrashevtsy as a group even though they were serving in different regions (e.g., the Caucasus, Orenburg, and Semipalatinsk).[1] In other words, the documents translated here help to situate Dostoevsky within various communities of exiles, many of whose members, like Dostoevsky, were conscripted into the ranks and sought to advance in order to reach the rank of a noncommissioned officer, thereby earning a return home.

Shared Biographies of Zaleski and Żeligowski

Bronisław Zaleski and his friend the poet Edward Żeligowski share acquaintances and a similar background of incarceration to Dostoevsky's fellow prisoner Józef Bogusławski, as they were arrested in connection with the student circles at Dorpat University linked to Hildebrandt and then became associated with the conspiratorial circle surrounding Dr. Renier and the emissary Röhr.[2] After their first arrests, Zaleski and Bogusławski were exiled and then released owing to petitions by their parents, but they returned only to be arrested again along with Dr. Renier with whom they shared a cell.[3] Whereas Zaleski admitted that he met with Jan Röhr, who consulted with him about potential support among landowners for an uprising in Poznan, Żeligowski was primarily visiting Dr. Renier's to make use of his library of forbidden books. For this reason, Żeligowski was initially released under secret police observation, and then subsequently rearrested and exiled to Petrozavodsk in 1851 for his drama *Jordan*.[4] Although Zaleski began serving in the Orenburg battalion in 1848, Żeligowski came to Orenburg only in 1853 before being reassigned to Ufa in 1854. Zaleski's letters to several exiles from the Orenburg circle, including Żeligowski, Shevchenko, Sierakowski, and Pawel Kruniewicz, as well as the writings preserved in the Czartoryski Archive in Krakow attest to the direct influence of the Orenburg experience on Zaleski's literary and artistic output,

1 Tret'e otdelenie Sobstvennoi Ego Imperatorskogo Velichestva kantseliarii. Fond 109, opis' 31, delo 133. Gosudarstvennyi arkhiv Rossiiskoi Federatsii.

2 Caban, *Z Orenburga do Paryża*, 22.

3 Ibid., 24, 37. Caban writes that Zaleski came to know Bogusławski well during their shared imprisonment and pities his fate in letters from exile (38).

4 V. F. Ratch. Fond 629, opis' 188, f. 45–46; Edward Żeligowski: Korespondencja Edwarda Żeligowskiego i zebrane przez niego dokumenty dotyczące zesłańców syberyjskich, Archiwum Hotelu Lambert. Rkps. 6972, II. Biblioteka Czartoryskich.

which he published in Paris after his emigration in 1860. Żeligowski, after his 1858 amnesty, initially settled in St. Petersburg where he associated with a multiethnic literary community—for instance, Shevchenko, his co-conspirator the historian Nikolai Kostomarov, the Russian novelist Ivan Turgenev, and Jozafat Ohryzko (with the latter he worked on the Polish-language newspaper *Word*).[5] Like Zaleski, Żeligowski first returned to the Congress Kingdom (after having been released from state service in 1860) and then emigrated to France, but he finally settled in Geneva where he suffered from poor health leading to an early death in 1864.[6] Zaleski, however, remained active in the 1860s and 1870s in the Parisian community of Polish exiles by publishing his own historical studies and developing his skills as a published artist.

Although Piotrowski was connected with the Parisian community, as evidenced by Klaczko's translation, his political activities were more removed from the community than Zaleski's.[7] Zaleski directed the Polish library in Paris, was a leader in several benevolent societies, and worked with the prominent aristocratic Czartoryski family.[8] Moreover, by the time that he wrote "Polish Exiles in Orenburg," Shevchenko and Żeligowski had died, and the prominent exile Sierakowski had been hanged in Vilnius for his participation in the armed uprising of 1863.[9] The impact of such personal losses is evident in Zaleski's correspondence with fellow Orenburg exile Pawel Kruniewicz, who describes Żeligowski's final illness as "a sickness in soul and body" and expresses his own disbelief at the destruction of this "beautiful life" that so openly bared his heart.[10] In the article, however, Zaleski strives to avoid an overly personal witness, since he prefers to describe a community in exile with the more experienced generation

5 G. Pisarek, "Rol' russkikh i ukraintsev v zhizni i tvorchestve Edvarda Zheligovskogo," in *Sviazi revoliutsionerov Rossii i Pol'shi XIX–nachala XX v.*, eds. V. A. D'iakov, I. S. Miller, and L. A. Obushenkova (Moscow: Izdatel'stvo "Nauka," 1968), 231–35.

6 V. F. Ratch. Fond 629, opis' 188, f. 65; Edward Żeligowski, Rkps. 6972, II.

7 There are seven letters to Zaleski from Klaczko preserved in Zaleski's correspondence. See Bronisław Zaleski. Korespondencja. Listy od osób różnych K-R, Archiwum Hotelu Lambert. Rkps. 6955 III, Biblioteka Czartoryskich.

8 Andrzej Zieliński, "Bronisława Zaleskiego wspomnienia z Kazachstanu (1848–1856)," in *Polacy w Kazachstanie: Historia i współczesność*, ed. Stanisław Ciesielski and Antoni Kuczyński (Wroclaw: Wydawnictwo Uniwersytetu Wrocławskiego, 1996), 140.

9 Bronisław i Bohdan Zaleski. Korespondencja. Listy Edwarda Żeligowskiego. Korespondencja do Bronisława Zaleskiego, Archiwum Hotelu Lambert. Rkps. 6953 II, Biblioteka Czartoryskich.

10 Bronisław Zaleski. Korespondencja. Listy od Kruniewiczow, Archiwum Hotelu Lambert. Rkps. 6946, Biblioteka Czartoryskich.

protecting the new arrivals, perhaps as a means of giving hope to the relatives of those newly-sentenced thousands on their way to the depths of Russia.

Zaleski on the Polish Question

Nevertheless, Zaleski also attempts to shape a transnational dialogue on the Polish Question when he rejects a political theology maintaining that deportees' suffering represents "divine justice" sent for "our final purification," even though he connects deceased exiles to the ecclesiastical tradition of the Roman martyrs. He expresses frustration at those idealists of the later generation who supported "the idea of fighting for sacrifice itself" as they embraced a "truth" that "lit up in Warsaw in 1861," but in doing so Zaleski also betrays a class bias, since he concludes that after 1850 political prisoners of the middle class start appearing in larger numbers. This preference for the nobility is reflected in his romanticization of the Bar Confederates, the learned exiles connected to Mickiewicz, or those deported after the 1830 uprising, which logically follows from his aristocratic émigré connections at the Hotel Lambert. Therefore, the noble attributes of faith, conscious, fortitude, and charity are imparted to the Polish deportees in apposition to heresy, instinct, debauchery, and savagery characteristic of the Russian soldiers. Such sentiments reflect his background as a landowner, which necessarily differentiates him from the former serf Shevchenko, but Zaleski still remains affectionate toward his Siberian comrade, comparing him to Saint Peter, writing of his love for children, preparing to send him money, and trying to help him through political and artistic channels.[11] Citing pangs of conscience over the eighteen-year grief of his mother, Zaleski initially renounces the artist's calling and distances himself from political activity in the late 1850s.[12] However, he visits St. Petersburg in 1859 where he meets with several of his fellow exiles, including Sierakowski and Shevchenko, and then goes abroad in 1861, where he encounters agitators in Parisian exile, which leads to his debate with Mikhail Bakunin—the famous Siberian escapee and a member of the progressive émigré circle of Aleksandr Herzen. At this point, in his 1861 booklet, *Michael Bakunin and His Appeal to Russian and Polish*

11 V. S. Borodin, *Listi do Tarasa Shevchenka* (Kiev: Naukova Dumka, 1993), 73, 79–80.
12 Ibid., 82.

Friends, the Polish community in Siberia appears less isolated than it does in his work after the 1863 uprising as he advances an exilic camaraderie between Russians and Poles: "We lived together with your exiles from 1825 in Siberia and in the Caucasus, with the victims of the Petrashevsky affair in the very same Siberia and Orenburg."[13]

All the same, unlike Bogusławski, Zaleski in his published writings displays a tendency to conceal personal relationships developed during his Orenburg experience, even though he continues to maintain contact with a number of exiles, including Shevchenko, Żeligowski, Kruniewicz, Sierakowski, and Vasilii Belozersky. This may be an aesthetic choice based on his own portrayal of his creative process as part of an expedition (with a pencil and portfolio in hand) to the river Neris, which flows through Vilnius, in order "to publish a description of the river in historical, archeological, topographical, hydrographic, and other relations" for an album of landscapes. In his diary pages on the Kokand fortress Ak-Mechet, which he helped seize in a famous expedition, as well as in his descriptions of Central Asia, which consciously engage an 1867 account in the French journal *Review of Two Worlds*, he applies methodologies of topography, anthropology, history, and military science to the tribes he has observed in the Russian Empire.[14] In other words, Zaleski chooses to blend the immediacy of an eyewitness account with an analytical approach, allowing him some distance from experience, and at times even with drawings that visually rather than verbally translate his observations to paper. Such an approach also permits him to avoid incriminating anyone—a problem to which he was sensitive given Shevchenko's experience—so Zaleski uses intermediaries to exchange letters with exiles, cautiously shares manuscripts of comrades in exile, and frequently avoids mentioning in his published writings relationships with the living, even in the more personal obituary written for Żeligowski.[15] Indeed, his allusion to foreign emissaries causing trouble in the Congress Kingdom may be an allusion not only to his own arrest for associating with Rhör but also to the seizure of correspondence linked to the Herzen Circle at the Russian border in 1862, which led to the arrest of

---

13 [Bronisław Zaleski], *Michał Bakunin i odezwa jego do przyjaciół rossyjskich i polskich* (Paris: W księgarni polskiej, 1862), 9.

14 Bronisław Zaleski. Dziennik (fragment), Archiwum Hotelu Lambert. Rkps. 6927, Biblioteka Czartoryskich; Bronisław Zaleski. "Absorption des peuple des assatiques [*sic*] par la Russie. Russification des Baschkirs," Archiwum Hotelu Lambert. Rkps. 6935, Biblioteka Czartoryskich.

15 This was published in the same issue as "Polish Exiles in Orenburg."

several radicals.[16] Hence, although the summary of the judgments of the Petrashevtsy, mentioned in Żeligowski's files and translated here, includes four of those sent to the Orenburg Line Battalions (Pleshcheev, Aleksandr Khanykov, Vasilii Golovinsky, and Petr Shaposhnikov)—several of whom interacted with the Orenburg circle—Zaleski does not provide details about their relations in "Polish Exiles in Orenburg."[17]

Networking and Publishing after Exile

Documenting the whereabouts of deportees and establishing a record of Polish exile history, however, was a preoccupation of many returnees from both Eastern and Western Siberia, as well as for Zaleski's friend Żeligowski. The translation of a document on the Petrashevtsy included here was found amid a collection of notes on Siberian exiles preserved in Żeligowski's files in an archive at the Parisian center of the Great Emigration, the Hotel Lambert. As Bogusławski clarifies in his section on the Omsk affair, if funds (~100 silver rubles) were available, it was possible to obtain copies of investigative summaries from the person who copied it. With his work as an official in the chancellery of the Orenburg governor, Egor Baranovsky and in the civil service in Ufa, Żeligowski would have had the means and opportunity to obtain this document, which lies in the same packet as a letter to Nazimov, responding to his request for information on deportees in an effort to discern who is deserving of amnesty. A similar "secret" document for the Tobolsk region, containing information on Bogusławski, Tokarzewski, and Durov, lies in the Ministry for Internal Affairs collection of the State Historical Archives.[18] The document amid Żeligowski's papers has no stamps or seals, so it is not official like some of the others he procured, but its presence in his files attests to the Orenburg circle's political and literary connections to the Petrashevtsy. Pleshcheev was, after all, well connected in Orenburg in Governor General Perovsky's circle (especially to Lieutenant Colonel Viktor Dandevil) as well as Governor Baranovsky's. Furthermore, Shevchenko wrote to Pleshcheev about publishing in the St. Petersburg journals, Pleshcheev alluded to Zaleski in his correspondence with Dandevil

16 This includes such prominent radicals as Nikolai Serno-Solovevich and Nikolai Chernyshevsky.

17 Bol'shakov, *Orenburgskaia Shevchenkovskaia entsiklopediia*, 94–95, 277, 350.

18 O litsakh, sostoiashchikh pod nadzorom politsii v Tobol'skoi Gubernii. Fond 1286, opis' 16, delo 387, chast' 1/I, k. 101, 102, 187.

(1854–56), and Pleshcheev published a translation of Żeligowski's lyrical poem, "Two Words" (1854) and several of Shevchenko's.[19] The summary of the Petrashevtsy's various crimes and punishments displays the arbitrary nature of the sentencing, alludes to some cooperation with the government on the part of conspirators (e.g., Speshnev and Palm), underscores official concern over the lithograph (connected to Durov and Dostoevsky), and shows an intent on behalf of the new tsar to focus on education, censorship, and surveillance as means of suppressing political dissent.

Zaleski addresses censorship in connection with Żeligowski in his obituary when accounting for Żeligowski's initial decision to establish himself in St. Petersburg: "The censor there was less suspicious, the proximity to the highest authority seemed to indicate security from the often severe persecution of lower authorities, and it was easier to familiarize oneself with the reforms that were introduced and already commencing."[20] Even while geographically distant from Russia's two capital cities, the Orenburg circle attempted to find publishers for their writings; for example, Zaleski met with editors from *Russian Messenger* on Shevchenko's behalf in Moscow.[21] Zaleski was well positioned to locate publishing opportunities not only because of his early return from Orenburg in 1856 but also since he had been working in library acquisitions in Orenburg since 1855—an occupation that contributed to his knowledge of the history of Orenburg.[22] Already in an 1857 letter to Dostoevsky, Pleshcheev wrote of submitting his work to *The Messenger* and the following year contacted Moscow editor Mikhail Katkov about publishing Dostoevsky's work.[23] Because those connected to Orenburg networked with each other while maintaining contacts with their co-conspirators, they enjoyed many opportunities for publishing, especially in St. Petersburg journals like Nikolai Nekrasov's progressive *The Contemporary*, the bilingual Ukrainian-Russian journal *Basis* edited by Shevchenko's co-conspirator Vasilii Belozersky, and the Dostoevsky brothers' *Time*.

Although Zaleski visited St. Petersburg in 1859 and worked with the former exiles in the editorial group of *Word*, he was primarily situating

19 T. Shevchenko, "Listi Shevchenka," *Osnova* 5 (May 1862): 7–8; A. N. Pleshcheev, "A. N. Pleshcheev: Pis'ma iz Ak-Mecheti (1/2)," *Russkii Turkestan. Istoriia, liudi, nravy*, LiveJournal, http://rus-turk.livejournal.com/221368.html, accessed August 13, 2017.

20 Zaleski, "Zmarli na wychodztwie od 1861 roku: Żeligowski, Edward," 371.

21 Borodin, *Listi do Tarasa Shevchenka*, 74.

22 Bol'shakov, *Orenburgskaia Shevchenkovskaia entsiklopediia*, 136.

23 A. S. Dolinin, ed. "Pis'ma A. N. Pleshcheeva k F. M. Dostoevskomu," *F. M. Dostoevskii: Materialy i issledovaniia*, ed. (Leningrad: Akademiia Nauk SSSR, 1935), 437–39.

himself in Polish exile circles in Europe, as he established himself with famous exiles, including the son of Mickiewicz (Władysław), the poet Cyprian Norwid, the revolutionary Agaton Giller, and the novelist Józef Kraszewski.[24] Identifying with neither of the two main nineteenth-century waves of emigration—following the failed uprisings of 1830 and 1863—he was empathetic to the noble sensibilities of the Romantic generation but concerned for the material well-being of the younger generation, which not only had fewer financial resources but also was educated in an increasingly de-Polonized nation. As an author he attempts to bridge this divide by showing the present as rooted in a tradition of political dissent that had begun under the reign of Catherine the Great and had continued not only with the two rebellions but also with intellectual circles connected to insurrections in 1825 and 1846. The following article was published in the same year that Zaleski participated in the public defense of Polish patriot Anton Berezowski, who, much to Dostoevsky's dismay, had attempted to assassinate Tsar Alexander II in Paris. Consequently, "Polish Exiles in Orenburg" indicates that the author's sympathies remain with the liberationists, whose obituaries he wrote for *Annual of the Historical-Literary Association in Paris*.[25] In this respect, Zaleski remains a transnational author, conscious of his status as a mid-century writer in Parisian exile, who is uniquely poised to analyze Ukrainian, Lithuanian, Polish, and Russian tensions within their historical contexts, ranging from the reigns of Catherine the Great to Alexander II.

24 Caban, *Z Orenburga do Paryża*, 85, 93, 198–99. Kraszewski is linked to Zaleski's Orenburg days when Zaleski had contacted him concerning the sale of Shevchenko's paintings.

25 Ibid., 194–95.

"Polish Exiles in Orenburg"[1]

For many years our history ran beyond the geographic borders of Poland. From the struggles of legionnaires to the attempts at renewed emigration in the West—everything depended on it and contributed to it both in the internal history of the country and in each of its provinces, and in one of her all-too-real parts is the history of our exiles, whose syllables are tossed in practically all the recesses of the extensive Russian nation. Without this part the image of the life of our nation continuously over the last hundred years would not even be complete; it increases in significance in measure to the growing number of victims. Today when that number has reached frightening dimensions, encompassing already almost an entire generation, it is even more worth scrutinizing the fates of our former exiles, so that it gives us a certain likeness to the current situation of our already almost innumerable brothers.

Wanting this image to be more or less exemplary, it would be necessary to run through all the years of our misfortunes, encompassing at the same time all of Russia, and above all Siberia, the Caucasus, and Orenburg as three main places of exile. Perhaps at some time the secret archives of the Third Section of the tsar's chancellery will provide these materials; now it is time for one to be almost content with that which is written in individual memories. Such stories about Orenburg will be the subject of the following pages.

Orenburg from almost the very beginnings of the anguish and our atonement seemed to belong to the privileged places of exile—and having excluded Siberia, whose significant spatial capacity absorbed a number of our brothers—perhaps there, for some time, they were sent in greatest numbers. Situated on the Eastern edge of the empire among populations of various tribes, mainly Mongolian and Finnish, this was indeed a suitable place for a living grave for us. There the government could fear the least

1 This is a translation of Bronisław Zaleski's article "Wygnańcy Polscy w Orenburgu," in *Rocznik Towarzystwa Historyczno-Literackiego w Paryzu* (1866): 75–107.

Polish impact and reckoned that we would miserably die out. But the name of Orenburg, alone, still does not describe the places of exile in these parts; it extended there even in measure to the continual growth of the nation, because sure enough, as if just from fatalisms attached to our wanderer's lot, we also had to travel step in step with the conquests of Russia. Anywhere the foot of the Russian soldier was set in the East—whether on the peaks of the Caucasus, or the borders of the Chinese kingdom, or the Pacific Ocean—immediately behind them had to walk a Polish exile with his pining and his tear. So, it was the same in Orenburg. In the first years, the edges of the Urals became the final border—after this time it moved farther and farther, deep into Central Asia; between 1840 and 1850 it was already based at the Aral Sea and the eastern shore of the Caspian Sea, in '53 it moved 500 versts to the east, along the banks of the Syr Darya (once the Jaxartes of old), and only during the reign of Nicholas did Russia acquire in these parts a space greater than France, Spain, and Portugal all taken together. Today it would be necessary to search for the borders of new provinces already in the heart of Bukharai and the Kokand Khanate—and these are temporary borders—because, as the Ministry of Foreign Affairs officially informed the border administration in Orenburg, Russia has no border to the East.[2] So even our exiles do not know to where in the end they can be compelled to go, not even when departing for their destination.

The first exiles for the national affair in Orenburg were the Bar Confederates. How many of them were there and how did they stray this way, we do not know. The memoirs of Benyovszki and General Kopeć cast a light on the existence of our compatriots and their suffering in Siberia; from Orenburg, no one, as far as we know, returned who could give testimony about this. But to this day stands a stone wall, surrounding the Orenburg fortress raised by the hands of our confederates, and this attests meaningfully that there must have been not a few of them and that there they were used for heavy labor, but many characteristics may be provided today to the one who knows the contemporary condition of this region's edge.[3] Russia not long ago transformed herself into a state seemingly European and was just beginning to settle down there; she brought with her the idea of tsardom, being at that time

2 Although it was only in 1876 that Russia acquired the Central Asian Khanate of Kokand, which neighbored the Khanate of Bukhara, the governor general of Orenburg appointed in 1851, Count Vasilii Perovsky, supported aggressive action against the former.

3 General Józef Kopeć fought in the Kościuszko uprising against Catherine, spent many years in Kamchatka, and wrote a diary about his Siberian experience, whose preface contains additional biographical information in *Dziennik podróży Józefa Kopcia* (Paryż: Księgarnia Luxemburgska, n.d.).

in full force, because she had such representatives as Suvorov, and brought the still coarse customs—only just having experienced the external European refinement—and found tribes still living a vivid and barbarous life with their entire family. After not many years, the established Orenburg was threatened not a few times by the Bashkirs and Kirgiz, the local Tatar tribe, and as there were masses predisposed to living on these expanses, it best explains the fact that exactly there Pugachev's gang came into existence and grew so well.[4] In the fight with them we even unwittingly took part. Once in Siberia, the confederates, conscripted into the army, came to the regiment in Orenburg at that time; 400 of them fell in battle with Pugachev—many together with the entire garrison in Trinity after the population of that city was slaughtered by him. Antoni Puławski, being with his colleagues and in Kazan only for the battle, owed him his return to his homeland. But after the utter defeat of these gangs, the community itself still did not rapidly change. The Bashkirs were not completely calm, and time and time again broke off with the army. The Orenburg governor general was alarmed not infrequently. Massacres, plunders, and conflagrations were daily events. It was not possible to pass through to the other edge of the Urals without danger, and often even the river did not defend from invasion; when it froze over, the Kirgiz often attacked unarmed people, kidnapped them, and then sold them off in Khiva, where such a slave was transformed into a shepherd—very often they made incisions in the heel and sprinkled in the wound fine chopped horse hair so that they could not run away.[5] Very often the entire homestead and even the settlement fell victim to steppe marauders. Each newly established Cossack station was a fortress; an embankment encircled it, and for this purpose a guard with blazing fires was maintained to let everyone know of attack or danger. Moscow with threat and force established its own order. After suppressing one of the Bashkir uprisings, Nepliuev hung 135 by the throat and about a dozen by the rib, beheaded 140, and sent 3,000 to hard labor, and several hundred were released to return home, after having had their ears and noses slit—everything was done under the authority of judicial sentences.[6] Our exiles were witnesses to such events and during this chaos they needed to live. Perhaps

4 Bashkirs identify as a Muslim people and are indigenous to the area of the empire between the middle Volga and the Urals.

5 Khiva is an Uzbek-dominated khanate, known for being a Central Asian slave market, against which Perovsky launched an expedition to insure the safety of Russian routes and confirm the empire's access to the Amu Darya River.

6 Ivan Ivanovich Nepliuev was a statesman favored by Peter I and the first governor of Orenburg, who had a fortress built there to protect the population from raids by nomadic peoples (Vladimir Semenov and Vera Semenova's *Gubernatory Orenburgskogo kraia* [Orenburg, Russia: Orenburgskoe Knizhnoe Izdatel'stvo, 1999], 46–60).

one among them looked for connections with rebellious tribes, because, for still a long time, they deluded themselves with the thought of finding allies, at least enemies dangerous for Russia there—as they evaluated, according to our own concepts, these tribes differing completely from us and not having anything in common with Europe, nor even allowing any European idea to be raised. Having been suspected of desiring to join the rebels, four of the confederates in Orenburg were hanged, but there were no more traces of even a similar intention. That they could not find either sympathy or understanding in the masses is not reliable information. The government used them for labor and violently seized them for line regiments in which it enforced the fulfillment of oaths of fidelity to the tsar with the lash; thus it probably had to conscript them into the class of Cossacks, because in Russia, just where it places a foot in the East, is formed the Cossack army, enlisting into it people from every class and origin. Many—not only isolated families but even entire settlements—met such a fate there voluntarily for the colonization of new arrivals; it is something more natural than those having been sent by violence, not bothering with ceremony. One meets now in the Cossack settlements names that are completely Polish, but just with a Russified ending, and they bear testimony to this origin; these are the grandsons and great-grandsons of our confederates, who, having been made Cossacks, were attached to the land. They were turned into a permanent local population and thus deprived of returning even at a time when Tsar Paul returned our exiles from Siberia, wanting in this way to reward Ilinsky for first bringing him the news about the throne that already awaited him. What is in these souls of our fathers still giving rise to freedom, having belonged to the supercilious Polish *szlachta* and combatants not long ago for the fatherland, but having died in Cossack jackets under the Central Asian sky? Who will say what they should have done? However, they had something to leave behind, and who knows whether their terrible pain was not the first trauma which the barbarity there needed so as to think through things completely foreign to it and through concepts unattainable in their entirety in order to understand moral suffering and compassion—didn't their life and death make the way there easier for their children and grandchildren?

And there must have been many successors to those in exile. In the first years of our century the great European wars paid attention to where else? Russia had just established itself on the Orenburg edge and had not made a conquest. Maybe one of our military POWs or some patriot was taken through Russia from the provinces and was sent to Orenburg; there must have been such misadventures—because, for example, in 1839 after the Khiva expedition, among the POWs returned with the mediation of

England through the Khiva Khan, was an exile to Orenburg, Adamowicz. He had been kidnapped by the Kirgiz and had spent close to thirty years in Khiva captivity, and when he returned for a final few years of life, he was assigned to one of the battalions, because before his abduction he had been a soldier and, according to Russian law, captivity did not count for a soldier as years of service; he still had not finished them so as to have the right to dismissal and a return trip. However, such examples must not be many, and after 1815 followed a time of rest, of political change with our Tsar Alexander, until the victims of Nowosiliec in Lithuania were first trod on, already growing dear to us there. Among them were the striplings from the school in Kroży, and counted among them was Jan Witkiewicz[7]—men existed and matured—university youth who mined science and above all virtue, like Adam Suzin, Jan Czeczot, and above all Tomasz Zan.[8] After them, were to come many others.

From the time of the Bar Confederates to the arrival of these new Polish wanderers, the Orenburg region underwent great changes. Life already long ago had been completely ruined; the exhausted Bashkiria became completely obedient and tame. Its regiments still attired, admittedly, in its nation's wolf caps and armed with bows and quivers with arrows; they had already held the road to Paris in the ranks of the Russian army—a wide strip of land called the land of the Orenburg Cossacks. Their divisions from the still great, not long past, Kirgiz steppe were now coming to an agreement on everything, with both tribes exceptional at making difficulties. The steppe itself calmed down. The Urals were already completely peaceful; on its other edge the Orenburg merchants expressed agreements with caravans from Central Asia. The Kirgiz sultans had already sat down with the Russian border administration. Within the gubernia the Muscovite element increased a lot; the wide, deserted but fecund expanse enticed colonists. Not just few of them arrived and for a short time simple settlements grew on great villages; in the Ural mountains, on land bought for almost nothing from the Bashkirs, newer and newer huts were raised, and the bathing of gold was established; the militia and army made short work of the greater and greater pacification of the region and created local

7 Witkiewicz was a legendary figure in Orenburg and Orsk, where he was sent to serve owing to his participation in a Vilnius conspiratorial circle, the Black Brotherhood. A talented linguist, he immersed himself in Central Asian languages and cultures, assisted the explorer Humboldt, and engaged in diplomatic missions, but when one failed, he was found dead, apparently by his own hand (*ZpIR*, 672–74).

8 These members of the Philoret Association (a secret organization within the Philomaths), with connections to the famous Polish-Lithuanian poet Adam Mickiewicz, were deported in 1824 from Vilnius (Ibid., 113–15, 584–85, 701–3).

organization in a short period of time. Thus, the Teptiari from the Cossacks were transformed into state peasants, and guards around the Cossack settlements were no longer deployed; the embankments around them often were already ploughed with a plough; everything was still and assumed a Russian form.[9] The official spheres were already completely organized; official life went on there as a matter of course throughout all Russia—as it was with the Finnish and especially with the Mongol population entirely; with an ease that suited itself they were converted completely to the Muscovite element.

Thus, the nation itself was here distinctly revitalized and strengthened; but next to this the ancient spirit—that idea of Muscovite tsardom—grew weaker. Awakened in 1812 with a spark unknown till now, political enthusiasm permeated these masses; the European wars, then the migration of the armies to Paris—all of this brought new opinions and conspiracies against the government throughout almost all Russia. And although only a certain stratum of society belonged to those conspiracies and the masses did not understand all the ideas over there, there was already proof of a turn beginning in shared ideas and a shaking of notions, fundamental up until now, on which were based mainly all tsarist authority.

All these transformations and changes also must have occurred within a few short decades and influenced the position of our exiles. The natural setting became something of the past. The population somehow was built up with the increased flow from Russia; there were not so many in these areas that they could change the internal physiognomy of the region—the impression of those arriving from Poland always remained the same. Everyone who underwent this road agreed that after traversing the Volga a deep sadness gripped them; they felt that they were entering into another world, as if the lid of a casket had fallen on them and separated them from their acquaintances and their own. And as to the matter at hand, there already in Central Asia it really begins: the farther he goes, the more the feeling of the desert encompasses a man; the expanse becomes wider and wider, flatter and flatter; stripped bare of forest, or the wide road, not overshadowed by any tree, goes through the desert and passes into eternity, where in some places one meets a village, also without a tree and shade. During the winter it is filled with snow, and settled by gloomy Finns or Tatars—their speech completely unintelligible, their different faces, and

9 The Teptiari is a name given to the part of the population living among the Bashkirs on their traditional lands who have non-Bashkir or multiethnic (especially Tatar or Turkic) heritage, according to the 2012 edition of the *Bol'shaia sovetskaia entsiklopediia*, accessed June 30, 2017, at: https://slovar.cc/enc/bse/2048017.html.

their foreign custom. The region between the Volga and the Urals is a kind of vestibule of the wilderness; beyond this last river is already the wilderness. At Orenburg itself, there is still a copse on the second edge of the Urals, but farther on by the Aral Sea on one side and by the Caspian on the other the steppe is silent and empty. In an expanse of a thousand versts there are tiny hills, a tree, and a ravine—like waves of the lightly rolling sea, they continue in endless progression with shifting sands, constantly poured by the wind and often filling passes a length of three hundred versts. Thin streams flow intermittently into small lakes that disappear into the earth, and this again glistens in many places like salt crystals, often widely covering it; the heavenly vault most often is dimly blue and empty, like the earth that it covers without hardly any small clouds amid the heat of the sun with the fantastic phenomena of a fata morgana, which colors the expanse for a moment. But when the gale storms, it is already a real steppe windstorm, stifling and obstructing breathing, and in winter even very dangerous. In the summer the heat is great and exhausting; in the winter it is far more biting than our frost. Like the surface of the earth, the shape of the sky is different, so there everything varies from ours; the different small plants and animals, apart from a horse and dog, are not like ours. There the long necks of the camels stretch out, herds of antelopes and wild horses run along the steppe, and a type of tiny kangaroo jumps from place to place. The lark even—that little birdie so dear to a Polish farmer—is different from those in Poland; it is two times bigger than ours and bears black feathers. And the people? The Kirgiz cling to a horse, with their own traveling tent, with their drink from mare's milk, with their entire nomadic life, and with Mongolian facial features. The landowners from these deserts from that time, who for many centuries left as a souvenir of their existence several wells dug into the earth and somewhat smashed sepulchral monuments here that our exiles chanced upon. Everything there is not only different, but completely varied and alien in both form and spirit. There was nothing around that would invigorate oneself, and everything forced one to retreat into oneself and to begin a new life.

Though the conditions of that life for everyone are different from their former one, they were still suited to the sentences that met the exile, which were varied. The degrees of punishment for the so-called political prisoners in Russia are tremendously numerous, and expanded, especially under Nicholas, whose entire reign was a constant persecution of us. Through the absence of every fixed right, through always exceptional courts, and through various war commissions issued and confirmed by the governor general, by the Viceroy of the Kingdom of Poland, and finally very often by the Tsar himself, the variety of sentences was infinite. On the judicial commission was admittedly always a so-called assessor, who had the right as a justice to make a change, but usually this was an empty formality. Szymon Konarski, for example, and all his fellow prisoners in Vilnius were judged according to the Naval codex. In general the degrees of punishment were as follows: exile for civilian service to the Great Russian gubernias was considered the least; then followed exile there in residence under police supervision or further in a settlement or as a soldier; still more to a so-called company of convicts or labor houses; and finally to hard labor in the mines. These degrees varied to eternity and so the place of exile could be one of the closer gubernias, where the Vologda grew moss, or by the White Sea lying at Archangelsk; it could be a provincial city or one of the poorest backwaters in the empire or situated around or beyond Petersburg in the north. One could have remained a soldier with the right of seniority and without it, with the retention of former rights, with the removal of all rights of station, or also with the retention of only noble station. The companies of convicts are also very varied, but hard labor can be at the salt works or by the extraction of metal—organized for several or a dozen years and sometimes again reaching beyond the bounds of human life. Nicholas sometimes made still his own additions to the sentences; so for example, for Shevchenko, the Little Russian poet and painter, he added to the sentence that he be condemned to soldier so that he must be held in a separate platoon and so that taken from him were: writing, singing, and drawing. Some of our compatriots were sentenced to being denied, after their atonement, a return ever to their homeland and, for others, any arrival at its capital. Also, everything changed again eternally, suited to the people charged with the execution of the sentence on whom the further fates of the condemned depended, because in Russia where there is not the least notion or sense of law or responsibility, almost everything depends on the will of individuals—their caprice or various instincts.

In Orenburg one could find people afflicted with all kinds of sentences—apart from the one being sentenced to the settlement—because these were always sent to Siberia. The convict companies in Orenburg had Poles within their walls, and the Orsk fortress lying near the mouth of the Or at the Urals, around 260 versts from Orenburg, had its own work house, which was considered hard labor, and with this was officially made an equal. However, for the most part the main number became soldiers. Nicholas provided them mostly in 1831, because he sent all of our military POWs to be soldiers in the Siberian and Orenburg Corps; they had to serve out their years of service there, and those who were from the fourth line regiment met a still heavier punishment, since they, from the moment of the reading of their sentence, were obliged to serve another twenty-five years. Until 1856–57, some of those for whom God extended life really waited until their release—the majority naturally died in the army. After 1840 when it was shown that conscripts sent to the Caucasus flooded the army of the Caucasus with a Polish element, Nicholas ordered some of them sent to Orenburg, and in this way the quantity of Poles in the battalions there grew again to a solid number of more than two thousand. The Philomaths were sent only for residence and with the condition of first spending a certain period of time as prisoners. The first newly trod the traces of the former confederates certainly more painfully than later arrivals had to feel their exile—there was no one with whom to speak in Polish, and they were completely alone amid this entire community comprised of various elements. But the then-governors of the region, Generals Suchtelin and Essen, were honest people, and, as for the rest, it was still the atmosphere of Alexander I—a time when their fellow prisoner and comrade Mickiewicz met so much sympathy in Russia.[10] For a certain time, they were rather more a subject of curiosity than of persecution—they were certainly mistrusted and were not understood unerringly but did not strive to oppress—while they slowly were capable of winning respect for themselves and certainly enhanced their position. Czeczot was in Ufa, Suzin and Tomasz Zan in Orenburg. These first of our new exiles immediately were drawn in two different directions, in two ways of comprehending the responsibilities and opinions of Polish exiles in Russia, who for a long time then found imitators among their compatriots. Czeczot, about whom the university youth sang: "If virtue is worthy of worship, who is better than Czeczot," decided to avoid all relations with the Russians, organizing only that which was most entirely necessary—that which would have allowed him to return the soonest. Zan, on the contrary, did not avoid them completely and was always and everywhere talking to those held and loved in a soul of truth. The former, wanting to obtain the favor of the governor, donated for free the instruction of his children in writing, reading, and arithmetic, saying that he possessed these sciences and with this marked out the rest of the entire hour, turning to his own education, relations with exiles, and correspondence with old friends. His sacrifice was readily accepted and after several years, when the

10 Petr Essen, awarded for bravery in the war against Napoleon Bonaparte, under Alexander I became military governor of Orenburg, where he promoted the education of Cossacks and more equitable Kirgiz-Russian relations. Pavel Sukhtelen was military governor of Orenburg and commander of the Orenburg Separate Corps during the cholera epidemic in the 1830s. For more on these two governors, see Semenov and Semenova, *Gubernatory Orenburgskogo kraia* (178–88, 191–200).

children had grown older and demanded sciences, Czeczot, fearing that he would no longer be retained as necessary, said he could do nothing more; he was believed and as a thank you was put forward for return—and he really returned first out of everyone. Zan became quickly acquainted with many people, he worked, and having indulged in natural science, mainly in geology, he did not render a single favor to the local authority—so rich in the region—about which it did not entirely know. He made frequent excursions to the steppe, and he loved the Kirgiz as a child of nature; he was also loved by them and was known in the mountain settlements under the name of *lover of stones*, because he collected them on his excursions. Universally respected by Humboldt, even after his travel to Central Asia advised Nicholas as to the greatest curiosity of these parts, Zan was in Orenburg close to twenty years and was scarcely able at that time with great effort to return through St. Petersburg. For Russian camaraderie, his affectionate, poetic nature inclined to mysticism was not clever—many called him a dreamer and rarely could someone really value the evangelical life; however, a dozen or so years after his departure from Orenburg people there came together, maintaining with enthusiasm that if there could have been five such people on the earth like Zan, then the entire world would have converted without spilling a drop of blood. Suzin went by way of Zan and won over some warm friends among the local population, but upon his return he also forestalled Tomasz, but not by much. The one and the other guarded an irreproachability of character and our national dignity—which every exile unwittingly found in the convictions among those here—held for themselves, but in manner the behaviors were, as we see, two different systems as in an old and new law. The first, the safer for the less developed and the one less certain, can even be more appropriate, while the second, for the weaker is full of temptation and more difficult for everyone but is without comparison higher. The first guarded the individual and perhaps more quickly returned him to his homeland, and the second, although slowly and not unfailingly, prepared the future victory of the national idea of truth and justice. Our compatriots later held both of them with various modifications, suited to individual strengths and shades of character, and they were the natural result of the condition of the Polish exile, whose leading thought was always and must be the homeland, under the loss of its great dignity.

Amid the quiet labor and pained and exhausting boredom, news about November 29 found its way to our handful there.[11] These souls had an inkling of the course of the nine-month fight. With what distances they

11 This date marks the beginning of the November 1830 Uprising in Warsaw under Tsar Nicholas I.

were separated from the nation, how they had been torn from it, how it happened to be a hundred times more difficult at that time every day in bondage, and how the new collapse of the affair must have been in the end for each—it is easy to understand. It was a resolute epoch in the life of the nation and certainly for the undead inscribed in letters in the soul of the exiles. And from then on, their position changed considerably.

Already before this the events of 1825 and its Petersburg gallows stunned Russian opinion and sent it in another direction; a violent and unrelenting reaction against the influence and idea of the West began on the side of the government.[12] Russia was directed anew along the path of passive, unconditional obedience and military discipline; everything was muzzled, and according to the pliability of the Muscovite character so easily disposed to the will of the one commanding. Nicholas very quickly in his organs of state, in the administrators of the provinces, and especially in the army had people near to his heart and way of thinking. The personal character of the monarchy set the tone, a coarse national instinct played along, an entire stratum influenced the top, and the government machine into which every screw, pressed anew, was squeezed with all its strength.

Still the first, the affair of the popularly condemned Decembrists was combined with the Polish affair, and the long and obstinate war called up plenty of emotion. The government added an element to this, awaking as much hatred as it could and sowing slander at us through all its various organs. Insults and contempt often met our POWs, and they were mocked; the crowd did not take us for Christians and tried to touch our soldiers, mocking national songs or calling out to them "that a Pole napped through Warsaw." At that time with the military POWs, crowds of various classes and ages immediately came after people exiled for participation in the uprising, and a systematic persecution of each national pulse began, which almost every year delivered new victims.

All of this was reflected in Orenburg. And there, as everywhere where we were, a quiet but incessant fight began—the right of the defenseless with armed violence, of human feelings with material force, of the Polish idea—represented by prisoners fitted with fetters—with the idea of the Tsar dressed in purple and propped on a bayonet—a fight in which we were obligated to prove how beautifully the poet expressed that "the stamina of the soul always consumes the stamina of steel" and in the end the victory

12 This is the year of the Decembrist rebellion led by army officers of the nobility seeking limitations on the authority of the tsar upon the occasion of the ascension of Tsar Nicholas I to the throne.

belongs to truth.[13] We are not a nation of saints or even Christian martyrs and in the life of our exiles not everything was purely spiritual or immaculate; the idea of fighting for sacrifice itself and truth in its entire brightness lit up in Warsaw in 1861, and certainly these solemn moments will not be forgotten. But no matter how they were the fruit of long national suffering, in the works of exiles a comparison of their position in Russia at the beginning of the reign of Nicholas and Alexander II is the best proof of how they, divested of everything and persecuted, achieved a great moral victory while their various courses would show that at almost every new stage it fell to us to pay with a victim or blood.

In the first moments of their stay in Orenburg, it was difficult to demand a complete resignation from military POWs. Taken from the field of armed battle, still with pulses almost trembling from it, with a highly developed feeling of military honor, deprived of their rank, and exposed to manners to which they were not accustomed, they often could not endure them calmly. They arrived in significant numbers, joined in this solidarity of arms given by commonality of arms, and even more by baptism by fire. Many times in this they found a stimulus, which drove them to dynamic activity and to speak with a fist; scenes were numerous in which they favored mockery with blows—hence new investigations, judgments—the situation of the individuals worsened by a lot and some completely perished—in general, however, it did good. So it is an undeniable thing that the Muscovite nature must be first physically humiliated and beaten in order to become softly human and that all these events impressed a *Moskal*. The government for its part found itself forced to put an end to them and to ban most severely everyone from the final battle of taunts conducted with ours; thus they dared not jeer and scoff any longer from then on. As if the army and local population were not enough, the then authority of this region, General Perovsky, had to learn the fact that all of Russia on account of Poland must suffer terribly; he had to feel shaken to the depths of his soul. One of the POWs was the officer Lewandowski—at the time a private in the Orenburg battalion—who was abused on the drill ground by the battalion commander; he was carried away with anger and tore his epaulettes on the spot. Handed over to military judgment, when Perovsky came to him, asking how being an old military man he could allow himself such a step, Lewandowski replied to him that if he had been the commander of the corps and had treated him as

13 This is a verse from nineteenth-century French poet Victor de Laprade's "Resurrecturis: Aux Polonais," which can be found as "Resurrecturis: Do Polaków" at: http://pbc.up.krakow.pl/Content/4857/0046_20140602_h_resurrecturis_do_polakow_w_t_ramingo.pdf, accessed February 24, 2018.

this colonel had, Perovsky could not have behaved toward him otherwise.[14] Angry with this description, Perovsky ordered that he be judged within twenty-four hours. Lewandowski, as a result of the verdict, was beaten with truncheons, but henceforth the general had no peace, could not forget this sentence, and felt obliged to repay this Pole. From this moment, indeed, began on his part an attentive occupation with their fate, and to this many exiles owe an easing of their condition and even then a return. Also, there were as always denunciations and prosecutions; in Siberia widespread ones were uncovered—for example, the conspiracy of Father Sierociński and Dr. Szokalski that ended in awful tragedy also left its traces in Orenburg. For the exiles brought in from all parts to the fortress, Perovsky appointed a Commission of Inquiry and took its chairmanship upon himself; thus they, already in the land of exile, found themselves anew in prison. But this gave Perovsky the opportunity to get to know them personally; with appropriate mental acuity and refinement of a solemn but proud nature, he assessed them, acquitted everyone, and several became closer to him. It was the beginning of his closer relations with Tomasz Zan and especially with Jan Witkiewicz whose abilities were said to be so widely developed, which were used later on important missions to the East and also ended tragically.

At that time, slowly, a change was taking place in the views of the Russian soldier himself. Our old comrades, drilled in the school of Grand Prince Konstantin, impressed the *Moskali* with their expertise in service and the precision of its execution; busy with holding up the soldiers as a model example, solemnity came to pass in the barracks. While telling colleagues about the state of the military men in Poland, they let them feel the whole atrocity of their position and the possibility of change—they awoke this desire. Slowly this edifice of absolutism, leaning on the foundation of absolute obedience, felt a desire for the authority that not long ago permeated the Russian soul, and began to take shape and to chip away at this hole. Instead of hatred we began to awaken curiosity first and later already a certain respect. The Pole, from a being not long ago disdained and low, became dignified and superior in the feelings of the masses.[15]

And contributing to this were new ones, the statutory exiles arriving from various parts of the nation as a result of various investigations and judicial commissions. To their brothers already there, they carried with them a

14 The cultured Count Vasilii Perovsky was military governor of Orenburg during its golden age in the mid-nineteenth century and successfully advanced Russia's control over Central Asia with his military expeditions (Semenov and Semenova, *Gubernatory Orenburgskogo kraia*, 201–214).

15 Here Zaleski inserts a picture of Father Michał Zielonka in the journal.

new reserve of strength and a constantly transforming national idea; there were witnesses to the lasting battle and new efforts in various areas; and for the Russian conscience just being awakened, they were a constant reminder of Poland. I must recall exclusively one of them here, because more than the others he influenced later the position of his brothers in Orenburg exile. He was Father Michał Zielonka. A former pupil of Vilnius University, a master of theology, and later a Dominican and professor in schools maintained by a congregation in Nesvizh; he was a prefect at such a school in Grodno, when today's renowned Muravev visited the governor there and conducted an investigation of the now-departed Michał Wołowicz.[16] Two other emissaries were also sought, the prisons were overflowing, and Muravev badly wanted to draw the school into the investigation. Zielonka with the power of a priest and with the personal courage of a civilian defended the children entrusted to him, not allowing them to be imprisoned and plied with questions in his absence. "I am father and mother to them," he said bravely to Muravev before whom at that time so many were terrified, "the parents entrusted these children to me, and not to everyone am I responsible, so ask me, sir, what you want." The children were saved, but Zielonka had to prove further the superiority of his character in order for him to remain in the country. He was sent to reside in Orenburg only for the influence that he had on the community, as his sentence expressed. In his white coat, branded with the mark of a political offender, he appeared in that place where the least of our laws are given no means of representation. From the beginning, he could not show himself on the street, because as soon as his habit was spotted, the street people gathered and guided him around, crying that the comedians had arrived. One day, Zielonka put on a long black frockcoat and appeared thus before Perovsky, announcing to him that henceforth he would be going around like this, because he did not want to subject his spiritual dress to ridicule. And from that moment, during some twenty years, no one saw him otherwise; his habit concealed—it was to serve him to the casket for his final clothing. Endowed by nature with a good head, he at once assessed his situation and means of staying useful; he abandoned books, which previously he had been taken with almost exclusively, but he commenced the practical life, and in a short time he had already extensive community relations. Thanks to them and to the respect with which he had graced himself at Perovsky's, he was allowed to celebrate church services

16 Grodno is a city in the province of Minsk in modern Belarus; Mikhail Muravev became known for his ruthless suppression of Vilnius conspirators participating in the 1863 Polish uprising, but he was also involved in the Russification of the Congress Kingdom after 1831.

and to deliver religious services to his compatriots. This was the first step. The Germans strove at that time to set up at the corps a permanent position for a Protestant pastor; Zielonka, already having connections, eased the way for them and when it succeeded, demanded immediately that the same be done for Catholics. Then, Perovsky himself asked that Zielonka be made chaplain of the Orenburg Corps. Having gone from an exile to a government figure thanks to his moral force and reason, it was already easier to go further; with his effort, a little Catholic church in Orenburg was finally raised. At first sparse and poor, slowly from offerings, to which even the *Moskali* contributed, it was supplied with everything needed, and it became a hotbed and a place of solace for everyone. Zielonka served every person; the name of Michał Fadiejewicz—because he was so called—was known later to every resident of Orenburg. From early in the morning, the doors of his house did not close, since Russians of every station, Bashkirs, Tatars, civilian and military clerks, and even Orthodox clergy arrived at the house of the recent exile for advice and help. He made everyone interested, and in this way, having become familiar with the life of each person, speaking often a harsh truth, and always rendering favors, he really acquired mainly a moral influence. Everything was permitted him; it was most strictly forbidden for a soldier to ride around town, but the *tarantas* that took Zielonka to mass and took the exiles back from the church was known to everyone. With it arrived letters from families, which according to the law should be surrendered to the military censor, and with every grievance and in every violent need it succeeded with this; very many times the *tarantas* lightened, and sometimes was capable of saving, someone from a ton. Zielonka led a very modest life: his famous black frock coat always lacked buttons, but his last groszy he shared with those in need, and his influence on the community there was so great that they repeated, that if they were free, many of them would convert to Catholicism. It was not for his theological treatises, because he did not get involved with these, and it was not for a gripping pronouncement, because he did not have this, but it was for his personal virtue, for a selfless, pure, and active life, consecrated to the service of those around him and so different from the spiritual life of those there. It happened often that not knowing him personally, the landowners of Orenburg gubernia chose him as executor of their wills and confided in him their complicated dealings—certain that no one as conscientious as he would fail to fulfill these responsibilities. Zielonka's parish included all sections of the Orenburg Corps; after the end of his stay there, it extended so far that just to travel around it, around the five thousand versts, in spite of his advanced age, had to take him a year. The respect such as he roused was so universal that many times during his travels while changing horses in Bashkir and Tatar villages Muslim inhabitants surrounded his vehicle, imploring him to stop by their homes if he wanted, because they would be blessed by this. In day-to-day life, he always loved children. With those whom he exclusively developed a liking and more whole-heartedly honored with affection, he spoke with pleasure about times when he became in charge of the small school in Grodno and then easily he moved on to exile. For the memory of these times they called him in Orenburg "priest prefect," because it gave him pleasure—by this name he was known by all the Poles there. He could return to his homeland, but although he, like everyone else longed for it, always with a rapidity of intellect and characteristics of self-abnegation he realized that he was more of a benefit to Orenburg than he was in one of the Dominican cloisters, and he remained. He died very soon after Alexander II's return of everyone, to whom he rendered so many services and who will certainly never forget him.

But this is everything that in a few words I can say here about Father Zielonka, and slowly, little by little occurred a redirection of efforts toward serving people, the work of many years—life then for the other exiles plodded along the usual course. For those who were in the army after the year 1839 a new horizon was left to be discovered. Russia, having sufficiently assimilated former dominions, pondered further annexed territories in Central Asia, and a project of a Chinese expedition matured, and they had to take part in it. Nothing at all in these plans could be immediate for us, and by the very nature of the thing, all sympathies had to be more readily for the opposing side; already the hope of expedition and danger—interrupting the tormented body and soul and the monotony of life in the barracks—was pleasing. In any case, for the exiles deprived of the rights of all station, it was always exceptionally desired; danger changes people, and before it disappears divisions and laws. Everyone above all is found to be a human being and returns, as it were, to the position to which he belongs according to his moral disposition in the hierarchy of true human souls. For this reason, in the Caucasus amid constant war, the situation of those sentenced to be soldiers was without comparison more tolerable than in the standing armies, peacefully and permanently occupying. For this reason in Orenburg many transferred their service to the steppe over to an ordinary internal regional garrison; finally, for this reason, even the time rife with cholera so terrifying everyone, was not awful for them. Comparatively the epidemic took exceedingly few victims among them, and everyone felt by comparison more free. Still, an expedition for one thing or two could bring one a promotion and beyond this a return to the homeland. This once, expectations were disappointed, and the expedition was turned into an awful disaster, which in very small proportion was, as it were, a repetition of the year 1812 for the Grand Armée. At that time, they still did not have the precise news about the steppe; it was known only that a great waterless expanse cut the road to China in two. Thus, for this reason the final days of spring were chosen for the beginning of the expedition, counting on the fact that by the time they would reach waterless places, the snow would replace the lack of drink for the animals and people. The winter is not in practice severe, like the one the oldest people in these parts did not remember, and it misled calculations; the snows suddenly fell so heavily and the frost was so intense that before the first managed to reach those waterless places, all their camels carrying provisions for the army from the winter perished, sickness unfurled in the ranks, and they had to return, not having even met the enemy. Before the units arrived at their place, they lost a significant number of people; those who were dragged there were decimated further by typhus and scurvy from excessive emaciation and the ensuing fatigue. More than one of our brothers found death on that road which a dozen or so years later was bleached with piles of bones. Disaster was universal; however, everyone was struck by the fact that not only were our soldiers numerous, but still relatively fewer died by comparison with the Russian soldiers. While those sons of the North from the age of ten are accustomed to cold and frost, in general the more strongly built bodies died like flies, and our armies violently driven here from under a native sky, and so many, already tested by pain and tragedies, withstood everything. The reason for this lay unfailingly in the highly developed soul and in the hardening of the will. The *Moskali* themselves attributed it to our moral superiority.

After the unfortunate expedition, General Perovsky was called back to Petersburg, his place was occupied by General Obruchev, and again followed ten monotonous and oppressive years, abundant in petty but acute suffering, in which especially for those who wore soldiers' overcoats, the situation was made to feel still more painful.

The soldier's life had its own exclusive conditions, which it is necessary to recognize in order to get an idea of it. The admission to it was naturally the road from a native land to Orenburg. For those sent from Lithuania and Russia, the road did not have in itself anything exclusively awful. The quick ride by day and night admittedly was torture, but for a man coming from a cramped prison in which he most often spent two or three years, it was peculiarly at first a certain type of pleasure. He breathed fresh air and had the heavenly vault over his head. Accustomed to a constant prison guard, the inseparable association with the gendarme was no longer so oppressive, and after several days this gendarme most often became familiar with the prisoner and even many times issued a kind word. There were examples that when for money intended for the prisoner's nourishment (2.5 kopecks or 5 groszy by our rate) it was possible to get only dry bread, the gendarmes who sometimes conducted the prisoners by twos and who for a silver ruble for every 100 versts collected nourishment, made it up themselves, beseeching insistently that the prisoners accept their offering, and they allowed themselves this little comfort. But with our brothers from the Congress Kingdom it worked entirely differently; those had to undertake the entire road from Warsaw or Modlin to Orenburg on foot, and this journey ranked unfailingly as a most terrible moral and physical agony. Told in detail, it would furnish entire volumes of main plots.

It is evident to everyone that nobody knows the Russian criminal code of capital punishment; there they really beat many times with bludgeons, but those are only soldiers or people sentenced by an exceptional military court like ringleaders of gangs of robbers or arsonists, etc. For the criminal offenders, it is the civilian courts, and most often they punish crimes with the whip and hard labor, and the less guilty they send to settlements in Siberia. They submitted to this fate the vagabond, and of such there were very many. This entire population came from all parts of the kingdom, and at the so-called Sparrows Hills a prison built for this purpose took them onward. On the wide roads everywhere stand the prisons, called by the name "staging points," waiting for those who are passing through; the changing escort leads them through several staging points and consists of a certain number of soldiers and officers riding on horseback. From Moscow one route, already called Siberian, leads everyone through Kazan to Tobolsk or Orenburg. Clusters—or, in official language, parties of reprobates—depart from there two times a week, and such a party is not less than one hundred people. To our final misfortune, when the population sent in masses ceased being divided into clusters capable of being housed in prisons on the road, the number of those sent at one time could not, according to law, be higher than 200 people. One walks usually two days, spending time walking from staging point to staging point—20 to 30 and 40 versts a day; on the third day they have a rest, and this is called "a day's rest." The one who never falls sick on the road, this one trekking in this manner reached Orenburg after seven months. For the weaker ones, who are left behind on the road in hospitals, this journey sometimes lasted a year and a half, and so our exiles had to be held up, because there was for them no difference; they went together with an entire mass of reprobates sent to Siberia.

Russia is a nation and society completely different from all European nations. Almost every man has there two different countenances: one formal and official and the other domestic-like, his own—and so it works with everyone. Under the formal external shell—under the form in which everything appears to be comprised—flows the individual, suitable to that social life and incomprehensible to people of the West wanting to assess it according to European concepts. From here even the parties of such reprobates differ immensely from crowds of people whom the law excludes from society in civilized nations. They emerged differently, have their own autonomous traits and customs, and could be recognized more closely for casting a great light on the state of the entire empire and its world, which awaited our exiles. They are usually assembled from the most varied elements and a reason for this is not only the diversity of the tribes entering into the composition of an enormous nation but also the nature itself of its institutions and the character of its ruling tribe.

One of the traits of Muscovite society, on which not long ago even the most enlightened Russians agreed, is the complete lack of conception of the law and thus of responsibility; there are no sophisticated precepts there, but there are instincts and not conscience. In people still so historically young, strong, and excelling at a rapidity of intellect and working of the heart, crude passions and sensual urges play a great role and develop with enormous force. There are admittedly fewer of those subtle crimes appropriate to an aged society from refined civilization, but on the other hand, there is a lack of moral foundation and a vague border dividing virtue from its execution, almost not existing in souls. Against such a moral background of social relations being an occasion of strength or violence, the artificial government machine, often hateful and assembling a multitude of circles and groups, itself shattered the concepts of the law and of foreign people. With universal lawlessness at the top, falsity is almost the sole defense of the weak, almost as a condition of existence. In such a state they reach the prisons in Russia and under judgment as not only ordinary prisoners—as brigands, arsonists, and thieves—but often arbitrary victims of the more powerful and strong, of officials and masters—often people not able to render an account of their own affairs or really commit an offense or not, etc. To add to this are still the vagabonds, whom the law judges and of whom in Russia there are more than anywhere else, because the Muscovite people love wandering and, aside from the one tied to the land, are almost unceasingly in motion. The government holds this entire mass of accused in common prisons, and then those it sentences, it exiles together.

The Russian courts have earned a universal and completely well-deserved reputation for independence and corruption; also people, feeling often instinctively disgusted at the injustice for the accused, do not trust the verdict of the courts. In any case, people themselves, not having developed principles, look differently at those condemned than everyone in the West. They call them "unfortunates" and always hurry to them with alms and help. The one who carries the alms knows that tomorrow he himself could be in a similar position, and he feels that from moral consideration, at least half of those there are completely equal to him.

The common prisons, with exceptionally long procedures and lack of any occupation for the prisoners, form among them a strict moral atmosphere in the end. Sustained injustices and wrongs degenerate into hatred, and the stronger natures gain the majority; a community of its own kind freely takes shape, which is its own goal in and of itself, in which an offense already becomes a mark of prestige, almost as an honor—in the end, this is the party of the condemned. On the outside, the community assumes forms suitable to the Russian people.

Serfdom developed in Russia a loyal community, and it spread throughout one's entire life. Peasants coming in large numbers for seasonal work, cart drivers transporting others' goods (often from one end of the nation to the other), and artisans occupied with various crafts there bond to form economic partnerships, so-called artels. This is one of the characteristic traits. The party of prisoners is also such an artel, a single solidary partnership. It selects a superior from among its own, a so-called elder, who is usually the most devious, the strongest physically, and the most frequent and greatest criminal; it will trust its interests to him and obeys him. He distributes charity, he settles arguments among the prisoners, and he fixes and carries out punishments; in a case of betrayal on his part, another—one newly chosen—stands in for him. The guard is also in a partnership of its own kind with a party that morally does not differ from itself; only being responsible for delivering the prisoners, it conducts and guards them, but looking at the party of prisoners like a wellspring of income, he is most often conspiring with it. He allows the collection of alms, and, on condition of its distribution, provides vodka and looks at various pleasures through the cracks.

During the long prison journey they learn each others' stories, because their story becomes an entire pastime; in all the little district towns on the road, they take up relations with still new prisoners and learn a multitude of details about all the prisons on their trek. Often there happens to be a regular in the party, who already once or twice was in Siberia, escaped from there, and again returns; such a one is usually the master. They arrange various projects and plots and undertake certain interests. At the staging points, they usually copy the names of the prisoners, and after some time chaos, not a solution, arises from this. Their number will remain the same but who is who—this already nobody knows. The prisoners change their names. For example, they conduct someone for a confrontation with some co-conspirator in a remote gubernia, and from Ivan he became Mikhei and goes there to where Mikhei was assigned, and in this way Mikhei comes to the place of Ivan. At the identity parade they do not recognize him, a new investigation is organized, and it is so endlessly. Someone needs to stop in a certain prison, because there he has some plan prepared; so he fakes being sick, and when this will not address it, he commits a crime. For example, he kills one of his fellow prisoners—the first he happens to come across; they leave him behind for a new investigation, and he benefits from several months of time. If he is cunning and well acquainted with procedure, then he can stretch the process out for an entire year. Such incidents occur not rarely. Many of our brothers undergoing this journey were witnesses to similar scenes. "How could you do this; why did you kill him?" asked one with outrage of the criminal.

"Leave me in peace," was the response, "Be thankful that it was not you; I had to do something in order to stay here, and I should have killed you, because you are not of use to us, but you slept so peacefully that I could not—from this you can see it was destined to be. It is all the same to me; I have already killed ten, and one more or less is just one and the same responsibility." Here it is possible to add that similar and like scenes usually happen there, where the guards of the prisoners more severely treat them. They are generally on their guard for this, as a rule, so as to save those who are better and more reasonable with them.

In such camaraderie and in such a moral atmosphere our exiles were forced to undergo this enormous journey. But it was not enough to go together; they usually chained the condemned to a single iron rod, and they had to walk thus. Until they learn to walk step in step, the physical pains are unspeakable. The elderly, the youth, girls, and people of the most varied strengths walk on with them. The nephew of General Dembiński had some gypsy sent to Siberia for a companion on this road. Every movement made not in time pulls and halts everyone; the hands rattle from the iron rings, here the frost is often a torment, and only by quick movement is it possible to avoid being frozen. Some died thus on the road, and the overwhelming majority reached their place of assignment. New agonies awaited the arrivals at this staging point; admittedly, they were unchained from the rod, but shut up in a cramped prison, from which under no pretext were they released before the morning. The air was awful, the filth indescribable, and the vermin in countless multitudes. Often there were so many prisoners that they could not be accommodated, and they had to be placed in two strata: one on the beds and the second under the beds. Happy was the one who was not alone and had at least a comrade with whom he could share thoughts or feelings. The ordinary offenders usually looked mistrustfully at our brothers, as at people not belonging to them and from whom in their intentions they often feared obstacles.

The one who had some money, he now and then succeeded at freeing himself for a time from his fetters and rod. If the clerk at the staging point in exchange for payment still left off the fetters at registration, then one succeeded even further until a new officer, the master and authority of the party, in a step of ill humor and already newly his own authority, did not order them shackled. But who had money? And how much of it would be needed on such a road! Of all the sufferings, hunger often increased because of the miserable kopecks allotted by the government—half remained in the pocket of the officer, and with the rest it was not even possible to get bread. On account of this, the prisoners found significant reductions already before having started from Moscow. In advance of the prison there on those Sparrow Hills the usual solace met them; always on hand to visit all the prisoners was an already eighty-year-old man, Doctor Gas—a foreigner who remained in Moscow after 1812. He then entered the Russian service and dedicated himself to the service of the unfortunate; having been respected for a long time by Alexander I, the doctor had importance in this prison. The dignified doctor always had ready printed copies of the gospels in every language, and he distributed them to the prisoners, providing words of solace for the road. When he established that there was in the party a Pole sent for a political affair, he lavished particular care on him. He always allowed him to stop for a break as much as he wanted and did not oppress him with strange sweetness and kindness. The copy of the gospel, a book for the service in Polish, and the heartfelt word warmed with divine love were his gifts, which certainly no one forgot, blessing him from their soul. The figure of this old man was like one beaming from a better world on this dreadful road. Thanks to Gas, for those who made the road from Warsaw to Moscow alone, there usually awaited the arrival of friends and comrades who still remained in prison.

After such a moral fortification material help arrived, because Moscow provides alms to all prisoners sent to Siberia. It is such a common custom that not one party was overlooked. For this reason, the escort strives to lead the party through as many numbers of streets in the eighteen-verst-long city as possible, and everywhere along the road people arrive—most often the merchants and their wives. Aside from bread and various victuals, they also give money in the name of Christ, as they say. Having arrived at the staging point, the elder divides them, the officer takes half, and the escort takes from the other half of the prisoners, from several to up to a dozen and sometimes up to 200 rubles, from each. This suffices for a long time. Having departed Moscow, the alms-giving is repeated everywhere, although naturally not so generously as in the great capital city; therefore, there is no longer hunger, but aside from this everything is as it was: the same camaraderie, the same such prisons, and the same pains and boredom. Only the climate is more and more severe, the frosts and blizzards greater and greater, and the road more and more empty and sad.

The arrivals to Orenburg are usually led to the general of the division, because the infantry of the Orenburg Corps comprises a single division. The one who was not exclusively ordered to prison, he was assigned to one of the line battalions and began already his soldier's life of the barracks and drill.

The army in Russia, especially under Nicholas, became a class at the forefront of society. The general, already satisfied with everything, could become trustee of a university, the administrator of a province, a scholar, an administrator, a judge, a member of the senate, a seaman—anyone at all. Every officer considered himself infinitely higher than all the others, even than the civilian officials—contemptuously called hazel grouses for their colorful dress different from the uniform—but was not treated like a soldier at all. Relayed to him is his true superiority over the agricultural class, from which, however, he came, and which was accustomed to despising him, but really he has become the lowest rung in the social hierarchy—*lower than grass, wordless as the earth*, as was the saying, which was repeated to him by regulation. Also to which, undeniably, belonged very unfortunate creatures. Tsar Nicholas, once while discussing the theories of Fourier, let it be heard that in every battalion he had a real phalanstery, and it really was a phalanstery, only governed by violence and based on force and the bludgeon. Various things flowed into the element there, that is aside from the usual recruit taken from various provinces and the bourgeoisie from everywhere were also people sent for various offences, because the army in Russia also substitutes as a place for reformatory companies in different regions—not only for political crime but also for a bad life, even for theft, it is possible to become a soldier there. Peasants and also landowners, as long as the handing over of a recruit belonged to them, usually sent the worst people there. They were the morally ruined segment, the poorest. Aside from these were soldiers' sons, in special units of so-called battalion cantonists, trained from infants as soldiers. They most often got by on account of service; they made the best weaponry, and from them for the most part came the aristocracy of the barracks: seasoned soldiers, noncommissioned officers, sergeants, and sometimes even, after many years, officers. In childhood they are torn from their families, and in the disciplined groove of army perspective they lost nothing with their connection from the people; the army sucked out their souls—they were the most passive and diligent instruments, without any moral foundation. Aside from all of this was the simple villager, torn from his family and taken from his wooden plough, who often left a wife and children at home somewhere and in his soul carried everything that is human in these social classes. Everything together is positioned depending on old boundaries unknown and is taken with regulations hindering every step not only in service but also beyond its boundaries. Everything is tormented by drills, which are taught with the most concocted meticulousness, and are fulfilled according to regulations, so as to think that there was no time from the perspective of long years of service, which at the least offense were prolonged in their infinitude, beyond the boundary of the grave and threatened daily by the bludgeons—this was the army. The more oppressive life is said to be, the better the fact lends to repeating often that soldiers committed murder with the only goal of freeing themselves from the grey overcoat and of setting out for hard labor, because for them it was more tolerable. A segment was completely and deeply ruined; those which the government itself raised, those who had no soul. A segment was completely thoughtless like that executioner Kaplinsky, preparing victims by flinging the noose on their neck with an almost bovine indifference. But there was also a segment almost suffering, which retained its wistfulness and goodness and often was beyond comparison morally superior to its officers. Mickiewicz in his lecture said that the Muscovite soldier under certain conditions recalls the medieval monks; and really in the souls of these poor Russian villagers attired in grey coats were always patience, resignation, simplicity, and often compassion, but the one who has lived with them for long would say that it is completely raw material, yet housing in itself much that is humane and good—whereas these people can withstand much physically, this has to define each of them.

The officers of the line battalions were usually deprived of every form, because this was the means by which if one did not go into the guard then at least one went into the army. They did not already have the good instincts that a soldier from stock brought; they had polish constituting their exterior while completely covering a moral nihility, lacking every principle, convinced of its eternal superiority over the soldier, and all of them thought only of themselves, their income and careers. In any case, in their notions and behavior as *Moskali*, they abided by the usual pliancy of will and the predilection of their commanders.

It was a world that received an exile sentenced to soldier and having led him to the barracks, immediately brought him a master—a so-called old timer, who acquainted him with a soldier's life, entered into the recruit's command, and put him in uniform; often already the morning after he served at drill. His first guard was a noncommissioned officer in the ranks and later a noncommissioned officer in the division, and then a sergeant. That one gave reports to the captain about his behavior and even his means of thinking (such was the command). These reports went to the battalion commander and from there by the headquarters of the corps to the tsar himself. The tsar was informed about the place of service for each of the condemned, and without the tsar none of them, even the noncommissioned officer, could be advanced, and for this advance that had been stubbornly denied usually it was necessary also to wait. A stay in the recruit's command lasted several months, sometimes a year or more; the older and weaker in strength with great difficulty came to the exercises and progressed for Nicholas to the highest pedantry, for it was necessary to learn the exercises, because the battalion commander visited the command, and if he was not satisfied with the progress, he ordered a beating of the noncommissioned officer by whom the one enlisted was taught, while repeating: "Watch—it is because of you that they beat him and so they will lash you." Having learned how to stand, to march, and then to make weaponry, he advanced to the front and already together with his company or battalion was enlisted as a guard and underwent drill and the entire service.

The one who thus attained the army had to, above all, hold great inner discipline and to descend deeply into himself; if he had such ancestral or noble pride, he had to cure himself of it and to pull himself together as a man. Because really his former life had completely ended; what he was in his homeland and whatever position and relations he had there—all of that meant nothing. If even in the final investigation he found himself well or poorly or if those whom he saved blessed him or cried over him, no one knew anything about this; that which surrounded him and those who were to constitute his further fate did not quite understand him. The officers knew that a rebel, a brother of the barracks under the name of a political prisoner, usually figured out a *police* violation; he could not speak to any achievement, because there were none in this community. If he had something, then it was repeated to him that all his learning was for nothing, that only marching and a rifle could make him a man, and didn't he see daily that hundreds of soldiers and seasoned soldiers surpass him a hundred times on that field. That even if he wanted, he would never equal them? It was necessary to extract from inside his moral strength, which gave the power to bear everything patiently, and at the same time to win respect and in time a certain position. This was the only path. Indeed, the older exiles helped the new arrivals in this, but each had to adapt his tone to it, and only such work stuck with everyone and over the course of entire years modified their position, developed respect for the Polish name, and made life possible for the exiles themselves. An arrival, even for his compatriots, was an unknown person; taken always with compassion, he still had to earn respect by his life among them. Here, in order only not to perish, every person had to flex all the strength of his soul.

The situation at every step was full of humiliations. When at the Commissions of Inquiry the prisoners were tormented and harassed—wanting in this way to get out of them some evidence and to find out about some names—they were sustained by the feeling that they were shielding others in this way, that they were bearing it for some idea. Those sentenced to being soldiers were reprimanded and reviled for the fact that they did not have, for example, their legs extended or did not move the rifle very deftly like a seasoned soldier, who is healthier by far and introduced to all this from childhood. "I know that you are an enlightened man," the battalion commander, standing in front of the row, called to one of them, "and I know that you are a good man, but until you make weaponry for me like a seasoned soldier, I will sentence you every day to blows of the bludgeons." And when at this the blood rose to his face, he added, "You still dare with your eyes to babble coarse things, and I will drive that Polish spirit from you" and so on and so forth. Similar things await everyone, and more than once or twice it depended upon caprice and disposition. The Muscovite soldier is accustomed to all this and knows that his superior must reprimand and beat—it is for this that there is a superior. When in the recruits' commands they expected the battalion commander, the noncommissioned officers studying to be soldiers to put on white shirts; when asked for what reason they were doing this, they responded that they knew that they would be beaten, but the colonel loved white linen, and they would get it two times harder if the shirts were not completely fresh. Not being able to have this slavish resignation, our brothers had to arm themselves with all strength of will in order to manage to bear everything calmly that they could encounter at such drills and at such an assembly with the superior. It often happened that at drills, the colonels ordered a *confirmed* Pole (as were called political prisoners whose sentences the tsar either fixed or *confirmed*) to come out of the line, and then the commander returning to the soldiers asked them what is with these people? And while talking, he explained that they are worse than thieves and robbers, than every kind of villain, because they are not only soulless but tsarless and that it is necessary to guard and watch them like the plague.

The battalion commander had wild fantasies sometimes—an example from the Urals: making the inspection of the lines before the drill, he had the custom to strike those soldiers who passed sullenly in the face with a fist, saying: "Look more cheerful!" When Perovsky again assumed the administration of the region and ordered the soldiers not to torment needlessly with drill, Colonel Chikhir arrived at the barrack of his battalion, and standing near the church he ordered them to conduct everyone in overcoats, only without arms, and had the following speech for the soldiers: "Children! I was convinced heretofore that every man without exception could march well and make weaponry, and for this reason I often tortured you with drill and training; I was convinced that God's exclusive favor necessitated this. I thought then that each person could learn literature (literature in the Muscovite army they are calling by a dozen definitions—that is soldier, noncommissioned officer, ensign, and so on, and these soldiers must be brought forward), and today I see that for this one needs favors from heaven. But in regard to (Christian) prayer, everyone without exception can do this, unless it is anathema (damned). So I have arrived to watch pure people and to see if you can pray; the one who will not be able will get 200 lashes. But children! My wife is sick, and I do not have time to dilly-dally with you; let the one who is not able come out front and collect what he deserves." After this speech, several lambs, feeling themselves guilty, voluntarily came out to the front, the rods were brought out, they undressed, and the flogging began. While they looked after the morality of subordinates, the commander circled the ranks while listening to every soldier one after another. After the examination, it was found that still a dozen or so were not able to do it well; they stood apart, awaiting their future fate. The God-fearing colonel again spoke to them: "I told you that I have a sick wife, and there is no feeling and no compassion in any man among you; you will get 400 rods for it." The exam showed that all the Polish conscripts could pray perfectly; the colonel ordered them to stand apart, and returning yet again to the accused, he added: "Look, they are who knows how far from their God; however, they are able to pray. And you live in God's house, under his very cathedral, and you cannot do anything—you guys are simply anathema (damned)." And he stood to the end of the execution, after which he departed for his sick wife.

Our exiles were often participants in such and similar scenes, and they paint the position of the Russian soldier at that time better than long case files.

Moreover, life together in the barracks, amid constant chaos, in the camaraderie of those so completely different by notions and by entire disposition was a thing exceedingly burdensome. For quiet natures and those more inwardly focused, it was one of the greatest distresses, but there it was appropriate to learn to get to know the sufferings of the lowest social classes—after some time respect for oneself was won, and then the tirades of the battalion commanders no longer made an impression on the soldiers. The one who conducted himself well—and for each exile this was an easy thing, because it was necessary only to not get drunk, to not lead a dissolute life, and to start no brawls—the one who remembered that his friends were not responsible for him, he especially succeeded in rendering some favor, in sometimes shielding himself from the punishment of the soldier, and in justifying it—this one already had respect for himself. The Russian peasant remembers the good. Aside from this, there was still inculcated in people from long ago a respect for the upper classes, supported in the army by this exceptional disparity that occurs between a soldier really deprived of all his rights and an officer owning every privilege. The soldier is together with the people, having not really developed moral impressions, looking in general at every criminal like an unfortunate, and is himself most often the one punished not for the reason that he stole, but because having stolen, he was not able to hide it away. More severely beaten for marching or the smallest contravention of a rule of service than for villainy and moral offenses in general, he did not fit completely into the motivations of those who were exiled and to those whose own moral position he was indifferent, but in our exiles he always saw nobility and felt that each of them, a soldier today, could tomorrow become an officer. It did not conceal thousands of unpleasantries, and even worse, envious natures; it awakened persecution many times, but in general it eased relations and brought in a certain relativity. When the commander informed someone that he would lash him with rods and for rudeness (uttered to him with a gaze), would fix him with fetters, or would order him hanged, the soldiers looked at him for a few days too familiarly, as at a man responsible for various corporal punishments among them, but his moral advantage soon returned, and in general it was for no one as bad as it could be and as it should have been, according to the will of the tsar. They were threatened with lashings, but there was really no example that it had come to this—not for the feelings developed in the officers but simply for general opinion and also for the conviction, enhanced by the military POWs from '31, that they would not have gotten away with it.

Anyway, the situation changed a lot according to the place where the condemned found themselves. The Orenburg battalions had permanent quarters, and they were spread out in the vast expanse of the region. Orenburg, itself, housed two battalions—one was broken up along the steppe fortresses, and the remaining four stood in Ufa, Orsk, Troitsk, and Uralsk, and several hundred versts of space divided one from another. If it were necessary only to live with the soldiers themselves, the differences would not have been significant, but exceedingly more depended upon the battalion commanders and all the elders—and this position changed endlessly. One of the traits characteristic of Russian tsardom is that lawlessness is met there at every step, and almost nowhere is the law carried out; if there is no authority so unrestricted and broad in principle as the authority of the tsar, then on the other hand there is, perhaps, none so often impotent. Almost everyone, provided with an order, carries it out in his own way; it is often the cause for horrible agony, but, after all, maybe in this Russia, as she exists is guilty, as she is for the people who live under this rule. The *Moskal*, as we already said, is flexible, complied with every condition and to the will of every superior, and is as they order him to be. Police Chief Vasilev in Vilnius for Nazimov naïvely expressed that first he was a devil, because it was demanded of him, whereas now he was ordered to be an angel, and therefore he became an angel.[17] In the latest national cases, many times people, named first for being very good-hearted and gentle, distinguished themselves with cruelty and even savagery. Every person who knows Russia is not astonished at all; such metamorphoses are there on a daily basis and are repeated constantly—the entire atrocity of it becomes a complete lack of principles. And in the Orenburg battalion, the same thing happened. The disposition of the colonel influenced the officers and imparted the tone for everyone concerned; the colonel again abided by that which reached him from the higher authority, or that which his company usually demanded of him. In Orenburg, he was a small figure, he had to examine all staff corps, divisions, and brigades for a host of higher persons, on whom he depended and before whom he strove to ingratiate himself. Often some excess dealing with Poles went around the town, conferring

17 Vladimir Nazimov was sent by Petersburg to serve on the Commission of Inquiry in Vilnius, which sentenced Zaleski in 1842, and in 1856, as governor general of Vilnius, he helped Zaleski obtain his decommission (Caban, *Z Orenburga do Paryża*, 23).

ridicule or poor opinion on him; he had to guard himself. Otherwise, in the smallest of towns, he was almost the main person; he was not afraid of anyone and more boldly relaxed the reins according to his own instinct. It worked similarly with the younger elders. Out of all this, the infinite variety of hues held influence, changing again for almost every wind in every place. Not one of those higher again readily made a concession and quietly allowed it, but he was terribly afraid and at the smallest denunciation cut his losses. Even the administrator of the region, Obruchev, did not have hatred for the Poles and, certainly, was often tolerant, but the word was Petersburg and the tsar had already taken over it with a thrill, and under this influence Obruchev returned a strict execution of severe regulations. For example, Obruchev, himself, ordered Shevchenko to paint views of the steppe fortresses, although he had been forbidden to sketch, and thanked him for them, but when he received the denunciation that Shevchenko was making portraits, Obruchev became frightened, handed him over to the judgment of the court, and informed the tsar; the poor poet spent more than a year in a filthy prison with Kirgiz. One of our compatriots met him in his house, also gave him work, and gladly saw that he drew this portrait of his children. When, however, one of the generals told him that he would be writing to the capital that in Orenburg the soldiers are being accepted into society, he became so frightened that he ordered all Poles not to place a step out of the barracks; this lasted for several weeks, and again it passed, like all orders of a similar kind, of which there were hundreds.

According to an order of Nicholas, it was not permitted for any Pole in the army to make use of writing or to allow him something after employment in frontline service; everyone had to be using only a rifle, although among those sent to be soldiers there were several who were lame from birth. Even the one who reached the rank of officer still did not obtain the right to be adjutant of a battalion; he was always supposed to guard the drills. In spite of this, some had orders freeing them for several months from drill, and, for example, a Pole often more capably fulfilled the duties of adjutant, only someone else signed the papers. Providing a lecture was even for many a means of satisfying one's needs for which the pay of the Russian soldier naturally could not suffice. One was paid not so very badly, but it was always in some groszy, and this always got down to relations, often private between oneself and another. The one who had some means and knew also some languages, music, and drawing, gave lectures in the better houses—most often free of charge—and found a courteous reception, a rest, and was really generously rewarded by this. Father Zielonka usually organized everything and helped on these occasions, and how happy was he when he could approve of someone, when one of his protégé compatriots was well sought after? It helped everyone, and it was precisely one of the means of shaping opinion. After years, there had been for a long time learned Poles as officers and officials; the number of people obligated grew, and relations unwittingly changed. In this way a profession was regulated. It happened, for example, that lectures were found at some powerful person's house or at some adjutant's division on whom the fate of many people depended; after some time relations were good, children made progress, the tutor was accepted as a friend of the house, and he had already succeeded in freeing some colleague out from under a captain oppressing him and in transferring him sometimes to another battalion. Then a great thing again happens in that the adjutant gets himself under judgment for the theft of government funds; they remove him, and the entire laboriously raised scaffolding collapses; it is necessary to build anew, and so it goes without end. But weren't we for many years condemned to this regulated delivery of constantly overturned buildings and scaffoldings? This is the life of an exile and by extension must be the life of a Pole.

Like the habitat for all staff and main administration of the region, in which enlightened people are concentrated, Orenburg was the most convenient city for our exiles; beyond it came other cities and villages. The condition of those sent to the steppe fortresses was again very different. There was no drill there, and a soldier was busy with the building of forts being erected; anyway, he enlisted in the guard, and with this everything was finished. Our brothers were not used for work; they were usually, in spite of the prohibition, officials of various sorts. When sometimes there were several, this one issued provisions, this one kept watch over the arsenal, and that one looked after the vegetables or the hospital. The freedom was comparatively great, but for all that the steppe is level and empty all around, and in the fortress are very often two or three officers, the commandant, and a dozen or so soldiers drunk every day. There are no books, there is no camaraderie, and it is scarcely possible to say that there are no expressions for such nothingness with which the surrounding desert infused the exile; life is brought to its most simple functions. The Kirgiz post twice a month conveyed papers from Orenburg, and then again it was silent. Being in Novopetrovsk, on the eastern shore of the Caspian Sea was fortunate during the summer; they had steamships arriving from Astrakhan that carried letters and news, but there again in the winter was complete silence. The sea freezes, and it is as though the paltry fortress is cut off from the whole world. The bobac, with its capability of sleeping through the whole winter, is envied. When a young man reached there, with his fiery imagination and warm heart—for example, the dearly departed Zygmunt Sierakowski, who spent his first two years of sojourn in the Orenburg Corps—he would indeed lose his mind from it or completely blow a fuse.

In general under such conditions, at such work and with daily small sufferings and fights passed the life of exiles. Some supported others. The greatest consolation was the camaraderie of fellow brothers. After drills they often gathered in the barracks for a shared feast. A letter from family or some news brought by a newspaper were the subject of endless discussions; and even if more than one of those present had to be laid to rest in some cemetery there, no one lost hope that after all he would still return to his homeland, while doubt about the future fate of the Fatherland certainly was not set in any mind. To have always hope, against hope itself, this was already our destiny, and this was our strength! Sierakowski, who just where he found himself, was a soul of such gatherings where he usually donated the milk jug to the assembled brothers, because the pockets of a soldier did not suffice for a more costly reception, and he called such gatherings *the great milks*. More than one certainly remained forever in my memory. In the beginning only the nobility themselves were sent, and people who amounted to something more or less; with time, with the broader awakening in the national life of the country, every free class began to have its own representatives. About the year 1850 and later, more and more burghers and craftsmen began to arrive, and in the end even peasants were among those sent for political affairs. Everyone together became one family. Everyone arriving had to pass through Orenburg, so everyone was known there; naturally this was a bonfire to which everyone headed with interest. Father Zielonka was the advocate of everything, and his care was felt everywhere. As usual, in every battalion and in every fortress was someone in mind or in heart who excelled above the others, and this one was like the head of the cluster and the caretaker of those poorer and weaker. He furtively kept his own little room not far from the barracks; there it was possible sometimes to take break, to have a rest, or to read some book. The one who returned to the homeland, he left his books to be held in common. In this way a little library formed freely, and the circulation of books to exiles in various residents often strengthened their spirits and even allowed them to educate themselves. A long life, given over to service and still more lectures in the end caused a desire for knowing our language and literature to be awaken in the local population. Women often studied Polish in order to be able read Mickiewicz, and there were times when it was the fashion in Orenburg to have wide coats in the salon; it gave way to change, like everything, but in general respect grew. No single exile could say that it was his own doing;

almost everyone contributed to this; each person, as a man, had his faults and deficiencies, but everyone represented the Polish idea—that through them, often even unintentionally, fought for and earned recognition.

In Orenburg our exiles met with still others of the condemned. There were a few Russians from the Petrashevsky affair, and there was Shevchenko, whom I already recalled. With them one very quickly came to an understanding. Shevchenko, the grandson of a Haidamak, who bearing in his warm blood a great hatred for the Polish nobility and dreaming of Little Russian sovereign independence, there reconciled with Poland, wrote verse to the friend of Lach, and rid himself of many old erroneous notions; yet he let our brothers recognize the entirely beautiful, wistful, and poetic side of the Ruthenian people.[18]

Women were almost never sent at that time; however, I saw in the Orenburg region a young Polish woman who arrived there to share the fate of her husband and whose heroism and self-sacrifice then brought tears to the toughest souls. Ms. Migurska with family from Galicia came to Uralsk, where her husband was a soldier. She spent several years there sweetening his life, so that in the end she thought to free him. The entire project that only a loving Polish woman could dare to execute was arranged. On a certain day Migurski disappeared; they looked for him in vain, since his coat was found finally on the bank of the Ural with a letter to his wife bidding her farewell and entreating that she forgive him everything that she bore for him and that she return to her family. An investigation was ordered, they searched, and finally it was believed that Migurski had drowned. He was at that time with his wife, concealed in the small storehouse, but only his wife and a good-natured servant, also from Poland, knew. After several months Ms. Migurska was allowed to return. She ordered that a traveling vehicle, a *tarantas*, be prepared with a double bottom; there at night she placed her husband and the coffins of the two children, whom she lost there, and she was already supposed to have gone, when upon her departure the local general gave her a Cossack for safety, as he said, on the road. Really he supposed that Migurski could have escaped, and the Cossack was supposed to stop him, when and where he met with his wife. The poor woman excused the escort, but she had to take it, not imagining, anyway, the secret instructions. They left in spring; the overflowing of the rivers hindered the journey

---

18 The Haidamaki (derived from *haydamak* or "to make an attack") are Cossack or peasant groups in Ukraine who struggled against Polish domination in the region in the eighteenth century; Lach is a way to refer to Poles (Joseph Wieczynski, *The Modern Encyclopedia of Russian and Soviet History* [Gulf Breeze, FL: Academic Internal Press, 1979], 13:233).

and often for entire days she had to stand in place; the poor thing did not come out of the carriage, guarding her treasure and trembling lest he be discovered by accident. Her husband had already poked his head out from his hiding place at times, and she spoke with him. Then, around Petrovsk, in Saratov gubernia, during a fast drive, the plank on which the postilion sat with the Cossack, broke under the weight and wounded the crushed Migurski's head. At the unexpected blow he cried out. This cry betrayed the one having fled; the ride was halted, and the secret was uncovered. Nothing—requests, money even—did not help. The Cossack, thinking that for this he would be advanced, took them both back to Saratov, to the governor's. A criminal investigation inquiring about the escape began. There was general sympathy in the town, but nothing could help. The intercession of the governor, struck by the entire affair, only elicited from the tsar that for this he reasoned only that Migurski be assigned to the Siberian battalions. The poor thing went there after her husband, but her strength was no longer holding out under these conditions; she soon died. A dozen or so years later, a poor Lithuanian woman, Suboczow, arrived there also on foot after her husband; for several years she prepared Polish dishes for the exiles and was happier than Ms. Migurska, because she returned together with her husband.

Aside from the exiles, there were still in Orenburg, as there were everywhere in Russia, many compatriots, so-called volunteers, looking for service and a hunk of bread; really, those driven out of their country and to this peregrination were forced by directives of Nicholas making every position difficult for us in our country and subjugating everyone to government service. They contributed very much to the alleviation of the fate of the exiles and soldiers. Their ideas and degree of education were varied, and during the continual growth of the Polish circle, each of them more and more felt themselves Polish; not one there really studied the homeland, and many of them took notes, always in their memories, for those who were really family. During the holy days of Christmas and Easter, the host and blessings were always prepared there for the brothers, and when it was allowed to exchange favors during times of sicknesses, in want, and in various needs, more than one name with a tear of gratitude would arrive for the exchange.

With General Perovsky taking up the administration of the region for the second time in 1851, conditions became still better. The personal temperament of the man of the nobility influenced the subordinates, drills in general became less onerous, and our compatriots were watched comparatively better. Among the people surrounding the governor general, they had a lot of friends; one of the highest placed officials often for entire nights read and poured tears over Mickiewicz's lectures with one of our soldiers. More often our brothers were given orders not with the frontline service, not having it in common; although exile was always exile and the grey coat did not stop being too tight, it was less arbitrary treatment and more and more hope of improvement of fate and even return. That desirable moment really was brought closer for some, greeted with joy even by the local population. When the expedition approached Ak-Mechet—the Kokand fortress on the Syr Darya situated about 500 versts to the East beyond the Aral Sea to the North and which later obtained the name of Fort Perovsky—many of our compatriots with the will of the governor general himself, took part in it. For a month and a half the columns went from Orenburg to the Kokand Khanate; the siege of the fortress lasted three weeks, because under the thick and high walls—although joined together only with clay and leaning on cannon balls—had to be planted mines. Those laying siege, like today's residents of Central Asia were well armed, but after the wall blew up into the air, the fortress was taken out in August of 1853. Two beloved young men well known and popular with their colleagues, Michał Bielikowicz and Karol Pogorzelski, found death during the storming, because everywhere the Polish grave must be built near the Russian flag, but for many this expedition was the beginning of liberation from the soldier's coat and then return, even. In 1857 with the liberation of almost everyone, the previous period of our martyr's history was supposed to come to a close; with this, also, today's story arrives at its close.

Running over it yet another time with the thought of those dozen or so years of calling up entire series of these victims who went there generation after generation and so often died unknown, the question involuntarily arises: Did the homeland make much of a profit on this; for what did everyone suffer and perish? Was the sea of tears spilt by our wives and mothers rewarded, and was all this lost strength and squandered lives? If another national direction, less painful and more beneficial had been sent, could they not have served it? And indeed, if there were fewer conspiracies, especially fewer emissaries from abroad, and more solid, domestic, and organic work, the fate of the nation today could be otherwise. But these speculations must today remain only speculations, to which it could be possible for others to respond anew. In this an entire generation took part—it was not the work of a few people; and with their strength it could not be altered. Our exceptional and outstanding generation drove us down this road. Actually, on the paths of exile and in the ranks of those condemned by the Russian government, people of all political persuasions and every hue met: from the Philarets, who thought about the education of youth and the edification of the people, to those who bore arms in their defense; from those establishing schools for peasants at their places to those conspiring against an existing regulation. Those who did not permit the inopportune uprising of 1846 in Lithuania, they there found themselves together with those who wanted to call for it. How many again were shackled only because they were Poles, because of sentiment itself, and were not defended anywhere else and did not yield to punishment? Having given still more thought as to how the Polish spirit was constantly tempted, having run through all the directives of Nicholas, having had school with Polish children, having left them for the cadet corps and later for service everywhere where we had to suffer, and having measured the abyss of moral and physical misery, such a degree of education only now for entire masses has already become accessible. We can stop being surprised that even many of those efforts were untimely and fatal, and we acknowledge that it could not be otherwise.

While comparing oneself to the armies of exiles since the time of the Confederacy of Bar and later, even since 1831 with those having arrived in the latest years, one could not fail to recognize the difference in them; not an individual among them was at all better or stronger, but their spirit was different in its measure of how under oppression they grew and matured in the nation itself. Differences of conditions were completely effaced, traditional habits were transient, and a stronger and stronger solidarity arose; the place often despaired at quarrelsome yet inspired projects, and the most solemn view substituted for duty and position. Each more and more stopped being only for himself and felt a member of the entire community of suffering; a shared opinion developed—national duties and the general good of exiles, and its consecrated interests and individual needs, being the goal above all. More and more seldom were the examples of those who were married in exile, and in the end escape itself was condemned, as it was possible to bring damage to everyone. The stronger and more popular strove also to graft good grain in the Russian community itself in order to bring relief to the suffering there. Turno was attentive to the greatest solace in life so that after many years of a soldier's service, having become an officer and finally an adjutant for the head of the internal guard, he saved about ten or fifteen thousand bludgeons a year as a soldier.[19] Sierakowski in Orenburg took up the idea of the moral elevation of the soldier—freeing him from

19 Ludwik Turno was arrested in 1846 in connection with the Krakow uprising and sent to the Orenburg line, where he also was linked to Sierakowski and took part in expeditions with Shevchenko and Zaleski (Zieliński, "Bronisława Zaleskiego wspomnienia z Kazachstanu," 137; Śliwowska, *ZpIR*, 640–41; Caban, *Z Orenburga do Paryża*, 57–61).

corporal punishment and labor—and devoted some years of his life to its exclusion.

Having taken a glance at this again, our exiles through long-standing suffering for themselves and for the Polish name in general improved within the Russian community, as much as they managed to rouse a conscience there; and seeing how today tens of thousands filled in the paths to exile as almost an entire generation of people set out there where they had worked and suffered, the isolated exile cannot rely on the thought that divine justice sent inexpressible suffering for our final purification and the awakening finally of those still slumbering there.

Be that as it may, for those who over the course of ten or fifteen years went there to suffer and to yearn, and with longing and suffering to wash away national sins and to buy something better for the great-grandchildren of the future, anything would be at their service, even life; we can always say with emotion that they suffered for Poland, and we were free to expect that their suffering influenced the scales of divine justice. From all these thousands, only a few names are written in the memory of the nation; their own families do not even know about a greater number, without comparison, of dead there. But it is possible to talk about those greater, more noble, and truly the already sainted believer of divine thought all the same, for the miraculous Roman inscription over the bones of unknown Christian martyrs says that their names are known to the Everlasting.

Correspondence about the Petrashevsky Affair

A List with Respect to the Minister of War for the Minister of Internal Affairs

December 22, 1849 no. 132[1]

By Imperial Order the following persons were judged by military court for criminal plots against the government: 1. Titular Counselor Mikhail Butashevich-Petrashevsky: 2. Landowner Nikolai Speshnev: 3. Lieutenant Nikolai Mombelli; 4. Lieutenant Nikolai Grigorev; 5. Staff Captain Fedor Lvov; 6. Student at SPb University Pavel Filipov; 7. Kandidat at SPb University Dmitry Akhsharumov; 8. Student at SPb University Aleksandr Khanykov; 9. Collegiate Assessor Durov; 10. Engineer-Lieutenant Fedor Dostoevsky; 11. Collegiate Assessor Konstantin Debu 1; 12. Collegiate Secretary Ippolit Debu 2; 13. Teacher in the Main Engineering School, Feliks Toll; 14. Assistant Inspector of Classes in the Technological Institute, Titular Counselor Ivan [Jan] Jastrzębski; 15. Nobleman Aleksei Pleshcheev; 16. Titular Counselor Nikolai Kashkin; 17. Titular Counselor Vasilii Golovinsky; 18. Lieutenant Aleksandr Palm; 19. Titular Counselor Konstantin Timkovsky; 20. Collegiate Assessor Aleksandr Evropeus; 21. Bourgeois Petr Shaposhnikov; 22. Honorable Citizen Vasilii Katenev;[2] 23.

---

1 Edward Żeligowski: Korespondencja Edwarda Żeligowskiego i zebrane przez niego dokumenty dotyczące zesłańców syberyjskich, Archiwum Hotelu Lambert. Rkps. 6972, III. Biblioteka Czartoryskich.

2 The following footnote is in the manuscript:

> According to the request of the mother of Katenev (who is located in a home for the insane) for permission to take charge of him, but Count Orlov in response to the Minister of Internal Affairs on June 22, 1855 did not agree.

Second Lieutenant Rafael Chernosvitov. After an examination of the affair they carried out at the adjutant general's, it turns out that criminal plots by the accused for overthrowing the existing governmental structure in Russia arose from a liberal turn of mind and from their assimilation of harmful socialist ideas from Western Europe. The first example of such plots is displayed by Petrashevsky, who already from youth having been penetrated with liberal understandings—which at the end of his university studies in 1841 had been even more strongly inculcated in him—conceived a criminal plot for the overthrow of the governmental structure. To achieve this goal he used various means; he tried to engender the pernicious beginnings of liberalism in the young generation by means of teachers. He, himself, tried to corrupt young minds with pernicious books and conversations, and since 1845, acting more intelligently in the spirit of propaganda, on well-known days gathered at his home teachers, literati, and students acquainted with him. In general he constantly aroused and directed judgments produced at these gatherings, leading to a flouting of religious convictions, to the condemnation of government administration, to the censure of government individuals, and even to the sacred person of His Imperial Majesty. In this way, he reduced his visitors to the point, that in many respects they received new views and convictions and left his meeting more or less shocked by their former creeds and inclined toward a criminal direction. Not satisfied with this, Petrashevsky at the end of 1848 for the more rapid achievement of his coup d'état, together with some of those having visited him, made attempts to form a secret society, independent of his gatherings, and under these conditions had secret conferences with the accused Speshnev and Chernosvitov about the possibility of an uprising in Eastern Siberia and in the Urals, and, following this, in the same such conferences with Lieutenant Mombelli and three other individuals about leading a secret society under the name of an association or brotherhood with the goal of transforming our civil way of life; however, this society according to a disagreement in deliberations did not come to be. After the example of Petrashevsky, at the end of that year 1848 and the beginning of 1849 similar gatherings were introduced at the place of literati Collegiate Assessor Durov and Titular Counselor Kashkin. At the gatherings at Durov's, compositions of a liberal spirit were read in manuscript form, and moreover it was proposed that articles against the government be written, and for their dissemination a secret lithograph be set up, which however was abandoned without being carried out. The gathering at Kashkin's, having consisted of not a numerous group, had the goal of studying the socialist and communist systems—chiefly the system of Fourier with the goal of their application to Russia. The characteristics of their system, as is evident from their conversations and the manuscript compositions of the accused, led to an overthrow of both religious and political convictions in the people, to the annihilation of rights of family life and the rights of property, to the production of work and industry in a social way through the union of landowners and peasants in one commune, and therefore led to the consequences of the destruction of the present order. Independent of aforesaid meetings and of the people having participated in them, there was still doubt introduced concerning Bourgeois Petr Shaposhnikov and Honorable Citizen Vasilii Katenev about criminal conspiracy against the government and about the intention to set about a rebellion, but this was not supported by examination. It was revealed only that Shaposhnikov, trying a harmful way of thinking and being incited by those former students Tolstoy and Katenev who had visited him, had criminal conversations about religion and the government with them in his apartment and discussed the possibility of introducing a republic to Russia. However, all these meetings described here, which have generally distinguished themselves by a spirit contrary to the government and a striving for change in the existing order, do not reveal a single activity; to the category of organized secret societies they also did not belong and that they had some relations within the government has not been proven by any positive data. All the criminal initiatives of the accused in their furthest developments could have had disastrous consequences for the tranquility of the government if there were not opportune forewarning for the government, and moreover, if perverse thoughts had been disseminated among the many people having found themselves in relations with the accused. The adjutant general on the foundation of the field of criminal law, sentenced the aforementioned persons without exception, as criminals of the state, to the death penalty by shooting. But Sovereign Nicholas I was pleased as the Most Gracious to replace this penalty with punishment in proportion to guilt: 1. Butashevich-Petrashevsky, for his criminal plot to overthrow the existing state structure in Russia, for attracting gatherings of different ranks (in large part, youth who were at his place), for disseminating among them pernicious ideas against the regime, for arousing in them a hatred of the government, and finally for an attempt to form with this criminal aim a secret society—deprive of all rights of station and send to convict labor in the mines without limit; 2. Speshnev and Mombelli, for criminally conspiratorial intent to produce reform of the social fabric in Russia and for the attempt to form a secret society with the goal of political and religious relations, and for Mombelli, for his placing in his manuscript composition an opinion, impertinent in the highest degree, about the Sovereign—deprive of all rights of station and send to convict labor in the mines—Mombelli for 15 years and Speshnev, in consideration of voluntary disclosures of some circumstances, for 10 years; 3. Grigorev, for participation in criminal plots and for writing and distributing articles with content that was outrageous in the highest degree under the heading "A Soldier's Conversation," which according to sense and its fascinating word, was suitable to the understanding of soldiers and intended to shake devotion to the throne and obedience to authority in the lower ranks—deprive of all rights of station and send to convict labor in the mines for 15 years; 4. Lvov, for direct participation in such criminal purposes to produce reform, especially for taking part in meetings about the formation of a secret society—deprive of all rights of station and send to convict labor in the mines for 12 years; 5. Students Filipov and Akhsharumov, for participation in such criminal purposes with an attempt to distribute compositions, impertinent in the highest degree and outrageous—deprive of all rights of station and send into the convict company of the Engineering department for four years, and then appoint to service as a private in the Caucasus; 6. Student Khanykov for such participation in criminal plots and for pronouncing at service in the presence of others an outrageous speech in which he censured God, the Sovereign, and our social structure—in consideration of his young years, deprive of all rights of station and appoint as a private in an Orenburg Line Battalion; 7. Durov,[3] for participation in criminal plots, introducing meetings in his apartment for this purpose and attempting to distribute a composition against the government by means of a domestic lithograph—deprive of all rights of station, send to convict labor in fortresses for 4 years, and then appoint to service as a private; 8. Dostoevsky, for such participation in criminal plots, distribution of the letter of litterateur Belinsky, filled with impertinent expressions against Orthodoxy and higher authority, and for the attempt together with others to distribute a

3 Here, the following footnote is in the manuscript:

> According to the petition of the governor general of Western Siberia on January 26, 1856, he was informed by the Minister of Internal Affairs in the Military about the permission for Durov to be appointed to the regional administration with the right of Chancellery official of the 3rd rank.

composition against the government by means of a domestic lithograph—deprive of all rights of station and send to convict labor in fortresses for 4 years, and then appoint to service as a private; 9. Deby, 1st, for participation in criminal plots and in meetings about the formation of a secret society, in consideration that he did not give his personal assent to the proposed measures—having deprived him of rank and decorations distinguishing irreproachable service and all rights of station, send into the convict company of the Engineering department for 4 years, and then appoint to service as a private; 10. Debu, 2nd, for such participation in criminal plots for the distribution of the pernicious social teaching of Fourier and for keeping at his place Akhsharumov's composition, outrageous in the highest degree—deprive of all rights of station and send into the convict company of the Engineering department for 2 years and then appoint him to service as a private; 11. Jastrzębski and Toll, for participation in criminal plots and for reading at meetings at Petrashevsky's—the first a speech announcing an absence of religious conviction and the latter a lecture about political economy in the liberal spirit—deprive both of all rights of station and send to convict labor at the factories: Jastrzębski for 6 years and Toll for 2 years; 12. Pleshcheev, for participation in criminal plots and in impermissible discussions about the government, which took place in meetings at Petrashevsky's, for sending Dostoevsky the criminal letter of the litterateur Belinsky, filled with impertinent expressions against supreme authority and the Orthodox Church—in consideration of his young years, deprive of all rights of station and appoint to service as a private in an Orenburg Line Battalion; 13. Kashkin, for participation in criminal plots for producing reform in Russia, for the adoption of the pernicious system of Fourier, and for the introduction of meetings at his apartment for this aim, in consideration of his very young children and narrative—deprive of all rights of station and appoint to service as a private in a battalion in the Caucasus; 14. Golovinsky, for participation in liberal conversations at meetings at Petrashevsky's and Durov's at which he himself explained the possibility of the liberation of the serfs without the will of the government, with respect for his young years—deprive of ranks and noble privilege and appoint as a private to an Orenburg Line Battalion; 15. Palm, for participation in criminal gatherings at Petrashevsky's and Durov's, with consideration that he himself did not personally participate in the liberal conversations and that he expressed repentance for his deeds, having blamed himself for his punishment and being held in custody—transfer at the same rank to the army;

16. Timkovsky, for the distribution of the pernicious system of Fourier with the goal of adopting it in Russia—having deprived him of all rights of station, send off into the convict companies of the Engineering department for 6 years; 17. Evropeus, for such distribution of the system of Fourier, in consideration that he was thoughtlessly captivated to it and expressed repentance for his deeds—having deprived him of his rights, appoint him to service as a private in the Caucasus Line Battalions; 18. Shaposhnikov, for criminal conversations in his apartment against religion and the government and about the possibility of introducing a Republican government in Russia, as having clearly betrayed an inclination for free-thinking and having incurred strong suspicion for pronouncing impertinent expressions about the person of the tsar—deprive of all rights of station and send off to the convict companies of the Engineering department for 6 years and then appoint to service as a private in the Orenburg Line Battalions and 19. As far as that which concerns Chernosvitov,[4] having reserved strong suspicion regarding him, send him directly, without pause, from the fortress in Kexholm to a settlement—without having, however, deprived him of the pension previously received by him.

On the occasion of the discovered circumstances surrounding the Petrashevsky affair, in a January 4, 1856 review to Minister Prince D., he communicated the Imperial will:

1. Strengthen the strict measures of observation on the part of the authorities of the educational establishment for social instruction: both concerning the spirit and direction of instruction in general and concerning the strict selection of teachers and verification of their teaching. 2. On the part of the censor, have vigilant surveillance of journal and newspaper articles. 3. Take the strictest measures in importing foreign works with dangerous contents, having an ability to disseminate a perverse way of thinking. And also have all possible vigilant surveillance on the part of the police authorities over private gatherings and meetings so that, during the present corruption of minds in the West and the contagion of harmful ideas, meetings similar to those discovered in relation to this affair could not be formed again in our country.

4 The following footnote is in the manuscript:
On the occasion of a review from the excellent direction of the Plats-Major of Kexholm fortress about Chernosvitov, he was transferred by his Imperial command to the city of Vologda on January 25, 1855.

Index

www.ingramcontent.com/pod-product-compliance
Lightning Source LLC
Chambersburg PA
CBHW070644100726
47907CB00007B/2096

* 9 7 8 1 6 4 4 6 9 0 2 2 2 *